The Early Middle Ages

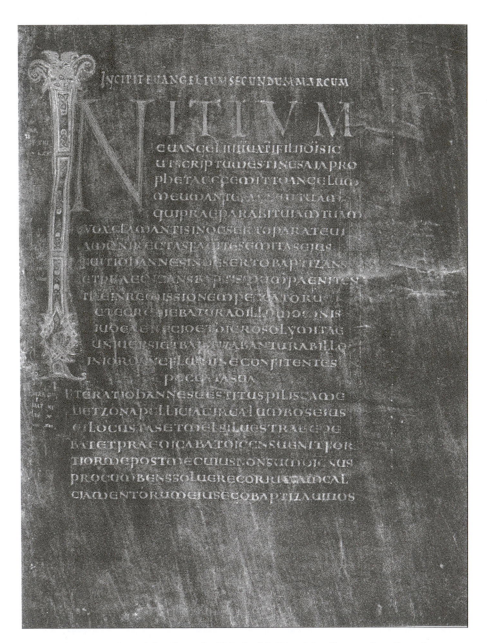

The beginning of the Gospel of Mark, fol. 77r of the Coronation Gospels, *c*.800 AD (Kunsthistorisches Museum, Vienna)

The Early Middle Ages

The Birth of Europe

Lynette Olson

palgrave
macmillan

First published 2007 by
PALGRAVE MACMILLAN
Houndmills, Basingstoke, Hampshire RG21 6XS and
175 Fifth Avenue, New York, N.Y. 10010
Companies and representatives throughout the world

PALGRAVE MACMILLAN is the global academic imprint of the Palgrave
Macmillan division of St. Martin's Press, LLC and of Palgrave Macmillan Ltd.
Macmillan® is a registered trademark in the United States, United Kingdom
and other countries. Palgrave is a registered trademark in the European
Union and other countries.

ISBN-13: 978–1–4039–4208–1 hardback
ISBN-10: 1–4039–4208–0   hardback
ISBN-13: 978–1–4039–4209–8 paperback
ISBN-10: 1–4039–4209–9   paperback

This book is printed on paper suitable for recycling and
made from fully managed and sustained forest sources.

A catalogue record for this book is available from the British Library.

A catalog record for this book is available from the Library of Congress.

10   9   8   7   6   5   4   3   2   1
16   15   14   13   12   11   10   09   08   07

Printed in China

To Michael and my mother

Contents

Maps

Illustrations

Acknowledgements

Over the years I have been privileged to teach in the Department of History of the University of Sydney, Australia, with a medievalist of exceptional insight and originality, John O. Ward. Only after writing this book did I realise the extent of the debt owed to his approach, which is nowhere greater than in the section on witchcraft in Chapter 7. I have also benefited from teaching and discussion with Ahmad Shboul of the Department of Arabic and Islamic Studies. Hilbert Chiu tactfully and efficiently procured picture permissions from nine different countries, and is owed thanks beyond the remuneration he received for doing so (I am grateful to the School of Philosophical and Historical Inquiry for assistance with the latter). I thank formally the copyright holders for permission to reproduce the images in this book and informally all of the individuals who helped in obtaining them. Andrew Wilson of the Archaeological Computing Laboratory designed the maps to my specifications with amazing technical skill. A debt is owed as well to a number of perceptive and interested students whose comments I have remembered. The two people to whom this book is dedicated have made specific contributions to its production and also given me their loving and wise support.

Prologue

In my second year of undergraduate study for a course on The Intellectual History of Medieval Europe, I had to choose a source written in the Middle Ages and write an essay trying to account for why its author had chosen to include what s/he did in the work. I eventually settled on the ninth-century *History of the Britons*, often but wrongly attributed to Nennius, and just before dinnertime on the day before it was due concluded my essay as follows:

> The study of the *Historia Brittonum* reveals a rather jagged kaleidoscope of the products of thought of many different peoples living at very different times. We have seen classical Christian[1] writings thrown together with crude annals and genealogies, Trojans in company with biblical figures in the far-off British Isles, and saints' legends full of pagan mythology. The close analysis of some of these factors has been carried out on the preceding pages; I wish now to look at the complete picture and what it means. While the effect of the complete picture is rather jarring, the fact that anyone would combine such disparate elements into a history of his people is significant. The early Middle Ages was a time in which many different ideas were still very much in the rough. One emerges from the study of Nennius with some conception of the wide variety of cultural elements which went into the making of the civilization of the Middle Ages and of the tremendous synthesis that went on as opposing peoples and their ideas came in contact with each other, whether they be Britons and Saxons, barbarians and Romans, pagans and Christians.

It was a recognisably defining moment at the time, and I wish undergraduate readers of this book one or more such of their own, and that all readers may share in the enthusiasm for the period which has been my specialty ever since. My interest in history in general had been awakened by my mother, and in early medieval history, in particular, by reading the right historical novel (Rosemary Sutcliff's *The Lantern Bearers*) at the right age (13); but now I understood what the early Middle Ages were: the birth of European civilisation which has become so large a component of the civilisation of the world as a whole. The great sin of Eurocentrism is to write as if all history (at least before 1500) is European history, and that is not done in this book. I hope that many of its readers are of other cultural backgrounds. The end of the period under consideration (after 1000) is placed in the context of world history in the Epilogue.

· ·

Introduction

The Frontispiece

This book begins by asking its readers to take a good look at its frontispiece, the
illustration opposite the title page. A detailed discussion of the manuscript page
of the beginning of the Gospel of Mark from the Coronation Gospels (AD *c*.800)
shown there will lead into explanation of what the book is about and of the
approaches taken in it. That is a pattern followed throughout: wherever appropriate, case studies and examples will illustrate overall developments. Sometimes,
always at the beginning of chapters (as here), the specifics will introduce the
general points. You are supposed to delight in the detail, not be bewildered by it
and worried that you have to learn it all, if you are a student. Its historical significance – what the data is *for*, what it is evidence *of*, will be explained. Developing
a sense of historical significance is important for people interested in the past at
any stage in their lives. What readers should understand, yes learn, are the overall developments. Still, details may persist in the mind and help in recalling the
big picture. For example, usually memorable, and a reminder to see Europe in
the early Middle Ages as part of a wider world, is Charlemagne's elephant
mentioned at the beginning of Chapter 5, who lived at the time when the
Coronation Gospels were made.

So, to the frontispiece. The original manuscript is written in gold ink on
parchment stained purple, which has a colour range of pink to blue. Purple and
gold was an imperial Roman colour scheme which was applied to glorify God
in early medieval Christian art. Look very carefully at the writing. The letters in
the main part, below the large word 'Initium', are rounder than those in the top
line of the page. That top line is written in rustic capital script, which, like the
large square capitals just below it, is an ancient Roman way of writing. The
rounder letters of the main text are uncial script, which emerged in the later
Roman Empire and continued into early medieval use. All of these styles of
writing, like the combination of purple and gold, are from the Mediterranean
South. Other features of the decoration, however, show the influence of the
way books were ornamented in the British Isles and are thus called Insular.
Look at the large initial 'I' that extends down the left side of the page and you

will see patterns of interlace transformed by the principles of ancient Celtic art. Notice as well the progression from the 'I' to the 'N', less than half its size, down to the rest of the first word of the Gospel (the top line is a heading). Those who study manuscripts call this the 'diminuendo effect', and it is characteristic of Insular manuscripts as well. In the vivid orange-red applied to the large initial, one can perhaps even glimpse the contribution of enamelled metalwork to manuscript art. Thus the manuscript page on the frontispiece is the product of cultural interchange between South and North, a major feature of the birth of Europe.

Both the manuscript page and the frontispiece on which it appears have things to say which need to be explained. The first line, in Latin 'Incipit evangelium secundum Marcum', in English 'The gospel according to Mark begins', introduces a sacred text of the Christian Bible, worthy of splendid and precious ornament and the time and effort to apply it. As well as the Christian 'good news' (which is what 'evangelium' and 'gospel' mean), the manuscript conveyed visual messages[1] of wealth and power and something more: it was deliberately old fashioned, deliberately Roman in the choice of scripts and, with the exceptions discussed above, their layout on the page. Here the manuscript fits its context. Produced at the end of the eighth century, it was associated with the court of Charlemagne, the greatest ruler in the early Middle Ages, king of the Franks and the Lombards. In AD 800 the pope crowned Charlemagne Roman emperor, a title not used in the West for over 300 years. So Roman revival was in the air. The manuscript comes at a high point in early medieval history, making it appropriate to feature as the frontispiece to this book.

Likewise, the frontispiece has visual messages, particularly about evidence and its uses here. Most of what we know about the early Middle Ages is from texts, from written sources, but some knowledge is from things, from artefacts. The manuscript page from the Coronation Gospels is both text and artefact. In the frontispiece the text can be clearly seen and can even be read, with care and patience in getting used to the form of the letters and knowledge of Latin to separate the words. Texts written in the early Middle Ages appear in the book you are beginning to read, which commonly includes quotations from medieval sources in translation, a few of them lengthy. These are here because they have something to say that cannot be got across in a paraphrase or allusion, and they should be read with particular care. The manuscript text in the frontispiece is about a still more distant time which early medieval people thought was the most important period in human history, when God walked the earth as a man, Jesus Christ, whose ministry was preceded, as the text in question points out, by that of John the Baptist. Thus, while the text itself does not refer to the early Middle Ages and can be found in any Bible, the manuscript page, as a medieval artefact of fine calfskin, powdered gold and purple dye, written on and decorated in a certain way, is far more important evidence.

What the Book is About

The text is nevertheless appropriate for the frontispiece because the word 'Initium' at the start of Mark's gospel, and written in large letters in the manuscript, means 'beginning' and the subtitle of this book is 'The Birth of Europe'. Its title, 'The Early Middle Ages', follows a historical convention as exasperating as it is misleading because the whole notion of an insignificant interval between the glories of Graeco-Roman civilisation and the Renaissance in which these were reborn is wrong. To say this is not to deny that the fifth through to the fifteenth century roughly defines a historical period, or the existence of Ancient accomplishments before the period or that of a self-consciously reviving and transforming cultural movement toward its end. Not even the applicability of 'barbarous' to aspects of the period is denied, although the strongly negative label 'Dark Ages', which originally applied to the whole period and not just its earlier portion covered in this book, is rejected because it conceals under gloom the immensely significant developments that were underway. The early Middle Ages (*c*.450–*c*.1050) saw the beginning of a European civilisation which has continued up to the present, influencing the whole world and having been more or less transplanted into certain parts of it by European settlers.

The change from the Mediterranean-centred Ancient world to a later, European focus is best understood by looking at North Africa, by which is meant the area extending east and west roughly from modern Tunisia. The Mediterranean Sea acted as a highway for contacts with the rich and sophisticated cultures at its eastern end, such as that of the Phoenicians who colonised North Africa. Eventually Rome conquered these areas (including Carthage, the Phoenician capital), and its Empire took in the whole Mediterranean coastline. The extension of Roman control over much of Europe away from the Mediterranean was significant for the later history of the region, but North Africa was an especially important part of the Roman Empire. It was, for instance, the source of Rome's grain supply. There, at the very beginning of our period, lived the greatest Latin Christian writer, Augustine, bishop of Hippo, who died in 430 during the siege of that city by the Vandals, Germanic invaders of the Roman Empire. It was natural that one of the post-imperial barbarian kingdoms was in North Africa (see Map 1.1 in Chapter 1). Strikingly, this was the only part of the crumbling Roman West that the Eastern Roman Empire tried to save in four unsuccessful military expeditions in the fifth century, and it was the first to be reconquered by the forces of Emperor Justinian in the sixth. The successful reincorporation of North Africa into the Roman Empire, which was then ruled from the East, separated it from the European West. This was confirmed when the forces of Islam took over North Africa in the seventh century. The current view of North Africa as 'non-Western' is ultimately the result.

This book does not claim that any particular identification with Europe developed in the period which it is about. The Ancient Graeco-Roman world knew Europe as a continent, named for Europa, mythical daughter of a

Phoenician king whom the god Jupiter took off to the island of Crete. It passed on this concept to the early Middle Ages. The Prologue to this book has already provided an example: the 'Trojans in the company of biblical figures in the far-off British Isles' to be found in the ninth-century *History of the Britons* are identified therein as descendants of Japheth, the son of Noah who got the part of the world called Europe after the biblical Flood. Yet what emerges by the end of the eleventh century is a strong territorial sense of Christendom, not of Europe. To return to North Africa for a moment, just after the end of the period with which this book is concerned, the coast there was briefly taken over by the Normans of Sicily, who did not say to themselves: 'Oh, that's not Europe, we can't go there' (Normans never put territorial limits to their ambitions, as will be explained in Chapter 7). From the beginning, the medieval concept of Christendom, nevertheless, was tempered by what can be called in retrospect a European perspective, even a Western European one. The crumbling of the Western Roman Empire narrowed horizons and intensified geographical isolation. Latin persisted as an international language, whereas Greek was dominant in the surviving part of the Roman Empire ruled from Constantinople (modern Istanbul) and Arabic spread with Islam from the seventh century on. Eleventh-century Western Christians wrote as if the Church that looked to the pope in Rome for ultimate authority was the only Church. Significantly, they did this while both knowing that there were Christians under the Patriarch of Constantinople whom they did not control, and being ignorant of the scatter of Christian communities all the way to China.

The kingdoms, societies and cultures of early medieval Europe developed in conjunction with each other rather than as the hinterland of a wider, Mediterranean world. The north of Europe moreover played a role most uncharacteristic of Antiquity, when conditions tended to become uncivilised the further one got from the Mediterranean Sea. Occasionally in the early Middle Ages civilisation can be seen to come out of the North in a reversal of the previous direction. Recall here the manuscript page displaying cultural features of both European South and North shown on the frontispiece. Given the proximity of the manuscript to the papal coronation of Charlemagne, also mentioned above, this can even be used to suggest the formation of a north–south axis between the papacy and the Franks of whom Charlemagne was king (that is termed 'the core of Europe' in Chapter 4). It should be clear by now that analysis via the geographical areas of north and south, east and west will be a feature of this book, and you are referred to the various maps which it contains for assistance.

There is more than geography to seeing the early Middle Ages as the birth of Europe, however. Its division into several states continues from that period, as does its linguistic diversity. Latin, which had replaced indigenous languages in much of the Roman Empire, now itself turned into Romance languages like French, Spanish and Italian. European, indeed 'Western' cities as economic powerhouses with some measure of self-government have an unbroken development out of the rise in population and agricultural production that occurred toward the end of the period. In the cities of the Ancient world, especially those planted away from the Mediterranean by the Romans, the administrative function was uppermost. The debt of modern Europe and its settler societies to Ancient Greece and Rome is by no means as great as is often thought. What about democracy, it may be objected, surely that is inherited from the Ancient Greeks? The roots of modern representative democracy, the great success story of the twentieth century, are mainly in feudal England, where vassal barons insisted on being consulted by the king. These do not reach back to the early Middle Ages, but in that period the soil was prepared in which they were to grow. As for the Renaissance, its context in the autonomous cities of northern Italy was essentially the product of the tenth century. Whatever was revived in the Renaissance, it was not the Roman Empire. The most instructive example of Renaissance distortion of the historical past involves writing and takes us back to the manuscript on the frontispiece one last time. Charlemagne, the greatest early medieval ruler with whose court the Coronation Gospels was connected, sponsored a reform of handwriting. The new, easier-to-read script, which is not shown in the manuscript on the frontispiece, owed a lot to the style of writing used in the British Isles, and separated the words with spaces. Romans literate in their own language could read words run together, but spacing helped those whose Latin was learnt more easily to read it. Much later, Renaissance scholars came upon this better writing and thought that it was Ancient. They imitated it in what is called Humanist script, which is the basis for modern typeface. Thus the very words that you are reading on this page testify to the early Middle Ages as the birth of European culture.

The early Middle Ages is a reasonably coherent historical period stretching from AD *c*.450 to *c*.1050. In this book it is thought best to include the whole fifth century and eleventh century, in order to show the transition which makes their ends look very different from their beginnings. A strong argument can be made that the seventh century saw a transition of great significance as well, as you will see in Chapter 3. It is important to recognise that historical periods are constructions placed upon the past. The shortcomings of the term 'Middle Ages' have already been discussed. Ask yourself what label will be attached to our own time 500 years in the future and you may see that historical periods are not at all necessarily self-evident to the people living in them. In a book with a chapter for each century, the arbitrary division of the past into periods of 100 years must be recognised. Nowadays we refer to centuries as if they had a life and character of their own, but at the point when this book begins they did not even exist. Dating from the birth of Christ, *Anno Domini*, 'in the year of the Lord', had not yet been applied to history.[2] AD dating was the innovation of Bede, a monk in eighth-century England. The fact that both this and the Islamic system of dating (see Chapter 3) originated in the period under study is evidence of its fundamental significance. Actually early medieval history lends itself to a century-by-century approach, which may have a virtue in its very arbitrariness rather than being based on interpretation of the past. The contents of each chapter are the result of interpretation, of course, and some bases of interpretation used here will be discussed shortly.

First, there is more to say about evidence, and even the lack of it, for the early Middle Ages. As already noted above, most is from texts, but some is from artefacts. The period benefits from interdisciplinary study, and archaeology in particular has much to offer by recovering and interpreting the material remains of the early medieval past. Those who use archaeological evidence in historical study need to recognise, though, that archaeology is a discipline with its own methodology. Here is one example of what it can contribute. Excavations at the major monastery of San Vincenzo al Volpurno in Italy have shown that its early medieval inhabitants lived surrounded by texts written on the walls of buildings there. While this is not unexpected given occasional textual references to and records of inscriptions elsewhere, the evidence for a literate environment is nonetheless striking. Archaeology is a source of brand new evidence for the early Middle Ages. There are others. Biological indicators like DNA are being used to testify in general to the stability of populations, a valuable corrective to written sources which emphasise invasion. Of course some people did move. Genetic study of the population of Iceland, which had no human settlement before the early Middle Ages, has indicated a majority component that was Scandinavian, but a sizable minority component that was Irish. This having been said, painstaking study of long-known texts continues to yield information of huge importance and implications. Scholarly research in the field of early medieval history is not easy. Periods of major transition are difficult to interpret even where the evidence is abundant. For example, the origins of the twentieth-century Cold War are murkier than is often realised. For the early Middle Ages, one takes the evidence that is available from any and all sources, combines it and does what one can with it, all with the greatest care. Readers may already be surprised that quite profound cultural conclusions have been drawn in this Introduction on the basis of changes in handwriting.

Approaches

There are certain premises and agendas that underlie the interpretation and choice of content in this book, and these need to be clearly set out. Early medieval texts are skewed in favour of the Christian religion, in many cases being written with the aim of getting people to think more about spiritual matters. An attempt will be made here to redress the balance, keeping the Church in its place and making sure that readers realise that there were large areas of people's lives that were taken up with other concerns, even though we may not be well informed about them. There was nothing Christian about blood-feud, or the value system of shame and honour which encouraged it, for example. This having been said, due attention will be given to conversion to Christianity, which before the last decade of the twentieth century received surprisingly little coverage in print given its staggering implications for the formation of European culture. Also, a deliberate attempt has been made to include the female half of the population in the history of the early Middle Ages, which is not difficult: one simply writes them in from the evidence that is there. Here is a case of what to avoid. In Chapter 5, on the ninth century, mention is made of a pious husband and wife who ransomed a beautiful gospel book, its pages ornamented with gold, from Vikings. In the contemporary account written on the manuscript page, both the man and the woman are named: 'I Alderman Aelfred and my wife Werburg'; however, a fairly recent book gives the man's name only and adds, 'and his wife'. One has to read the script in the illustration to find her name, even though the whole thing could have easily been her idea. This is not the only example in which modern authors are more sexist than early documents. Knowing that women of Werburg's time had better access to wealth through inheritance and marital arrangements than they did in later eras compounds the exasperation and strengthens one's resolution to show that the early Middle Ages was one of the most interesting periods in women's history.

Anthropological insights have contributed to the way in which early medieval history is presented in this book. Neither of the noted anthropologists Mary Douglas and Robin Horton was concerned with Europe in the early Middle Ages, but their work provides analytical tools of use in understanding its society and religious change, respectively. The influence of Douglas is particularly profound, and can be introduced by a brief anecdote. The writer of this book once had the good fortune to teach a seminar which included two quite exceptional students. Both went on to brilliant careers, but at this stage they were a contrast. One was a model student who did almost everything right, but the other was not. He worked at an all-night pancake restaurant, and used to come in early before the seminar to read in the library (being a very good student), only, not surprisingly, he sometimes fell asleep and came very late to class. On one such morning the teacher (your author) was summing up early medieval society as conformist, with little religious dissent to speak of, for example. This student said no, it had not struck him that way. He proceeded to explain that society in the early Middle Ages was loosely organised, lacking the definition that leads to identification of dissenters and their persecution. Indeed, there was more opportunity for groups who would be denied access to power in better organised societies where people knew the rules and kept to them. In about ten minutes he transformed my understanding of my own period of study, and in the years since then this way of viewing early medieval society has been repeatedly confirmed.[3]

To explain further, the early Middle Ages can be studied profitably with the following three types of society in mind. Again, these are analytical tools not pigeonholes into which actual societies must fit.

Type 1. Authority is clearly and coherently articulated. People are controlled by a public system of rules; obeying these is seen to bring success. Within the society there is a strong sense of 'us' and 'them': rejects are sharply defined by internal boundaries.

Type 2. Authority is weak, incoherent, inarticulate, ambiguous, even where there are unrealistic statements to the contrary. It is not clear why some people succeed. There is lots of social mobility, roles are ill defined, and identities are fluid.

Type 3.   Authority is strongly articulated, but very simply so by impersonal rules. Society is divided into a few leaders, normally male, who live by a code of shame and honour, and a great mass of subjects.

Noting the presence or absence of characteristics of each of the above helps to place the period in an even wider historical context. The absence of Type 1 characteristics distinguishes the early Middle Ages from Europe after the eleventh-century transition, but not from the later Roman Empire; however, these characteristics were present in the early Roman Empire. Type 2 characteristics are a feature of the early Middle Ages. Type 3 characteristics appear more in the second half of the period under study. This way of looking at early medieval society underlies statements made in the following chapters, which is why it has been set out at the beginning.

The contribution of Robin Horton's theory of conversion is more specific.[4] He argues that people's religious needs vary according to their circumstances. The needs he describes as being for explanation, prediction and control (one could think of others); the circumstances he analyses as being somewhere on the continuum from microcosm to macrocosm. The microcosm is the small world of isolated subsistence settlements, and religious orientation there is to the familiar local spirits. Now, as circumstances change, bringing people more into contact with the wider world, the macrocosm – whether they go out into it or it comes to them – their religion will show greater orientation to a supreme deity who has charge of everything. This process might modify an existing religion or facilitate adoption of a universal religion like Christianity or Islam. Horton's way of thinking about religious change focuses attention on the convert's creative role, and away from notions of mere imitation or combination of religious beliefs and practices. Its application to early medieval Christian conversion is fascinating because, while Christianity spread through contacts, especially of leaders, with a wider world, most converts and their descendants continued to live in the many small worlds of a profoundly rural Europe. So Christianity itself changed to meet their religious needs. We are about to see an example.

Finally, two cases will be considered in which diverse cultural components are found side by side in the way already set out in the Prologue. One is a text, the other an artefact; both are illustrated here. Sometime in the tenth century, someone at the monastery of Lorsch wrote in an early form of German, upside down at the bottom of a page of a manuscript of Latin sermons (see Figure 1), a charm to settle a swarm of bees:

> Kirst, imbi ist hucze. nu fliuc du uihu minaz. Hera
> fridu frono. In munt godes gisunt heim zi comonne.
> Sizisizi bina inbot dir sancte maria hurolob ni habe du. ziholce
> ni fluc du. noh du mir nindrinnes. noh du mir nintuuin
> nest sizi uilu stillo vuirki godes uuillon.

Christ, the bee-folk is out! Now fly, my cattle, back
In holy peace, in God's authority, so that you arrive home hale.
Alight, alight, bee: St Mary commanded you. May you have no leave:
To the wood flee not, nor escape me, nor deprive me of anything
Sit quite still, work God's will.

Note that the aim is not to drive away the bees, but to keep them where one wants them, producing honey which was highly valued as the only sweetener available at that time. The texts on the manuscript page are a contrast in both their language, Latin and German, and also, more subtly, their nature. There is a long tradition in Christianity of preaching sermons in order to teach people about the religion and guide their actions. The charm continues to meet religious needs,

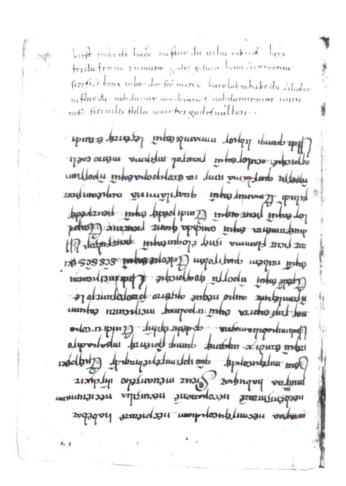

Figure 1 Lorsch Bee Charm, Vatican MS. Pal. Lat. 220, fol. 58, inverted in the photograph. (©Biblioteca Apostolica Vaticana [Vatican])

Figure 2   The Franks Casket (front), originally from northern England, juxtaposing the Christmas story on the right with the legend of Weland the Smith on the left. (©The Trustees of the British Museum)

and represents a way of meeting them, that were present in pre-Christian religion. Only here, at the time the charm was written, in what was a vital distinction to believers in real supernatural power, the Christian God and holy people were invoked. The placement of the texts on the page is intriguing, as the charm represents the underworld of Latin Christian culture of the early Middle Ages.

The other case of cultural juxtaposition is on the Franks Casket (Figure 2), carved on whalebone in northern England in the seventh century. In the scene on the right, the three Magi (labelled in runes above) approach Mary and the Christ child with gifts, while the Christmas star shines overhead. The scene on the left represents the legend of Weland the Smith, hamstrung by a ruler who wished to retain his skilled services, and taking a terrible revenge. Weland murdered the ruler's sons and seduced his daughter Beadohild, shown facing the smith, who supports himself against the edge of the scene on the far left. As a result she gave birth to a hero. While decidedly unchristian, it was too good a story not to keep telling.

Study of the early Middle Ages is particularly interesting because it provides an opportunity to watch the original formation of Europe out of such different elements. Ultimately these would fuse into a distinctive medieval civilisation, and develop further down to the present day. This book will show where Europe came from, its beginning, its birth.

The Fifth Century: Kingdoms Replace the Western Roman Empire

From Empire to Kingdoms

In 414 Galla Placidia (see Figure 3), daughter of Theodosius I, the last emperor to rule both the Roman East and West, married King Ataulf of the Visigoths. She had been in the custody of the Visigoths since just before their sack of Rome four years earlier. Subsequently they (with Galla Placidia) had trekked down through Italy, heading for North Africa, but then, when their king Alaric died and was succeeded by his brother-in-law Ataulf, they had turned round and gone back up through Italy, over into southwest Gaul (not yet France) and eventually down to northeast Spain. Galla Placidia is specifically praised by an eyewitness for the wise counsel she gave Ataulf. They had a son who was also named Theodosius after her imperial father. The fifth-century chronicler Hydatius saw them as fulfilling biblical prophecy that the King of the North shall marry the daughter of the King of the South, but their offspring shall not survive. Little Theodosius died as the Romans were blockading the Visigoths in Barcelona; much later, Galla Placidia had his body brought in a silver coffin and reburied with emperors in Rome.

Galla Placidia deserves to be better known to history, as do others of her time. Normally the only fifth-century figure of whom anyone has heard is Attila the Hun. His people, the Huns, had expanded westwards out of central Asia from the late fourth century on. They destabilised settled populations like the Visigoths north of the Roman Empire, which at that point stretched unbroken from Britain to what is now Iraq. Many Visigoths sought refuge across the River Danube in the eastern part of the Roman Empire, but were eventually deflected westwards. Their sack of Rome in 410 did not mean the end of the Roman Empire, which was ruled at the time by an eastern emperor in Constantinople and a western emperor in Ravenna in northeast Italy. Rome was no longer an administrative capital, but people knew where the Empire had come from. No

Figure 3   Image of Galla Placidia on a coin that has been given an ornamental surround and made into a piece of jewellery called a bracteate. She wears a diadem and the monogram of Christ on her right sleeve. The abbreviated titulature on the coin is also imperial. (Bibliothèque nationale de France)

hostile army had entered Rome for 800 years. If we put ourselves in their shoes, thinking of what happened 800 years ago and of where we live as having ruled and prospered during all of that time, we may have some idea of the shock that people felt. And this was one of many disasters for Romans in the western part of the Empire in the early fifth century.

The political situation in which Galla Placidia found herself was unprecedented. Every part of the Roman West was under attack except North Africa, which was where the Visigoths were heading when King Alaric died. Britain was raided from the sea by Saxons, Picts and Scots. Vandals, Sueves, Burgundians and others crossed the River Rhine frontier into Gaul, where the expansion of the Franks down from the northeast was underway. Spain was not protected from invasion by the mountains of the Pyrenees, nor Italy by the Alps. The Danube was beginning to change from a frontier into a barbarian thoroughfare. For those whom the Romans lumped together under the negative label 'barbarians', it was a time of great opportunity and fearful insecurity. Uprooted folk on a long trek, the Visigoths were looking for settlement in the best possible conditions. Meanwhile, they had to eat. As for Roman leadership, Galla Placidia's inactive half-brother, Emperor Honorius, had gone to ground in Ravenna at the very time there were several would-be imperial usurpers. In these circumstances a direct link of barbarian power to Roman imperial legitimacy was attempted in the marriage of Ataulf and Galla Placidia.

Whatever barbarian-Roman 'condominium' Ataulf (who was soon murdered by a servant) and Galla Placidia (thereafter restored to the Romans) had in mind for themselves and their very significantly named son, it was not the way the West actually developed. Roman control there was temporarily restored via a kind of internal foreign policy which settled or recognised the settlement of various barbarian groups under their own leaders in defined areas. A number of early medieval kingdoms originated from these early arrangements as the Roman Empire crumbled away[1] in the fifth-century West. The legitimacy of the kingdoms was nominally established at the outset by a treaty with the Romans. This was the case with the Burgundian, Visigothic and Vandal kingdoms (see Map 1.1) and probably the Suevic as well.

Even in Britain, where Roman control had, exceptionally, not been restored after the despairing provincials took matters into their own hands, their invitation to the Saxons to come and fight against other barbarians is described by the sixth-century writer Gildas in familiar terms of treaty and regular supplies to the settlers. In Italy, the ethnically mixed 'Roman' army requested settlement by treaty and when this was refused, rebelled, made Odoacer, one of its number, king and deposed the last Roman emperor of the West, Romulus Augustus, in 476. Last but not least, it is by no means clear that any treaty lies behind the kingdom of the Franks; the great success story of the post-imperial West, as we shall see.

The emergence of these kingdoms within the crumbling Roman West is where early medieval history begins. It set the pattern of a Europe divided into

Map 1.1   Barbarian kingdoms at the end of the fifth century, showing extent of linguistic change on the Continent (shaded area)

several separate political units which lasted until this century. It is by no means the whole story, even politically, of the transition from Antiquity to the Middle Ages, but there is eloquent fifth-century testimony to its significance. Sidonius Apollinaris was a Gallo-Roman aristocrat, public official and, finally, a bishop, whose letters from the third quarter of the fifth century have been preserved. Written in a flowery rhetorical style and often light in tone, the letters contain much of value about fifth-century circumstances and attitudes. In one of them, the reason given for irregular correspondence (hardly an exciting topic) is nevertheless interesting: 'we live in different realms', wrote Sidonius to another bishop in the 470s in what had been Roman Gaul, 'and are thus prevented from more frequent contact by the rights of conflicting governments.' The letter welcomes the making of a peace treaty between Visigoths and Romans, pointing out that now letters between the two bishops will no longer be regarded with suspicion. It ends with a prayer that Christ 'illos muneretur innocentia, nos quiete, totos securitate' ('may bless those people with guiltlessness [Sidonius took a dim view of barbarian fidelity to treaties], ourselves with peace, and all with freedom from fear'). The replacement of one, long since defensive, Roman Empire by several expansive kingdoms meant narrowing horizons and greater insecurity.

The Need for Protection

In an earlier letter Sidonius Apollinaris goes into considerable detail about a family in trouble, providing us a glimpse of the reality underlying political maps like the one here. This is just one case of what the lack of security meant.

Travellers were attacked by bandits called Vargi[2]; a man was killed and a woman abducted. Her kinsfolk traced her and discovered that she had died as the slave of a man whom Sidonius calls 'my agent'. There were market records of her sale and these gave the name of a third party to it, Prudens, said to be living in the city of Troyes. Now, Sidonius wrote that the relatives of the dead woman had travelled a long way to reach his city of Clermont in the Auvergne, which at the time was still a Roman enclave between the expanding Visigothic and Burgundian kingdoms. Troyes was to the north, in Frankish territory. Thus the case involved at least two, very likely three and possibly even four (since we do not know where the bandits attacked) different political units. These circumstances would not have been favourable to success of the criminal prosecution which Sidonius says the family was considering. Instead, he sent them with a covering letter to Bishop Lupus of Troyes, asking that eminent person to arbitrate the matter, 'lest this quarrel, as is the natural tendency in this quarter and in these times, should in the end develop a character such as now at the beginning it threatens to assume'. This is probably a reference to blood-feud: distressed and frustrated families taking matters into their own hands in the absence of law and order.

In such circumstances it was especially important to have powerful protectors. What we have been discussing is a letter of patronage, a fragment of the network of influence and benefit that mainly structured power in the early

Middle Ages. Note that although it is written from one bishop to another, the contents of the letter are entirely secular, 'this-worldly', although motivated by that concern for social peace which to us is the most attractive feature of the early medieval Church. These men had become local leaders in a power vacuum. Twenty years previously Lupus had turned Attila the Hun from the gates of Troyes, and Sidonius was no slouch in defence of Clermont either. But anyone could be a patron who had sufficient resources and/or connections. Women's participation in patronage, or more especially clientship, was limited primarily because they did not fight[3] and were thus excluded from the military relationships between lords and followers that were ultimately institutionalised into what historians have come to call 'feudalism'.

The rise of private power over public power is a major theme in the history of early medieval Europe. As the Roman Empire in the West failed in its duty to defend and its ability to compel, lords opted out of it for life on their estates with their private armies and dependent peasantry. In a poem, Sidonius Apollinaris describes the fortified villa of a friend, Pontius Leontius. This was sited on a crag above the estuary of the River Garonne, and was called a *burgus* (a Germanic loanword borrowed into Latin well before the fifth century), a fortified place. Pontius' 'burg' was elegant, being nicely furnished with Roman baths; strong with its walls and towers atop the natural defences; and self-sufficient, having granaries and weaving rooms. 'Methinks I see the future that is in store for thee, O Castle (for so thou shalt be called)', says Sidonius, and indeed this was the elite home of the medieval future. Sidonius hopes that his friend's place, which was then in the Visigothic kingdom, will once again be on Roman soil, but it was in any case a private power base.

In securing their own protection, lords could also offer it to others. They looked after their military retinues of *bucellarii*, 'biscuit men', in more ways than just supplying their rations. Moreover, rural patronage (*patrocinium*), which involved by far the largest number of people, flourished, binding peasants to lords in return for a protected place to live. Another Gallo-Roman writer of the fifth century, Salvian, presents rural patronage as an abuse by the greedy aristocrats (his intended audience), who always wanted something in return. It is easy to say that Salvian misses what *patrocinium* could offer to desperate, impoverished people: a little farm on which to subsist away from the impossible demands of a shrinking tax base. Yet what he sees and objects to is their loss of personal liberty. As *coloni* of their lord they were technically free tenants, but had to stay on their land, and this applied to their descendants as well, who eventually will number among the medieval serfs. Obviously the need for protection benefited those who could provide it.

Fluid Identity

These complex informal arrangements do not mean that the new political super-structure of kingdoms was unimportant. Nothing shows its significance more than the ethnic re-identification that took place as people gradually took on the identity of their ruling group. To appreciate this we must examine the composition of these kingdoms. Ethnically identified rulers had taken over parts of the Western Roman Empire. They were referred to as kings of the peoples shown on Map 1.1, for example *rex Burgundionum*, king of the Burgundians; however, most of those under his authority were not Burgundians, and the same applied in the other new kingdoms. Roman citizenship had long since been extended to everyone in the Empire and as far as we know Roman identity was universal by the fifth century. As the Empire crumbled in the West, times were hard but there was a massive survival of the indigenous population, Romanised people who had been there all of the time, at all social levels. The newcomers, moreover, destabilised by the expansion of the Huns northeast of the Roman Empire and by their trek into it, were themselves more fragmented than is indicated by the usual ethnic labels, which conceal splinters of peoples and indeed freelance individuals in warbands.

The aristocracy of this mixed society, oriented as such people were to power and thus to rulers as its source, is probably where the re-identification began. Basically those, of whatever ethnicity, who had acquired estates through treaty, or other means fair or foul, settled in with the Romans to become landowners and lords together. For the Romans, the disrupted conditions could mean reduced circumstances or ruin but also the opportunity to become powerful protectors as set out in the previous section. The customs of the new settlers dovetailed with the developments outlined there. While private lordship remained important in the kingdoms and potentially a challenge to royal power, kings mattered. In Italy, near the end of the fifth century, Odoacar, whose followers were so heterogeneous that he simply bore the title 'king', was defeated and killed by Theoderic king of the Ostrogoths, whose followers were by no means homogeneous. King Theoderic wanted to deny legal and property rights (*Romanae libertatis ius*, 'right of Roman liberty') to Romans who hadn't come over to his side quickly enough. There were many of these people. At the request of those in his region Bishop Epiphanius of Pavia persuaded Theoderic to relent, at which the king asked his palace official Urbicus (a Roman name) to issue an amnesty. Kings were not only a force to be feared, they were a positive attraction. The extent to which aristocrats of Roman background opted into the kingdoms needs to be realised. They did not just live on their estates and/or go into the Church; as just seen, they can be found serving the kings. The tendency toward identification with their rulers will be discussed further in the section 'A Warrior Aristocracy'.

Our sensitivity to culture and the relationship of power to it enables us to see identity as a fluid concept, in contrast to old-fashioned, indeed early medieval, explanations of how one population replaced another by killing off, enslaving or at best intermarrying with its predecessor. The latter will not do. Mass slaughter was not unknown: the Hispano-Roman chronicler Hydatius says the Siling Vandals were *extincti* as a result of the Visigothic campaign against them in Spain in 418. Otherwise, where we are at all well informed about the fifth-century West, the picture is very different, as described in the preceding paragraphs. Yet change in identity did occur. The ethnic mix in the kingdom of the Franks was originally remarkably varied, but by the eighth century the people in its north were Franks.[4] In the southeast, the Burgundian kingdom did not last a full century before being absorbed by the Franks in the 530s, but it was long enough to fix the identity of the ruling group as predominant, and again by the eighth century the people there were Burgundians. Gregory of Tours, himself of 'old senatorial family', provides massive evidence of the progress of acculturation in sixth-century France in his *Histories*, while the settlement of the Burgundians can be described from a variety of evidence as relatively congenial. If there was one place where the barbarians certainly didn't kill all the Romans, it was Burgundy. The following case may clarify the processes at work.

Further to the east, the origin of the Bavarians revealed by careful investigation of archaeological as well as written sources has implications for the formation of identity itself. They lived across the Danube from the great Roman fortress of Regensburg. With the disintegration of the Roman frontier defences which they had helped to garrison, the Bavarians made Regensburg the centre of their power. From there they expanded their control over all sorts of people between the Alamans to the west and chaos to the east, where the Danube had become a sort of barbarian thoroughfare. They were not very numerous, but they were in charge and set the tone for the region, and the people already living there ultimately took on their identity. We first hear of the Bavarians in the sixth century, when they were ruled by dukes (from Latin *dux, duces,* 'leader[s]') under a Frankish protectorate. Later, dukes of the Bavarians ruled autonomously, before Bavaria was incorporated into the Frankish kingdom toward the end of the eighth century. Note that the Bavarians did not migrate from elsewhere, but rather their identity grew up on the spot. A similar process may have seen the earlier emergence of the Franks themselves on both sides of the lower Rhine.

This way of accounting for the formation of identity is sometimes called ethnogenesis, and it provides a useful model of cultural change to set beside the traditional intrusive one. Extreme cases of movement of people and their interaction with others with whom there had been no previous contact are the coming of the English to Australia and the Spanish to the Americas. These were attended by terrible outbreaks of disease among the native populations, and have no counterpart in the period we are studying, in which intrusive elements are nevertheless to be seen. Thus the Gallo-Roman Paulinus of Pella, author of the best of all fifth-century sources for showing what elite life was like at the time, writes of the days in his life when two bad things happened: his father died and the barbarians arrived (the former was the worst, he says). If the intrusive model on the one hand and the ethnogenesis model on the other are both borne in mind when considering the so-called barbarian invasions or migration period, the reality of ethnic change will often lie in between the two, but on the whole closer to the ethnogenesis model. Given their role in setting the tone for the regions of Europe so that people already living there took on their identities, those whom the Romans regarded as alien, 'the other' must be examined.

Barbarians

What was a barbarian? This Roman (originally Greek) negative cultural construction appears in verses by Dracontius, a fifth-century poet in Vandal Africa:

> Inter '*eils!*' Goticum, '*scapja mazja ja drincan!*'
> Non posset dignos edicere versos.
>
> Among Gothic 'Cheers! Let's get down to eating and drinking!'
> No one can write worthy verses.

Clever lines, to fit a foreign language (in italics) into Latin metre, and if they are awkward, that's the whole point! Barbarians didn't speak Latin, or not well, and were people whose idea of the ultimate pleasure emphasised basic animal pursuits; their presence interfered with civilised ones. The Ancient, Graeco-Roman world privileged culture as ours privileges technology in separating those who know how to live from those who do not but, unlike our society, lacked racism. An educated upbringing ensured acceptance; for example, there is no hint of barbarism in the distinguished career of the fifth-century soldier and orator Merobaudes, despite his Frankish name. Above all, barbarians were ignorant, and this extended even to the Christianity that was spreading most widely among them.

Romans were remarkably unmotivated to convert barbarians, although where a Christian community existed among them, a bishop might be sent. In the mid-fourth century, when Christianity was becoming the Roman state religion, Ulfila, who was descended from Christian Roman prisoners of the Visigoths, took considerable steps to convert them, including translating the Bible, or most of it,[5] into the Gothic language. As it happened, Ulfila's contacts with the Roman East came at a time when Arian Christianity was in imperial favour. There Ulfila picked up this Christian heresy named for Arius, an early fourth-century Roman priest whose theological teachings emphasised the humanity over the divinity of Christ. The Arianism of Ulfila and other missionaries ensured that this was the version of Christianity that spread and spread among the barbarians long after the Romans had rejected it for good. To Salvian, writing *On the Governance of God* in the mid-fifth century to explain to his fellow-Romans how God could be in charge when the barbarians were winning, Arianism was the barbarians' Christianity. He explains the theological difference over the Trinity and the nature of Christ within it nicely:

> We are certain that they do injury to the divine begetting because they say the Son is less than the Father. They think we injure the Father because we believe the Father and Son are equal.

He says they got it wrong because of corrupt texts and ignorant teachers. God tolerated them and the pagans because they didn't know any better; but not the Roman Christians, who did, yet still kept on sinning.

On the other hand, the success of those who were taking over the Roman West brought them enormous prestige. So there was not only cultural cringe towards superior Roman civilisation which they admired and were prepared to learn from (especially codification of law) but also pride in what they were. Initially, most were Germanic-speaking (see below). Arian Christianity with its scriptures and liturgy in Gothic, an East Germanic language, and its native teaching tradition became a sort of cultural badge. And the barbarians had their own negative cultural construction: Germanic *wealh*, foreigner in the derogatory sense (= Welsh/*walisisch*/*welsch*, readers can probably think of modern-day equivalents), was applied to Romanised Celts not only in Britain, where the Welsh language is still spoken, but on the Continent. Probably the best known example of the latter is reference to the Welsh of Chur, a city in what is now Switzerland, inhabitants of a region which long remained a sub-Roman enclave with distinctive government and law. As indicated in the previous section, identity was fluid, created and claimed, but this was compatible with its strong assertion. In the eighth century someone wrote into a manuscript in Latin:

> Stulti sunt Romani, sapienti Paiorii.

> Romans are stupid, Bavarians wise.

Pride in being Bavarian would have helped the assumption of this identity by people of various backgrounds including Romans, who could even have been the scribe's ancestors!

Within what had been the Roman West, change in spoken language was remarkably limited in the long run. Most of the barbarians spoke one of several Germanic languages.[6] Yet there were only two sizeable areas of the former empire which became permanently Germanic-speaking: the region south of the Danube (including Bavarian territory – was the writer just quoted an unhappy student of Latin?) and eastern Britain, where English, the language in which this book is written, was established. Two things follow from this. First, contrary to what is so often said, Latin did not die. It merely turned into Spanish, Portuguese, French, Italian, Romanian and little known Alpine languages such as that still spoken in valleys around Chur. This regional evolution, already underway in the Roman Empire, was enhanced by the narrowing horizons after it crumbled in the West. Second, the barbarians mostly gave up their own languages. It is thought that the religious use of Gothic may have prolonged its life, in other words that Latin-speaking barbarians going to their Arian churches together heard the old language only in worshipping there. Yet Arian Christianity did not persist for all that long in the face of the Catholic majority, as we shall see in the next chapter. This situation, where barbarians who provided rule and thus identity at the beginning of the Middle Ages nevertheless took on the language and religion of the Romans they had conquered, shows indeed the tremendous synthesis from which Europe emerged. Their contribution was still more fundamental, however.

A Warrior Aristocracy

The enduring, most historically visible and important legacy of the barbarians to early medieval Europe was a warrior aristocracy. As already stated, the elite at the beginning of the Middle Ages was in fact mixed, and mixing. Those of Roman background continued to be major landholders. Some of them went into the Church, but others served barbarian kings in both a civil and a military capacity. Sidonius's son Apollinaris did all of these things. Of a wealthy landed family which was not only senatorial but imperial (his grandfather Avitus had briefly ruled the Roman West in the mid-fifth century), Apollinaris held office under the Visigothic king Alaric II. He was praised by a contemporary for his military deeds, and remembered in the next century for having brought a force to fight for Alaric against the Franks at the Battle of Vouillé in 507. Only in the last year of his life did Apollinaris become bishop of Clermont. The career choice is neatly illustrated by the two sons of Paulinus of Pella, both of whom were drawn against their father's wishes to Bordeaux, where the Visigothic court was located and where the family owned property. One became a priest but soon died. The other, writes Paulinus, 'enjoyed both the king's favour and then his enmity, and after losing almost all of my goods came to a like end'. This fifth-century Gallo-Roman family was not a success, but according to Paulinus others did better: 'since we see many prospering full well with Gothic favour'.

The barbarian elite settling on to estates had never had such good fortune. Appearance, dress and ornament proclaimed their success and the military accomplishment by which it had been secured and had to be maintained in difficult times. Sidonius illustrates this, and its appeal, in the following letter to a Roman friend, Domnicius:

> You who are so fond of looking at arms and armed men, what delight, methinks, you would have felt if you had seen the young prince Sigismer, decked out in the garb and fashion of his nation, as the chosen lover or as suitor paying a visit to the palace of his lady's father! Before him went a horse gaily caparisoned: other horses laden with flashing jewels preceded or followed him. But the most gracious sight in the procession was the prince himself marching on foot amid his runners and footmen, clad in gleaming scarlet, ruddy gold, and pure-white silk, while his fair hair, glowing cheeks, and white skin matched the colours of such bright dress. The princelings and allies who escorted him presented an aspect terrifying even in peace-time. Their feet from toe to ankle were laced in hairy shoes; knees, shins, and calves were uncovered: above this was a tight-fitting many-coloured garment, drawn up high, and hardly descending to their bare houghs, the sleeves covering only the upper part of the arm. They wore green mantles with crimson borders. Their swords suspended from the shoulders by over-running baldrics pressed against sides girded with studded deer-skins. This equipment adorned and armed them at the same time. Barbed lances and missile axes filled their right hands; and their left sides were protected by

shields, the gleam of which, golden on the central bosses and silvery white round the rims, betrayed at once the wearers' wealth and ruling passion. The total effect was such that this bridal drama displayed a pageant of Mars no less than of Venus. But why say more about it? This fine show lacked only one thing – your presence. For when I saw that you were not seeing the sights your eye delights in, at that moment I wanted not to feel the want of you. Farewell.

Notice that Domnicius (who elsewhere is said to enjoy a good game of dice) liked this sort of thing. The idea that late Romans were uninterested in the military and left fighting to the barbarians is misleading, not least for the formation of the early medieval aristocracy. Fifth-century Roman commanders are not hard to find. Aetius, greatest of the military strongmen of the fifth century, who balanced various peoples bound by treaty to the Romans against each other for a quarter of the century and defeated Attila the Hun at the Battle of the Catalaunian Plains in 451, was a Roman, and another example is given in the next paragraph. If Roman fathers encouraged their sons to follow gentler pursuits, it does not mean that their sons listened to them, given attractions like the above.

Favour and success were attractive to everyone oriented to power. In particular, court culture was focused on the ruler and encouraged imitation, and this extended to the Romans. A more hostile source than the poet Dracontius quoted at the beginning of the section on 'Barbarians', Victor of Vita's *History of the Vandal Persecution* tells us that 'a huge number of our Catholics who served in the royal household used to go in dressed like Vandals'. If this happened in Vandal Africa, where Roman–barbarian relations were at their least congenial, how much more likely is it to have done so everywhere! And warrior culture could be beguiling: in the Roman court Galla Placidia is said to have gone around with a large bodyguard of barbarians, not only because of her marriage to King Ataulf but also because of her subsequent marriage to the Roman general Constantius, who had commanded many barbarians in Roman service. While the aristocracy of the new kingdoms was of mixed background, the barbarians set the tone for it in the most important respect. The establishment of barbarian control over what had been the Roman West ensured that the mounted warrior shown in Figure 4 was in the future of the dominant class there, whether speaking a Latin-based, Germanic or a Celtic language. There was an alternative, however.

The Church

The most historically visible legacy of Rome to early medieval Europe was the Church, which represented a career choice not only for elite Romans. A fifth-century monk of particular spiritual accomplishments, Bonosus, was remembered as being 'by birth a barbarian' in the *Life* of St Severinus of Noricum

Figure 4 Grave marker from Hornhausen in Germany, *c*.700. (Landesamt für Denkmalpflege und Archäologie Sachsen-Anhalt)

(roughly modern Austria). 'Catholic' means 'universal' and the Church welcomed all, but it was identified with Rome. Christianity had originated within the Roman Empire. The authority structure of bishops developed within Christianity to minister to its faithful and foster and protect its teaching tradition reflected the urban basis of Roman society and, indeed, the importance of particular cities. For three centuries the religion was illegal, its followers liable to sporadic persecution. Then at the beginning of the fourth century, after a particularly severe persecution, the Roman emperor Constantine converted to Christianity, which he protected and fostered. By the fifth century Christianity was the Roman state religion, and its authority structure survived the Empire intact.

The Church, both in the broader sense of all Christians and the narrower sense of an institution of professional clergy, was ruled by bishops based in the cities:

Today when you see Bishops as worthy of the Lord as Emperius of Toulouse, Simplicius of Vienne, Amandus of Bordeaux, Diogenianus of Albi, Venerandus of Clermont, Alithius of Cahors and now Pegasus of Périgueux, you will see that we have excellent guardians of all our faith and religion, however great may be the evils of our age.

(Paulinus, quoted in Gregory of Tours, *Histories*)

Such a proud list of names that no one has ever heard of is even a little amusing, but this contemporary recognition that bishops were one thing that the fifth century was good for is noteworthy. Such men, in this case from southern Gaul, ordained priests and lesser clergy, consecrated new church buildings and administered church finances. As we have seen from the letter of Bishop Sidonius Apollinaris about the slave woman, their activities could go beyond the religious sphere. In far-off Ireland, Bishop Patrick penned an angry letter of excommunication to the soldiers of the British ruler Coroticus, who had attacked Patrick's Irish converts. He contrasts their actions with 'the custom of the Roman Christians in Gaul: they send suitable holy men to the Franks and other peoples with so many thousand *solidi* [coins] to ransom baptised captives; whereas you kill them or sell them to a foreign people who does not know God; you commit the members of Christ as though to a brothel.' He condemns Coroticus and his soldiers, 'who allot poor baptised women as prizes, for the sake of a miserable temporal kingdom which will in any case pass away in a moment'.

Overall the Church kept up morale in difficult times. Our sources are often part of that process, and need to be evaluated as such. The passage quoted in the extract above is an example of positive propaganda, the most effective kind. The overwhelming evidence for the emergence of bishops as local leaders in the fifth century needs to be kept in perspective. Would that we were anywhere near as well informed about secular leadership, and not so often reliant on hints such as those dropped by the likes of St Patrick! Within the Church, not all leaders were bishops. The above-mentioned St Severinus, who numbered the barbarian Bonosus among his disciples, was a monk. Monasticism (see below) was supposed to entail withdrawal from ordinary society, but Severinus, moving between his monasteries on the River Danube, was paradoxically well-placed to help people with this-worldly as well as other-worldly concerns. He secured the release of captives, organised poor relief, counselled on defence, and brokered agreements with the barbarians, to whom he also provided advice. In near chaos, not only his holiness/charisma but also his organisational ability inspired confidence and hope, in other words, they raised morale.

The Church reinforced patriarchy but also provided limited opportunities for women. Writing in the next century, Gregory of Tours gives us a picture of a fifth-century bishop's wife. Her husband St Namatius built a large and beautiful church decorated with marble and mosaics, and she built a church too. 'She used to hold in her lap a book from which she would read stories of events which happened long ago, and tell the workmen what she wanted painted on the walls.' The appearance of this old lady in black was so humble that a poor man, 'who had not understood who she was', gave her a piece of bread as alms. She had some authority, too: as a holy person of ascetic lifestyle (who could read, note), as the bishop's wife and as a wealthy donor. This couple were clearly people of means. A bishop could be 'a man of one wife' (remarriage was a disqualifying sign of enthusiasm for the pleasures of the flesh), but as Gregory writes of an earlier bishop: 'He was a married man and, according to the custom of the Church, his wife lived as a religious, apart from her husband.' In this case, however, his wife turned up at the church-house and insisted on her marriage rights. As a result they had a daughter, who became a nun.

By and large, the characteristics of the medieval Church were already in place in the fifth century. A focus on the holiness of particular people had led to the cult of the saints and monasticism. The latter involved asceticism, a self-denying regime of training for sanctity (little food, no sex, poor clothing, much prayer) undertaken in isolation from ordinary society. Christians became monks and nuns in order that they might follow Christ more perfectly, and often placed themselves under the guidance of masters of what they sought. Monastic communities were societies reconstituted along new, super-Christian lines. As well, a papacy claimed power for the bishops of Rome in terms that could be picked up and used centuries later. The prestige of Rome was coming to rest on its being the place where the apostles Peter and Paul were buried. As the Roman West crumbled, the claims to highest authority of the patriarch of Constantinople, the capital that Constantine had established in the East as a new, Christian Rome, grew stronger. Against these claims, in the middle of the fifth century Pope Leo I asserted that the pope was the representative of St Peter, the apostle to whom Christ had committed the Church, and had the *plenitudo potestatis*, the 'fullness of power' in the Church. By the end of the century, when there were no longer Roman emperors in the West, Pope Gelasius I innovatively declared that the power of bishops was separate from, and superior to, the power of the secular ruler. Only at the end of the period covered in this book will the pope begin to rule the Church, however. Finally, the Church inherited a political dimension and compulsory nature from having been the Roman state religion. Their ideologies dovetailed nicely: in theory the Roman Empire was universal, and 'universal' is what 'Catholic' means. Henceforth it will be assumed that Catholic rulers will have Catholic subjects, with the reluctant exception of Jews.

Yet Christianity had far to spread and missionary zeal was lacking. In northern Italy Maximus of Turin urged landlords to end the pagan practices of the peasants on their estates, whose souls they would be responsible for at the Last Judgement. The conversion of the countryside, where the vast majority of people lived, was just beginning; the catch-all term 'pagan' derives from Latin for a country dweller. In faraway Ireland Patrick piled biblical quotation upon quotation to justify his conversion of 'enemies who do not know God'. Like Ulfila, there were special circumstances behind his efforts: he had been enslaved by Irish raiders, escaped and, he says, in a dream was literally called back by the Irish to bring them the faith; unlike Ulfila, the Christianity he brought was acceptably orthodox. Conversion brought Latin textual literacy to Ireland, where it flourished. This is an early case of the transforming effects of Christianity with its Roman cultural baggage on a society beyond the old imperial frontiers, a major theme in the birth of Europe. Christianity itself would be transformed in meeting the religious needs of country folk who accepted it under compulsion from the authority figures in their lives, on whose lands they subsisted, and by native cultural elements in the British Isles as will be seen in Chapter 3.

From Roman to Medieval Culture

Another legacy of Rome to early medieval Europe is much less historically visible, but no less important. Beneath Roman elite civilisation was a cultural underworld. Over the centuries Romanisation had proceeded apace in the provinces, as the Romans consolidated their conquests by what today would be called cultural hegemony. Yet the reverse also occurred, as elements of indigenous cultures persisted and worked away from beneath, sometimes rising to the surface as happened in late Antique art and was the case with Christianity. When the empire crumbled in the West, the Roman superstructure was stripped away and what had been the underworld in the sense described above went on to form the basis of medieval culture over a wide area. An illustration is provided by a little word, or pair of words, with a great medieval future. Around the turn of the fifth into the sixth century it surfaces in the phrase *vassus ad ministerium* to designate a high-level slave like a steward. Over the succeeding centuries *vassus* and *vassalus* rose on the social scale along with what they came to represent: the military follower of a lord. We shall see a defeated duke become the vassal of a king in the eighth century, and vassalage develop into one of the most important relationships in medieval society. Consider, *vassus* and *vassalus* are Latin loanwords from Celtic *gwas*, 'boy' or 'servant', and thus come from the underworld of Roman Gaul, having been borrowed in obscure circumstances when Latin was replacing Celtic speech there.[7] They are clear evidence of deep processes at work in the making of European culture.

To conclude this chapter, two points, one geographical and the other chronological, need to be made about acculturation in the original formation of Europe, with which it has been concerned. Only part of the lands with which this book deals had lain within the boundaries of the Roman Empire. Scandinavia together with most of Germany and of Eastern Europe had always been outside them, as had Ireland and the far north of Britain. True, Rome cast a long shadow of cultural influence especially beyond the Rhine and Danube rivers. In a museum here at the University of Sydney, where this book is being written, is a brooch from Poland based on a Roman prototype, for example. Borderlands could be zones of great cultural fertility, as we shall see, and as such are of particular interest. Yet the societies that grew up in the crumbling Roman West were a template for the rest of what would become organised Christian Europe. At the top of these societies were Roman-influenced Germanic kings and a multicultural aristocracy, bound and supported by relationships that owed much to the Roman underworld from which the bulk of the dependent population continued to come. At first the newcomers tended to keep their distance in matters of religion, as we have seen, but that would change at the turn of the century with the conversion to Catholic Christianity of King Clovis of the Franks, with whom the next chapter begins. This completed the pattern that would be followed by rulers engaged in top-down conversion and/or conquest in and beyond the lands the Romans had controlled.

In their ill-defined and ambiguous authority structure and fluid identity, these societies also show continuity with the later Roman Empire, perhaps due to the extent of ongoing cultural contact. Theories, rules, labels might say one thing, but people might do, or be, another. For example, aside from a Christian notion of the spiritual equality of men and women which people found difficult to divorce from women's relative physical weakness, late Antique and early medieval attitudes about women were not at all enlightened. Yet, in the later Roman Empire, women had better access to wealth than previously, in part from their ability to inherit. As well, via what is called the reverse dowry, the more significant payment in making a marriage came from the man to the woman. The need for legislation to limit the size of the reverse dowry hints at deep social processes at work. And so it continued, and not only where Roman law was immediately influential, as in Spain. In barbarian customary law the ability of women to inherit improved over time in areas as far apart as France and Ireland. The reverse dowry dovetailed with the Germanic bride-price as the latter came to be paid to the woman. Only toward the end of the period of this book will these trends be reversed, one of a number of contrasts of late Antiquity and the early Middle Ages with better organised periods before and after them.

The Sixth Century:
The West Goes Its Own Way

Clovis and Theoderic

At the beginning of the sixth century King Clovis of the Franks wrote to King Theoderic of the Ostrogoths in Italy and asked him for a harper. In King Theoderic's name, his Roman official Cassiodorus referred the request on to Boethius, a fellow Roman in the service of Theoderic, because he was an expert on music. This is an interesting point of cultural contact. What Boethius wrote about, as part of a project to produce textbooks on the liberal arts, was Ancient Graeco-Roman music. That is probably not what King Clovis had in mind. Evidence survives not only of the performance of Germanic song and story accompanied on the harp but even of the instruments, although we have no idea what the music sounded like. The replica shown here (see Figure 5) is of an example found virtually complete in a warrior's grave near Oberflacht in Germany.

Technically a lyre, it shows southern, Mediterranean influence, recalling the direction from which the harper was dispatched to Clovis. 'He will perform a feat like that of Orpheus, when his sweet sound tames the savage hearts of the barbarians.' To Cassiodorus, Clovis was a barbarian, and presumably Theoderic, in whose name Cassiodorus wrote the letter, was somehow different. Yet Theoderic was Clovis's brother-in-law, and is celebrated in Germanic legend as a hero. Clovis, who actually established the longest lasting barbarian kingdom, never achieved a mention in the Germanic tradition. Be that as it may, both were great kings and their kingdoms make an instructive comparison, which will occupy the first part of this chapter.

Relations between Kings Clovis and Theoderic were not confined to the diplomatic exchange just mentioned. Theoderic was married to Clovis's sister Audefleda, just one of the Ostrogothic royal family[1] connections that reveal a world of barbarian power. These can be followed with reference to Map 1.1 in the previous chapter, which is a good way of reviewing the successor kingdoms to the Roman Empire in the West. Theoderic's sister Amalafrida was married to the king of the Vandals; his daughter Ostrogotho Areagni to the king of the

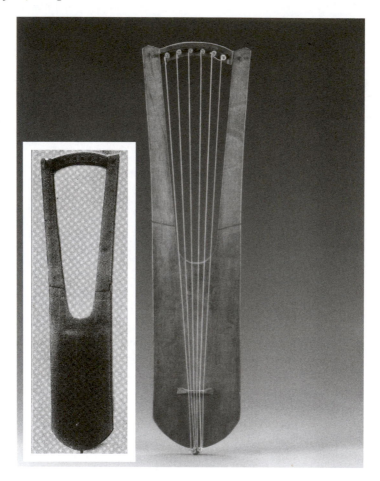

Figure 5 Lyre (rotte, after fifth–seventh-century German type), late nineteenth century. Oak; dimensions: 78.5 x 17.3 x 2.8 cm (30 7/8 x 6 13/16 x 1 1/8 in.) (Museum of Fine Arts, Boston. Leslie Lindsey Mason Collection, 17.1767. Photograph © 2006 Museum of Fine Arts, Boston). The inset photograph shows the original lyre found near Oberflacht in Germany and destroyed in World War II. (After *A History of Music in Pictures*, ed. Georg Kinsky, London: J. M. Dent & Sons, 1930)

Burgundians; another daughter Theodegotha to the king of the Visigoths; and his niece Amalaberga, daughter of Amalafrida, to the king of the Thuringians, another people on his northern border. When war threatened, Theoderic wrote to the Visigothic, Burgundian, Thuringian and Frankish kings, invoking marriage kinship, in an effort to avert it, but to no avail: Clovis soundly defeated the Visigoths under King Alaric II, Theoderic's grandson, at the battle of Vouillé and drove them from southwest France to Spain. The husband of Theoderic's daughter Amalasuintha was not a king but the direct descendant of one,

Ermanaric, ruler of the Ostrogoths when the Huns attacked in the late fourth century, who committed suicide because he could not protect his people but lived on in tradition for centuries afterwards. With such a marriage, Theoderic hoped to secure the royal succession, for he had no son and this was a serious problem which soured the end of his long reign in Italy (493–526).

Up to that point, wrote a Roman in the mid-sixth century about Theoderic:

> whatever he did was good. He so governed two races at the same time, Romans and Goths, that although he himself was of the Arian sect, he nevertheless made no assault on the Catholic religion; he gave games in the circus and the amphitheatre, so that even by the Romans he was called a Trajan or a Valentinian, whose times he took as a model; and by the Goths, because of his edict, in which he established justice, he was judged to be in all respects their best king.

Our leaders would give anything to be remembered thus! The praise is only qualified by the religious difference, which helped to maintain the essential distinction between Goths and Romans. Nowadays, Theoderic would be described as 'proudly Arian'. Continuing the imperial tradition of ornamented building at Ravenna and its use as a capital, he built a church there decorated with marble and mosaics. The frieze along one side of the nave began with his palace, but all that is left of the figures that originally stood within it are a few of their hands on the columns after they were replaced by curtains in circumstances to be considered later in the chapter. Also from northern Italy in the same period have survived most of the Christian gospels in Ulfila's Gothic translation and script written on purple-stained parchment in silver and occasionally gold ink, evidence of patronage at a very high level. The circumstance of Goths going off to church together and venerating the gospels written in their own language should be kept in mind. Yet Theoderic's Italy was a very Roman place. Aside from the change to rule by an Ostrogothic king, Roman administration in Italy was intact and so was its senatorial aristocracy, many of whom continued in public service. Cassiodorus and Boethius are examples.

The essential difference of Clovis's kingdom is the integration of all his subjects under his rule instead of the separation of Goths and Romans as under Theoderic. The roots of this contrast are long. Theoderic's Ostrogoths in Italy were a long way from Ermanaric's earlier kingdom in what is now Ukraine.[2] When that had been smashed by the Huns, many Ostrogoths had fled westward, those who did not enter the Roman Empire becoming tributary to the Huns. They subsequently, after the death of Attila and the consequent break-up of the Hunnic empire in the mid-fifth century, had entered into treaty arrangements with the Romans. The circumstances that brought the Ostrogoths (and others) under Theoderic from the Balkans to Italy have been touched on in Chapter 1 and will be further considered a little later in this chapter; the point to take here is that the Ostrogoths were still an intrusive identity in sixth-century Italy. By contrast, the Franks never lost touch with their homeland. Map 2.1 shows the

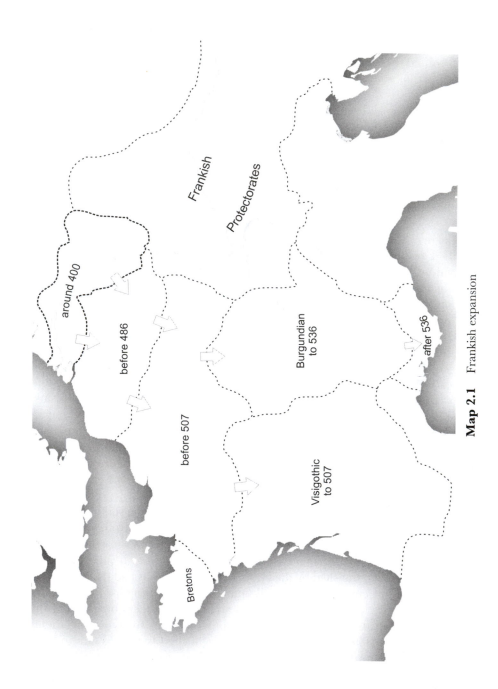

Map 2.1   Frankish expansion

around 400

before 486

before 507

Bretons

Frankish

Protectorates

Burgundian
to 536

Visigothic
to 507

after 536

contiguous nature of their expansion. Frankish identity was extended from its origin on the lower Rhine over a larger and larger area, especially through the efforts of Clovis, who founded France. Additions made in his reign (481–511) included the *Tractus Armoricanus*, as the Romans had called northwest Gaul. In the mid-sixth century the Roman historian Procopius wrote that its inhabitants, whom he called the *Arborychoi*, had resisted conquest by the Franks but agreed to intermarry with them: 'And in this way they were united into one people, and came to have great power.' This is as close as early sources can come to ethnogenesis. The Franks were already an inclusive identity in sixth-century Gaul-turning-into-France.

Frankish inclusiveness extended to religion. Sometime around AD 500, Clovis converted to Roman, Catholic, Christianity, initiating a top-down conversion that removed rather than maintained religious distinction between his subjects. Indeed, Procopius wrote that the *Arborychoi* willingly intermarried with the Franks because both peoples were Christians; and the same sort of Christians, one would add. Although Clovis's sister Lantechildis, who converted to Catholicism when he did, had been an Arian and the sister who married Theoderic probably was one too, there is no evidence that Clovis was other than pagan before his baptism. Religious diversity in ruling families was known elsewhere: Theoderic's own mother was a Catholic and in the Burgundian kingdom, which lay between the Ostrogoths and the Franks, the royal family was split between Arians like the kings and Catholics like Clovis's wife Clothild. To her the later sixth-century historian Gregory of Tours attributed the conversion of Clovis, with the assistance of Bishop Remigius of Reims. Clovis was 'like some new Constantine', wrote Gregory, referring to the Roman emperor who had converted to Christianity in the early fourth century. Clovis and Constantine were alike also in their concern for the unity of what they respectively ruled. Whereas Constantine sought to restore and preserve the Roman Empire, Clovis was putting his kingdom together for the first time. He was a particularly ruthless centraliser, ensuring that whereas the Franks had been ruled by a number of kings at the same time, in the end their only ruler was himself. The unified Christian kingdom under Clovis's rule was in conformity with the Roman model of a Christian state, as in all subsequent cases of top-down conversion in Europe.

Once converted, Clovis got the authority structure of the Church – articulate, literate, organised and linked by a network of communication as in the example of Sidonius's letter cited in Chapter 1 – fully on his side. To appreciate the significance of this one must realise the extent to which early medieval rulers would use the Church in governance and how eagerly Church leaders complied in that role. Some may see the Church as having used the kings rather than the other way around; however, writers at the time had no doubt about who was in charge. Letters of Bishop Remigius are illustrative. He did not even wait for Clovis to convert, but offered him advice on how to rule as soon as Clovis became king of the Franks after the death of his father Childeric in 481, including that he 'should defer to your bishops and always have recourse to their advice'. Shortly after Clovis' death in 511, Remigius, bishop for more than 50 years, wrote to answer a critic who alleged that he had been in the king's pocket when he ordained a certain priest:

> I made Claudius a presbyter, not corrupted by gold but on the testimony of the very excellent King, who not only strongly asserted but defended the Catholic Faith. You write: 'What he ordered was not canonical. . . .' The ruler of the country, the guardian of the fatherland, the conqueror of nations enjoined this.

This whole-hearted endorsement of Clovis should be compared to the judgement of the anonymous mid-sixth-century writer about Theoderic quoted earlier, as is also seen elsewhere in the same source:

> King Theoderic went to Rome and met Saint Peter [i.e., his successor Pope Symmachus] with as much reverence as if he himself were a Catholic.

Theoderic was a good king – for an Arian.

The contrast with Ostrogothic Italy is especially apparent at the level of the Frankish kingdom's city territories. These were all that survived of the Roman administrative structure there, comprising very small urban centres with their rural hinterlands, which formed a network that covered the whole kingdom. In each city territory (*civitas*) the royal official known as the count of the city (*comes civitatis*) wielded authority over everyone regardless of ethnic background.[3] There was no equivalent of the count of the Goths (*comes Gothorum*), a royal official in Italian cities, nor was access to countships ethnically specified. Likewise, with Catholic Christianity established as the religion of the Frankish kingdom, the bishops in the cities were bishops of everyone in their dioceses, which were coterminous with the city territories. Although Jews were usually tolerated, pagans could be forced to convert (if, one might add with respect to the rural population, the bishops or anyone else got around to it). And men with Germanic names appear among the bishops, especially in the north. Again, the operative word is inclusion. In these respects the Frankish kingdom differed not only from that of the Ostrogoths but also from the dual administrations of the Visigothic and Burgundian kingdoms, as well as from Vandal Africa which lacked officials like the counts of the cities linking the rulers to the ruled. In short, the Frankish kingdom differed from all of the other kingdoms shown on Map 1.1 which had Arian rulers.

One last contrast between Theoderic's Italy and Clovis's France-in-the-making is in their relations with what remained of the Roman Empire in the Eastern Mediterranean, which must now be properly introduced as the most important participant in the sixth-century history with which the present chapter is concerned. From this point on, historians call it the Byzantine Empire after Byzantium, the Greek city refounded as a new Rome in 325 by the emperor Constantine, whose name it came to bear as Constantinople. Yet its inhabitants always considered themselves to be Romans, so that in the language of the Turks who conquered it 1000 years later, the word for 'Greeks' is 'Romans', a usage which has not quite died out in Greece itself.[4] The strength of their identification is hardly surprising given that the lands around the eastern Mediterranean already had been under Roman control for four centuries, more or less, by the time when this book begins. The notion that the Roman Empire, all of it, fell in the fifth century is very widespread, due not least to the influence of Edward Gibbon's eighteenth-century masterpiece, *The Decline and Fall of the Roman Empire*, even though Gibbon took his study right up to the capture of Constantinople by the Turks in 1453; but it is wrong. When, as we have seen, the western half of the Roman Empire had been replaced by barbarian kingdoms, the eastern half was still there. Indeed, things were looking up: the emperors in Constantinople were strong and even militarily able, and there are signs of rising prosperity in what in any case had been the wealthier part of the Empire by the start of the sixth century.

Although the barbarian invasions had begun in the northeast in the late fourth century; now, a century later, Theoderic's Ostrogoths were the latest in a series of deflections of such people westwards. Theoderic lived as a well-treated hostage in Constantinople from the age of about 8 to 18. He then became king of the Ostrogoths while also receiving high imperial rank, military command and the consulship. The Ostrogoths' existence within the Empire was uncomfortable for all concerned, and in 488 by agreement with Emperor Zeno Theoderic and his people went off to conquer Italy from King Odoacar. Odoacar had acknowledged a theoretical control which the Empire never relinquished, and Theoderic also did this. Evidence like the gold medallion shown in Figure 6, struck in Italy in the early sixth century, shows that the delicacy of Theoderic's position was fully appreciated. Issuing such an object was the sort of thing emperors did, but the inscription gives Theoderic's initial title as simply *rex*, 'king', without specifying of whom or what. It also calls him *princeps*, 'the first one, chief', a word that was applied to emperors but had wider meanings and thus perfectly covered the ambiguities of Theoderic's rule. His head is bare, without royal crown, imperial diadem or even a military helmet which would suitably accompany his armour and cloak. Whoever designed the medallion has carefully observed distinctions so as to avoid a direct challenge to the Roman emperor in the East.

For King Clovis of the Franks, on the other hand, the Roman Empire in the East was remote. This is not to say that he had no communication with it. After he further extended his control to the southwest by defeating the Visigoths at the Battle of Vouillé in 507, he was given an honorary consulship (whereas Theoderic had had a real one) and made the most of the contact:

> Letters reached Clovis from the Emperor Anastasius to confer the consulate on him. In Saint Martin's church he stood clad in a purple tunic and the military mantle, and he crowned himself with a diadem. He then rode out on his horse and with his own hand showered gold and silver coins among the people present all the way from the doorway of Saint Martin's church to Tours cathedral. From that day on he was called Consul or Augustus.

Figure 6 Gold medallion of Theoderic, who holds a little winged Victory bearing a palm and holding out a laurel wreath. The reverse of the medallion has another Victory and an inscription calling King Theoderic *victor gentium*, 'conqueror of the (barbarian) peoples', from whom he was again apparently regarded as somehow different. (Photo: Deutsches Archäologisches Institut, Rome)

The passage, admittedly written much later in the century by Bishop Gregory of Tours in his *Histories*, blurs distinctions in a way that would have been inconceivable in Ostrogothic Italy. So does the title of the chapter (II.38) in which it occurs: 'Concerning the Patriciate of King Clovis'. To be consul was not to be emperor, 'Augustus'. The patriciate was not an office but a rank, the highest in the empire, which was held by Theoderic and the king of the Burgundians, and may well have been bestowed on Clovis, too. By the time of Gregory of Tours, the Roman Empire had actually come closer to the kingdom of the Franks than it was in Clovis's day. A great deal had happened in the Mediterranean to which we must now turn.

Justinian's Reconquest

In 527 an extraordinarily able emperor, or rather imperial couple, came to power: Justinian and Theodora. While the great church of Holy Wisdom in Constantinople (which still stands, see Figure 7) and Justinian's codification of

Figure 7 The interior of Hagia Sophia, built in Constantinople in 532–37, is still better caught by an artist's eye than a camera's. (After G. Fossati, *Aya Sofia*, London, 1852)

Roman law (which is still used) are well recognised legacies, the effect of Justinian's Reconquest of western Mediterranean lands in ending the Ancient world and defining medieval Europe has only recently been appreciated. The aforementioned architectural and legal projects were underway when Justinian sent a military force against Vandal North Africa, to be followed by the invasion of Ostrogothic Italy and eventually of Visigothic Spain. His motives for doing so are not certainly known. Clearly the Reconquest began at a time of marked imperial energy and resource, aided by the full treasury that Emperor Anastasius left to his successors. The usual explanation of Justinian's overall strategy, if he had one, is that he was attempting to restore Roman boundaries, but it has also been suggested that he was crusading against the Arians, picking off their kingdoms one by one. True, the Catholic Frankish kingdom was not attacked, but Frankish–Byzantine relations can be otherwise accounted for, as will become apparent later. When looking at the fullest extent of the Reconquest (see Map 2.2), one is tempted to conclude that the Roman aim was to get back all of the coastline of the Mediterranean and make it again *mare nostrum*, 'our sea'.

Be that as it may, the initial attack on the Vandal kingdom in 533 is not surprising. Already in the Introduction mention has been made of how back in the fifth century there had been four unsuccessful East Roman expeditions sent to get the Vandals out of Africa, but not in aid of any other part of the West. Justinian's was the fifth, and under the command of his great general Belisarius it succeeded in sixth months. The eyewitness historian Procopius has Belisarius tell his troops that the emperor had attacked the Vandals in order to relieve the suffering of the formerly Roman population (extensively plundered and dispossessed under Vandal kings who, in contrast to Theoderic and most other Arian rulers, persecuted Roman Catholics). Procopius also quotes a letter from Justinian to the Vandals saying that all the Romans wanted to do was to overthrow a tyrant usurper and restore their rightful king. When the usurper Gelimer had his deposed predecessor Hilderic killed as his enemies approached, the Vandal kingdom was brought to an end by the victorious Byzantines. In what we would call cultural genocide, the Vandals were shipped out of Africa, many of the men to serve in the imperial army against the Persians in the East, and were lost to history as a people. As had been the case in Vandal Africa, so next in Italy a royal dispute gave the imperial forces occasion to intervene. There it was to avenge the murder of Amalasuintha, daughter of Theoderic and niece of Clovis, who after the deaths earlier of her husband Eutharicus and eventually of her son Athalaric was left in a difficult position, which the murder of her Gothic opponents did not improve.

The Byzantine reconquest of Italy took many agonising years (535–54, with additional problems until 561) and by the end of it the senatorial aristocracy, which had survived the difficulties of the fifth century and flourished under Theoderic, had been smashed. Paradoxically, restoring Italy to the Roman Empire meant the end of Roman Italy, inasmuch as its elite had set the cultural tone. Procopius gives this account of conditions in Rome itself after it fell to the Goths in 546:

> And thus the Romans in general, and particularly the members of the senate, found themselves reduced to such straits that they clothed themselves in the garments of slaves and rustics, and lived by begging bread or any other food from their enemies; a very notable example of this change of

Map 2.2 Justinian's Reconquest

fortune being that of Rusticiana, the daughter of Symmachus, who had been the wife of Boethius, a woman who was always lavishing her wealth upon the needy. Indeed these wretches went about to all the houses and kept knocking at the doors and begging that they give them food, feeling no shame in doing so.

He says that the victorious Gothic king Totila was praised for protecting the women of Rome from rape. The city was to change hands twice more between the forces of Belisarius and Totila, most successful of the Ostrogothic kings during the reconquest before his death in battle against an imperial army under Narses, Belisarius's replacement. In northeast Italy the city of Ravenna fared better. There the beautiful church of San Vitale bears mosaic portraits of Emperor Justinian and Empress Theodora on either side of the apse leading to the altar. Back in Theoderic's church of Sant' Apollinare Nuovo, the Ostrogoths were 'mosaicked out' of the picture as we have seen. Ravenna ultimately became the headquarters of the exarch, an imperial official combining civil and military responsibility.

A useful perspective on the Reconquest is provided by following the extraordinary career of Liberius. It began under King Odoacar, after whose death in 493 Liberius served King Theoderic and his successors, including in a military capacity, until in 534 as an envoy to Emperor Justinian from King Theodahad, husband of Amalasuintha, he told the emperor that the king had imprisoned her. After this Liberius switched to Roman service, first in the East but later in the West. There he commanded the last phase of Justinian's Reconquest, the invasion of the Visigothic kingdom in 552 (again an intervention in a dynastic dispute) which led to the establishment of a Roman province in southeast Spain. Finally, Liberius had a major role in setting up the Roman administration in Italy in accordance with Justinian's Pragmatic Sanction of 554, and died there at the age of 89. Liberius was one of many Roman aristocrats who served barbarian kings. Secular office-holding came naturally to such people. In particular he illustrates the continuity of the senatorial aristocracy in Italy; his son was a consul. Clearly a survivor, Liberius is representative of an exodus of this elite from impending disaster in the Ostrogothic kingdom, though others stayed longer than he. Note that a career in the Roman East was open to him, a little like someone from a settler society serving in the British Empire, perhaps in Britain itself, a century or so ago. Liberius's last activity holds out the promise of a real restoration of Roman rule in Italy.

Yet Justinian's Reconquest reveals the extent to which the Western kingdoms had begun to go their own way. The aristocracy of Roman background had made the necessary accommodations. With the exception of Vandal Africa, Arian rule was not that bad for them. In fifth-century sources we read only of regret at the end of Roman rule, but when Roman rule was reimposed in the sixth century there is little sign that it was welcomed – it meant a more efficient tax regime, for one thing. Initially, of course, reconquest meant invading armies with danger to property if not life. Procopius stresses, including by what is cited above, the efforts of Belisarius, not always successful, to keep his troops from despoiling the North Africans, lest they make common cause with the Vandals. The following cases from Spain and Italy are suggestive. Although they were from Cartagena, which became part of the Byzantine province, the family that produced two leading lights of Spanish Catholic culture, Isidore and Leander of Seville, preferred life in the Visigothic kingdom. Leander wrote to his sister counselling her against going back 'where Mother is afraid'. (Isidore of Seville will be discussed in the next chapter.) The other takes us back to Cassiodorus, who wrote the letter for Theoderic to Boethius about the harper with which this chapter began. He continued to serve in the Ostrogothic kingdom after the reconquest of Italy began. Eventually he, like Liberius, overstayed on a diplomatic mission to Constantinople but did not enter Roman service; after the Reconquest he too returned to Italy, where, however, he founded a monastery and cultivated learning.

Having mentioned monasticism, and before gauging further the effects of Justinian's Reconquest, we must pause to remark, as is often not done, that Italy at that time contained the monasteries of Benedict of Nursia, whose practice would eventually become standard in Western monasticism. To appreciate the significance of this, some deep background is necessary. In the earliest centuries of Christianity there were ascetics, individuals engaging in exercises intended to cultivate the spirit at the expense of the body (much prayer, no sex, reduced food and an overall simple lifestyle) in their own homes. Monasticism entailed a further separation of ascetics from ordinary society. Originating in the desert of Egypt around AD 300, the monastic movement spread to the West later in the fourth century. Christians renounced the world and, isolating themselves from it, became monks and nuns in order that they might follow Christ more perfectly, and often placed themselves under the guidance of masters of what they sought. This guidance could take the form of a defined set of instructions for communal living, the monastic rule. While the authority of abbots and abbesses over their monastic communities was absolute, there was little if any control over their arrangements; indeed, the relationship of monasticism to the institutional Church was ill defined. Nevertheless, the spread of monasticism was accompanied and accomplished by enthusiasm, and the Church valued its enthusiasts. By the time Benedict wrote his Rule, around 535–45, there were various monastic rules in existence and, not surprisingly, he seems in part to have reworked someone else's. Yet, in setting out how monastic life was to be structured, Benedict showed genius.

The Rule of St Benedict is practicable. It tells how to set up a community along lines conducive to the salvation of its members: regular praying together to God, a self-denying ascetic lifestyle, humble obedience to others, occupation in manual labour, and edifying reading. The appeal of this Rule is often attributed to its relative moderation. It says of the monastery: 'We have, therefore, to establish a school of the Lord's service, in the setting forth of which we hope to order nothing that is harsh or rigorous' (Prologue). It says of the abbot: 'He must know that he hath undertaken the charge of weakly souls, and not a tyranny over the strong' (ch. 27). It says of the monks: 'And if the needs of the place, or their poverty, oblige them to labour themselves at gathering in the crops, let them not be saddened thereat; because then are they truly monks, when they live by the labour of their hands, as did our fathers and the Apostles. Yet let all be done with moderation, on account of the faint-hearted' (ch. 48). Yet even more impressive perhaps was the ordered completeness of the Rule of St Benedict. At the end of the sixth century it was endorsed by Pope Gregory I, by the beginning of the ninth century it was insisted on by the Carolingian rulers of much of Europe, although there were fringe areas to which it still had not spread by the end of the period covered by this book. Out of the wreck of Roman Italy the Rule of St Benedict passed on Roman organisation to medieval Europe.

To return to the effects of Justinian's Reconquest, there is a paradox that campaigns supposed to restore the empire in the West in fact contributed to the end of the Roman way of life there. The ultimate key to the paradox is that most of the area reconquered could not be held. The Byzantine Empire was increasingly preoccupied with attacks of Slavs, Bulgars and Avars from the north into the Balkans and with renewed conflict with the Persian Empire. In 568 the Germanic Lombards entered Italy from the northeast overland and quickly established themselves in the north and south, leaving to the Byzantines a diagonal belt of territory from Ravenna to Rome, a scatter of coastal cities and the far south of Italy. Lombards had fought in the last stage of the Reconquest as allies of the Byzantines and presumably had seen Italy as a land of opportunity to be grasped. Between the Lombard kingdom in the north and Lombard duchies in the south, central Italy was none too secure, Already by the end of the sixth century the bishop of Rome was stepping into the power vacuum in the part that looked to his city, with Pope Gregory the Great describing himself in a letter as 'the emperor's paymaster in Rome'. We will return to Gregory later in this chapter. It is worth pointing out that today's Vatican City is the direct descendent of these arrangements: the last little bit of Roman Empire that was never again conquered by anyone else. In Spain the Byzantine province shrank and did not outlast the first quarter of the seventh century, when the peninsula was unified for the first time under the Visigothic kings, who were now Catholic. More will be said about Visigothic Spain at the end of the Chapter 3; for now suffice it to say that the Visigothic kingdom was stronger rather than weaker after the Roman incursion.

Justinian's partially failed Reconquest contributed importantly to ending Mediterranean unity, and in this sense to ending the Ancient world and defining medieval Europe. As we have seen, the coming of the Lombards added fragmentation to the ruin of Roman Italy, and what happened in Italy mattered a great deal in the birth of Europe. There are signs of a wider fragmentation of the Mediterranean world in the later sixth century. Here archaeology can help by providing humble and prosaic evidence for changes of great historical significance. In late Antiquity the wealthiest people used silver dishes, a step below that was glass, and between glass and wood was pottery tableware. Finds of the latter, looking to the untrained eye like pieces of flowerpot, occur extensively on archaeological sites around the Mediterranean. The distribution of types of this late Roman pottery, after earlier Mediterranean-wide expansion from centres of mass production in Asia Minor and North Africa, breaks up into regions in the later sixth century. Politically and to some extent culturally, the partial success of the Reconquest split the Mediterranean more or less diagonally between the part that looked to Constantinople and the part that did not. For a Western capital was never re-established and the reconquered lands remained on the periphery of an Eastern-focused empire. Finally, nothing shows better the different European perspective that will develop than the view of North Africa, which was successfully reattached to the Roman Empire. As already mentioned in the Introduction, it went from being the part of the West most worth reconquering to non-Western. That change starts here.

Coinciding with the Reconquest, but affecting a greater area, was an outbreak of bubonic plague. While many people have heard of the Black Death of the late Middle Ages, few know that the period began with its equivalent. Disease in the past is difficult to identify, but this had the key features of bubonic plague: swellings in the groin and armpits and recurring outbreaks. According to Procopius, who gives a long and detailed account, the plague appeared in Egypt in 542 and spread in the next year to Constantinople, where he was present. Procopius records the enormous mortality and the utter bewilderment of people (including doctors) about the causes of the disease, which did not seem to spread from the sick to people caring for them, but inexplicably struck down others. Human-to-human transmission of bubonic plague is indeed uncommon, and the animal vectors of the disease (fleas) were not understood. Procopius also stresses the universal spread of the disease: to the Roman Empire, the Persians (with whom the Romans were also at war) and the barbarians. The Mediterranean Sea would have acted as a conduit, and Procopius reports, doubtless rightly, that the plague always spread from the coast to the interior. It would have protracted the wars of the day. A description by Gregory of Tours of a later outbreak in 590 in the Rome of Pope Gregory the Great brings out the lethal quality:

> My deacon, who was present, said that while the people were making their supplication to the Lord, eighty individuals fell dead to the ground. The Pope never stopped preaching to the people, nor did the people pause in their prayers.
>
> (*Histories*, X.1)

Whereas the Black Death struck in the fourteenth century when Europe's population had just peaked, the sixth-century plague came when population was already low.

Quoting Gregory of Tours brings us back to the Frankish kingdom, which was never attacked in Justinian's Reconquest. In 534, the year after that began, the Franks absorbed the Burgundian kingdom to their southeast. In 536, the year after the Italian campaign began; they took over Provence with imperial and

Ostrogothic agreement. This gave the Franks a Mediterranean coastline for the first time. Sometime between 539 and 547, the Frankish king Theudebert wrote to Justinian:

> You have deigned to concern yourself with the question of who we were and in what provinces we lived . . . By the grace of God we have conquered the Thuringians, acquired their territory and destroyed their royal family; the Swabians [Alamans] are now subject to our majesty; the Saxons and the Eucii have placed themselves voluntarily in our hands; our domain stretches as far as the Danube, the borders of Pannonia, and the ocean.

In context this reads like assertive posturing in the face of a potential aggressor: 'don't attack us, we're too strong'.[5] As it turned out, the Byzantines were to need the Franks as allies in attempting to hold Italy. The Franks took the imperial gifts and followed their own interests, which did not favour long-term involvement in Italy yet. The success of the Franks is a major theme in the history of early medieval Europe. At the beginning of the sixth century Clovis's and Theoderic's kingdoms were roughly equally balanced, but in the middle of the century the latter was destroyed by Justinian's Reconquest and by century's end the Lombards controlled only parts of Italy. The Franks had taken over the Ostrogothic protectorate along the Danube and established one of their own along their eastern frontier (although any claim to Saxony was wildly exaggerated). With good reason you are told to watch the Franks!

Frankish Society

Gregory of Tours's long and detailed *Histories* offers a valuable contemporary view of society in the Frankish kingdom in the later sixth century. Background on this author and source will be provided in a comparison with the *Chronicle* of John Malalas of Antioch in the Eastern Mediterranean which follows later in this chapter. Here we will do as Gregory does, and jump straight into an episode, which is quoted in full. As you read it, ask yourself: 'who are the authorities in this situation?'

> VII.29. In the meantime King Guntram sent a certain Claudius with these instructions: 'If you will go and drag Eberulf out of Saint Martin's church, and then either kill him with your sword or load him with chains, I will reward you richly; but, whatever else you do, I enjoin you not to damage the sacred building itself.' Claudius set out for Paris immediately. He was an empty-headed and greedy fellow. His wife came from the Meaux area. He debated with himself whether or not he should go to see Queen Fredegund. 'If I do see her, she, too, may give me some reward. After all, I know very well that she is the personal enemy of the man whom I am sent to kill.' He did visit the Queen and he was immediately loaded with presents. What is

more, he elicited from her the promise of much more, if only he would drag Eberulf out of the church and kill him, or capture him by some subterfuge or other and load him with chains, or, indeed, even cut him down in the vestibule of the church. Claudius went back to Châteaudun and ordered the Count to put three hundred men under his command to garrison the gates of the city of Tours. In effect, once he reached Tours, he was going to use these men to destroy Eberulf. The local Count called up three hundred of his men and Claudius made his way to Tours. While he was riding along he began to look out for auguries, as the barbarous Franks always do, and his conclusion was that they were unfavourable. He also questioned a number of people as to whether or not Saint Martin had recently exercised his miraculous power against those who had broken faith, and especially as to whether vengeance was exacted immediately from anyone who did wrong to those who put their hopes in the Saint. He rode on ahead of the men who were supposed to give him support and came to the church. Without more ado he went up to the ill-fated Eberulf. He gave Eberulf his solemn word, and swore by all that he held holy, and even by the miraculous power of the saintly Bishop whose remains lay just beside them, that no one could be more faithful to his cause and no one could represent that cause so well to the King. The pathetic creature had formed this plan in his mind: 'I shall never get the better of him unless I trick him by swearing these oaths to him.' When Eberulf heard Claudius promise these things and swear oaths about them in the church itself and in the portico and in the other vener-ated parts of the vestibule, the poor fool believed the man who was perjur-ing himself. The next day, when I myself was staying in a country manor some thirty miles away from the city, Eberulf was invited to a meal in the church-house. Claudius and a number of the citizens were present. Claudius would have struck Eberulf down there and then with his sword, if the man's servants had not been so close. Eberulf was unobservant and he noticed nothing. When the meal was over, Eberulf and Claudius walked up and down the forecourt of the church-house, swearing faith and friendship to each other, with a running exchange of oaths. As they were chatting, Claudius said to Eberulf: 'It would give me great pleasure to come and have a drink in your lodging, if the wine were mixed with spices, or if you, my noble friend, would order up a stoup of stronger drink.' Eberulf was delighted when he heard this. He said that he had exactly what Claudius was thinking of. 'You will find all that you want in my lodging', he said, 'provided, my noble lord, that you will deign to enter the poor hovel in which I live.' He then sent his servants, first one and then another, to fetch more potent wines, those of Latium and Gaza. When Claudius saw that all Eberulf's servants had gone off and that he was left alone, he lifted up his hand in the direction of the church and said: 'Holy Martin, bring it about that I soon may see my wife and my relations again!' The wretched man was now on the horns of a dilemma: he was planning to murder Eberulf in the vestibule and he feared the miraculous power of the saintly Bishop. One of the servants of Claudius who was stronger than the rest seized Eberulf from behind, clasped him tight in his powerful arms, and held him with his chest stuck out so that his throat could the more easily be cut. Claudius drew his sword from his baldric and aimed a blow at Eberulf. Although he was gripped so tight, Eberulf drew a dagger from his belt and prepared to strike Claudius. Claudius raised his right hand high in the air and stuck his knife into Eberulf's chest. With a great effort Eberulf planted his own dagger under Claudius armpit and then withdrew it and with a lunging blow cut off Claudius's thumb. Claudius's servants then came running back from all directions with their swords drawn and stabbed Eberulf in a number of places. He slipped out of their hands and started to run, although he was already mortally wounded. They struck him a mighty blow on the head with a naked sword. He fell down, with his brains scattered. It was too much for him to expect to be saved by Saint Martin, for he had never known what it was to pray to the Saint with a contrite heart. Claudius was terrified by what had happened and sought refuge in the Abbot's cell, seeking protection from one whose patron he had never had the sense to reverence. The Abbot was there and Claudius said to him: 'A frightful crime has been committed and if you do not help me I shall be killed!' As he said this Eberulf's men rushed up with their swords and spears at the ready. They shattered the glass panes and hurled their spears through the windows in the wall. Claudius was already half dead and they transfixed him with one of the blows. His own men were hiding behind the doors and under the beds. Two of the church-men present seized hold of the Abbot and dragged him out more dead than alive through the line of naked swords. The doors were opened wide and the band of armed men marched in. Some of the beggars who regularly received alms at the church and a number of other poor folk were so incensed at the crime that they tried to pull the roof off the cell. Then certain men who were possessed of devils and a number of other wretched creatures seized sticks and stones and rushed to avenge the violence done to their church, bearing it ill that such atrocities as had never been witnessed before should now have been perpetrated there. What more can I tell you? Those who had taken refuge were dragged from their hiding-places and cruelly put to death. The floor of the Abbot's cell reeked with blood. The dead bodies were pulled out and left to lie naked on the ground. The killers seized what loot they could and disappeared into the darkness which had now fallen. The vengeance of God was not slow to fall on those who had defiled His holy house with blood; but the wrong-doing of the man Eberulf, whom Saint Martin had permitted to endure all this, was certainly very great.

King Guntram was furious at what had happened, but he calmed down when he learned the full details. All the property of this unhappy man, his personal possessions and the real estate which he had inherited from his ancestors, Guntram distributed among his own supporters, who left Eberulf's wife, now reduced to penury, to the care of Saint Martin's church.

Their near relations carried away the corpses of Claudius and the others, and buried them in their own country.

The authorities, in order of appearance, are as follows. King Guntram gives instructions and offers reward for the assassination of Eberulf. At the end he confiscates and gives away the property of his victim to his supporters. Queen Fredegund, who is approached separately, gives reward and promises more. Claudius by virtue of his royal mission gives orders to the Count of Châteaudun. He commands 300 soldiers who are to support him. Later mention is made of his servants and men. The Count had command over the soldiers which he transfers to Claudius. Claudius credits the authority of pagan auguries when he looks to see if they are favourable or unfavourable. Saint Martin of Tours is a supernatural character in Gregory's *Histories*: he is three times said to have miraculous power, could have saved Eberulf but permitted his death, and is the patron of the abbot. The authority of what Claudius held holy validates his oaths. Eberulf has servants to send on errands and men to avenge his death. Gregory's audience would have recognised the abbot as an authority figure, the absolute leader of monks; what the passage shows is Claudius's expectation that he could offer protection. Even the possessed were held to wield a weird kind of authority in Gregory's world, for they could make known the will of the ultimate authority, which extended even over demons. This was God, to whom Gregory left vengeance, but King Guntram did not: he wanted Eberulf dead, as Gregory had explained a few chapters before, in order to avenge the death of his brother whom he thought Eberulf had killed.

The point is that there were various, sometimes conflicting authorities in this disorderly society. Authority structures were not clearly articulated. Formal, public ones (king and count) existed beside, and intermingled with, informal, private patronage and the need for supporters. As bishop of Tours, Gregory himself had to utilise every available back-up, including writing passages like this one, to his ecclesiastical office, which was not secure in authority. Telling of how the power of God through St Martin was exercised in a messy situation at Tours reinforced the position of Gregory, sixteenth in apostolic succession to St Martin as bishop of Tours. Social structure was fluid. Queen Fredegund had the necessary connection and wealth to be a patron, but she was originally a slave. So was Leudast, former count of Tours, at this point deceased and unlamented by Gregory. Not only did rules say one thing and people do another, but conflicting sets of rules sat side by side for the same people: Christian morality and the ethos of family vengeance were not compatible. Lest the latter be thought of as something that came in with the barbarians, it is instructive to see who is feuding in Gregory of Tours's *Histories*. Some of their names are Roman and some Germanic, and while these may not indicate ethnic background – Claudius who acted 'as barbarous Franks always do' had a Roman name – in a couple of cases the feuding parties were Jews, who are most unlikely to be of barbarian descent. Rather, family vengeance is best seen as a general social response to the breakdown of law and order, as was suggested for the initial case study in Chapter 1, which would happen more quickly in modern societies than we would comfortably admit.

An episode in which vengeance affected Gregory's own family (*Histories* V.5) reveals a small world of ill-defined social relationships and intense competition. Here the context is ecclesiastical, but the motivation is by no means always religious. Gregory's brother Peter was a deacon under Gregory's saintly great-uncle, Bishop Tetricus of Langres. Peter was also what would be called nowadays a 'whistleblower', having helped to get a fellow-deacon, Lampadius, dismissed from his position on the grounds that he was taking from, rather than giving to, the poor. Lampadius proved to be a dangerous enemy to Peter when the episcopate of Langres was destabilised by a set of unrelated factors: Bishop Tetricus had a stroke, his replacement ran afoul of a king and was exiled, and the new bishop-elect, Silvester, another relative of Gregory and Tetricus, died of epilepsy before he could be consecrated. Silvester, apparently not yet a priest when chosen bishop, had a son, who was provoked into taking vengeance for his father's death by Lampadius' accusation that Peter had killed Silvester by magic. The idea was that Peter wanted to be bishop himself. Although Peter swore formally before witnesses that he had done nothing of the kind, he was eventually killed by Silvester's son. Gregory of Tours left vengeance to God, but it took a curious form: the son later murdered another man, whose avenging relatives killed him in turn! Gregory does not seem to be altogether immune to their way of thinking. The murky situation outlined here is just the sort liable to have produced accusations of witchcraft, which were not made only against women. Magic and attitudes to it in the early Middle Ages are discussed in Chapter 7. For now we will leave this glimpse of 'the alien cunning of small, face-to-face societies in a distant past', in Peter Brown's wonderful phrase from his lecture cited in a note to the Introduction, and look at a much bigger picture.

Gregory's *Histories* and Malalas's *Chronicle*

A good deal can be learned about the Byzantine Empire and the West in the sixth century by comparing the context, content and perspectives of these two historical works written in this period, one in the Frankish kingdom and the other in the Byzantine East. While extensive use has so far been made of the *Histories*[6] of Gregory of Tours, the *Chronicle* of John Malalas of Antioch (present-day Antakya in Turkey) will become known through a comparison that can start with the authors. Judging from their respective historical coverage, Gregory was a much younger contemporary of Malalas. They lived 2000 miles apart and never got much closer. Both men had access to others who had travelled more widely, in Gregory's case to those who had been to Constantinople and even Antioch, while Malalas had informants about Persia and the Arab south. Both men lived in cities. There were counts in the worlds of both: Gregory had the above-mentioned Count Leudast and refers to many more in his *Histories*, while Antioch was the headquarters of the Count of the East, a very important Roman official.

Malalas was a bureaucrat probably in the office of the count of the East; Gregory was bishop of Tours (573–94) and a more important man than Malalas. The ancestors of both men were Romans, but for Gregory the empire was a memory and a distant presence, while for Malalas it was a present reality. Malalas lived in a very old world: he could look back on 800 years of uninterrupted history and culture at Antioch. His is a real voice of Late Antiquity, of Hellenistic Graeco-Roman culture. He was a Christian who delighted in fitting Christian and old Greek history, including lots of pagan myth, into chronological order. Gregory of Tours does not have this Hellenistic inheritance. His Roman content is very Christian, and he gets through it quickly.

Both Gregory and Malalas wrote major historical works: Gregory's *Histories* is twice as long as Malalas's *Chronicle*. Both of them start with the creation of the world and go on to their author's own time, which is covered in Books 16–18 by Malalas, but in Books 4–10 by Gregory, who obviously provided much more contemporary history. Gregory wrote in Latin, Malalas in Greek, but there are similarities in the sort of Latin and Greek that they wrote. Gregory's Latin is substandard and full of grammatical errors; in other words, it is beginning to turn into French, a language structured on different principles. For contemporaries like Procopius, the historian of the Reconquest, who could and did write in the language and style of classical greats like Thucydides. Malalas's Greek would have been regarded as far too colloquial, closer to what ordinary people were speaking. Gregory of Tours's *Histories* is more religious in content, John Malalas's *Chronicle* more secular. This is true even though Antioch had religious prestige and saints to rival Martin of Tours: the apostles Peter and Paul as well as Simeon Stylites, but Malalas doesn't go on about them. In part this is a contrast between the writings of bureaucrat and bishop, but also a reflection of the greater secular element in learned culture of the (very religious) Byzantine Empire. There is much more about women in Gregory of Tours's *Histories* than in Malalas's *Chronicle*. The latter's passing reference to the formidable Boa, queen of the Sabir Huns, pales into insignificance beside all that Gregory tells us about Fredegund, or, much more positively, Radegund (see Figure 8), whose holiness and skill with patronage networks made her also formidable, and whose lengthy letter on behalf of her monastery at Poitiers Gregory gives us in full.

The two historians have in common a focus on their own region and city. Gaul is featured even in Book I of Gregory's *Histories*, which after that is almost entirely about Gaul, especially Tours. Malalas brings in Antioch where he can, and eventually Constantinople, so much so that it is thought that he actually moved there. Both works are full of cities, and the similar late Antique nature of these can be seen by comparing two episodes. In the *Histories* (V.18), a Frankish king was angry when Gregory of Tours was reported to have opposed his interests at a church council. His consequent threat took an interesting form: he would assemble the people of Tours and give them a bad slogan to chant about Gregory, thereby undermining the bishop's position. In Malalas's *Chronicle* (XVI.19), the people of Constantinople rioted against an emperor's religious innovation. There the slogan of the mob was nothing less than: 'A new emperor for the Roman

Figure 8   There is nothing against the traditional attribution of this carved wooden reading desk, preserved at the Couvent des Dames de Sainte-Croix at Poitiers, to Radegund, who founded the monastery for women there in the sixth century and obtained for it a relic of the Holy Cross from Emperor Justin II and Empress Sophia in Constantinople; indeed, the reading desk may have been an associated Eastern gift. (Photo: Editions Gallimard, Paris)

state!' Yet Antioch (even more so Constantinople) and Tours were very different places, like comparing one of our major cities with a country town. Antioch had been founded by one of the successors of Alexander the Great, part of the spread of Greek civilisation in the Near East that is referred to above as 'Hellenistic'. Rome had acquired Antioch by bequest not conquest, and Antioch flourished as one of the greatest cities of the Roman Empire right up into the sixth century, when it suffered repeated devastation by earthquakes and the Persians. Tours, on the other hand, was tiny by comparison. It had been the Roman administrative centre of the territory of one conquered Celtic tribe, the *Turones*. Places like Tours are a testimony to the extent of Romanisation in northern Europe. Its significance began with the cult of its saintly bishop and monk Martin of Tours (d.397).[7]

Most importantly, what does each historian know about the other's region? Malalas does not say a lot about the West, and what he does say tends to be about Italy. In the first, mythological book of his *Chronicle*, Picus Zeus, presented as a man misunderstood as a god, is said to have 'reigned over the West, that is, Italy'. Malalas's statement that Emperor Claudius 'built Bretannia, a city near the Ocean' shows the geographical limitations of his knowledge – so much for Roman Britain! The crumbling of the Western Roman Empire gets a little attention. According to Malalas's *Chronicle*, Alaric harmed no one when he sacked Rome in 410. Gaul is not mentioned before the fifth century and the closest the chronicler gets to Tours is when, in connection with the formation of a Roman–barbarian alliance against Attila in Gaul, he alludes to the latter's attacks on cities there. The Vandals' sack of Rome and subsequent negotiations with the eastern Romans get particular attention; note the interest in North Africa. If one knows the history of the Reconquest one can follow it in a sketchy way via Malalas. The greatest space he gives to anything Western, however, is his account of an Italian showman who toured the East (presumably including Antioch) with trick dogs who could recognise the emperor's picture on coins and identify adulterers in a crowd – and never made a mistake!

Gregory writes more about the East than Malalas about the West. He mentions several emperors there including Anastasius, who made Clovis an honorary consul, and Tiberius, about whom he says the same sort of things as his Byzantine contemporaries did. Gregory is a source for Byzantine–Frankish diplomacy, including those gold payments for help against the Lombards, although he only mentions Justinian's reconquest of Spain. Then there is the fascinating episode of Gundovald the Pretender, who, not acknowledged by the royal Frankish father he claimed, went to live in Constantinople from where he was enticed to return by trouble-making nobles in France. Gregory knows of a doctor from Constantinople, and hermits who relished herbs imported from Egypt. Finally, while Malalas never mentions Tours, Gregory does mention Antioch: its early bishops and pillar-sitting saint Simeon, who was considered to be an inappropriate model for a holy man in a northern climate, and its contemporary sack by the Persians. Gregory is unclear as to where Antioch is located, placing it at one point in Egypt and at another in Armenia (it was really in Syria), which is worrying, but his source of information is really interesting. Gregory has spoken in Tours to a Bishop Simon who had been captured by the Persians, was ransomed, and had come West seeking assistance. And here he includes in the *Histories* (X.24) an Antioch earthquake story such as one reads in Malalas's *Chronicle*. Thus, this comparison has indicated that for Gregory of Tours the Eastern connections are still there and his world looked to Constantinople to some extent. John Malalas of Antioch, on the other hand, looked to Constantinople or further east, not to the West.

The World of Pope Gregory the Great

This chapter will conclude with another Gregory, whom we have already glimpsed as pope paying imperial soldiers and raising morale in plague-stricken

Rome, for his career sums up various developments we have been considering. He was one of the last to hold the ancient office of Prefect of the City of Rome, which like the Senate ceased to exist before the end of the sixth century; from 590–604 he was pope. Over the fifth and sixth centuries, Rome had been changing into an ecclesiastical centre, and as bishop of that city Gregory ornamented the graves of the apostles Peter and Paul there. After all that Rome had suffered, it was still, as *The Book of the Popes* makes clear, a repository of wealth in silver and gold and precious fabric. As pope, Gregory was responsible for some new beginnings. His phrase 'servant of the servants of God' is still used by popes to describe themselves. The first monk to become pope, Gregory favoured the monastic Rule of St Benedict, drawn up in Italy during the Reconquest as already stated, and he patronised the codification of church music which still bears his name as 'Gregorian chant', although the Europe-wide use of both of these was due to their promotion in the Frankish Empire two centuries later. Nor was this all, as we shall see. Note that Gregory, although he was born and died in Rome and spent almost all of his life there, before becoming pope himself had been a papal representative in Constantinople, where he lived as a monk and did not learn Greek. Pope Gregory the Great belonged to the Mediterranean world, and he had to live with the consequences of Justinian's partially failed Reconquest. Of necessity this meant that he had to engage with the barbarian West.

As *de facto* ruler of the region around Rome, Gregory, despite imperial disapproval, entered into diplomatic negotiations with the Lombards, who sought to extend their control over Italy, and about whom something will be said here. He cultivated an alliance with their queen, Theudelinda, and gave her a gospel book, of which the jewelled golden covers have survived.[8] She was not a Lombard, but Bavarian. Yet it was said that she was so respected by the Lombards that after the death of her first husband, their king, they allowed her to pass on the kingship to the man she chose to marry. This was Agilulf, who appears on a plaque (Figure 9), which once decorated a helmet. He has the long beard for which his people were named, and sits enthroned between two Latin Victories (female personifications holding signs saying VICTURIA so that viewers will know what they are) that, in a wonderful example of cultural fusion, bear Germanic drinking horns. To Theudelinda we owe more information about Lombard appearance, as described from visual evidence by the historian Paul the Deacon two centuries later:

> There also [Monza, near Milan] the aforesaid queen built herself a palace, in which she caused to be painted something of the achievements of the Lombards. In this painting it is clearly shown in what way the Lombards at that time cut their hair, and what was their dress and what their appearance. They shaved the neck, and left it bare up to the back of the head, having their hair hanging down on the face as far as the mouth and parting it on either side by a part in the forehead. Their garments were loose and mostly linen, such as the Anglo-Saxons are wont to wear, ornamented with broad

Figure 9 Helmet-plaque of King Agilulf (ruled 590–615). This would have been attached across the front of the helmet, above the eyes. Gilded copper. (By concession of the Ministero dei Beni e le Attività Culturali; further reproduction is not permitted)

borders woven in various colours. Their shoes, indeed, were open almost up to the tip of the great toe, and were held on by shoe latchets interlacing alternately.

(*History of the Lombards*, IV.22)

It is interesting to see an early medieval writer making use of material remains of the past in this way. Pope Gregory stopped these people from taking over Rome; mainly by buying them off, drawing on revenues from the extensive papal estates, including 500 pounds of gold to Agilulf to end his siege of Rome.

Queen Theudelinda was Catholic, but King Agilulf was not; their son was baptised a Catholic. From the end of the sixth century Arianism lingered on only among the Lombards, whose kingship well into the next century would pass back and forth between adherents of these two versions of Christianity. By contrast, at the beginning of the sixth century only the Frankish kingdom had a Catholic ruler, Clovis, with whom the chapter started. If you turn back to Map 1.1 on page 13, the extent of religious, political and cultural change in this respect over the course of the sixth century can be appreciated. The Arian Vandal and Ostrogothic kingdoms had been eliminated in the Reconquest. The Burgundians and Sueves had converted from Arian to Catholic Christianity before their kingdoms were absorbed by powerful neighbours, the Frankish and Visigothic kingdoms, respectively. The Visigothic king, Reccared, instituted a top-down conversion of Arians in his kingdom in 589. Removal of this religious distinction was both part of and facilitated the merging of people under the common identity of their ruling group. Increasingly the Roman template of a Christian state was transferred to the kingdoms of early medieval Europe. Yet, in a previous section of this chapter, our examination of Frankish society has shown how poorly defined and weak authority structures were in one of these

Catholic kingdoms. It is important to realise how limited the power of the early medieval papacy was: aside from Gregory's qualified success with Theudelinda and the Lombards, none of the aforementioned developments, right back to the conversion of Clovis, had anything to do with the bishop of Rome.

At the end of the sixth century, however, Pope Gregory the Great, citizen of the Roman Empire, looked further afield, away from the Mediterranean and up to the northwest. In 597 he sent Augustine with a party of other monks to Britain to convert the pagan Anglo-Saxons to Christianity. This was a papal initiative and a tremendous innovation, the first 'mission' (which means literally 'a sending') to a pagan people, and it was to have consequences which will be considered in the next chapter and beyond. Here is how Gregory was remembered by the Anglo-Saxons. Among the extensive writings of this the most literary of all popes, which circulated widely and early and were fundamental to medieval thought, was a book of advice for those who have governance (Latin *regimen*) over the Church, its bishops. It was composed by Gregory soon after he became bishop of Rome and, most unusually for a Western work, translated into Greek a few years later. King Alfred the Great, who translated it into Old English, the language of the Anglo-Saxons, at the end of the ninth century, knew it as 'the book which in Latin is called *Pastoralis*, in English "Shepherd-book"'. The title derives from the image of the bishop as a shepherd (Latin *pastor*) of a flock of sheep, the Christians under his care; in modern English the book is usually called the *Pastoral Care*. King Alfred included the following preface in his native poetry, relating the book to the mission and praising its author in imagery that echoes the praise of warriors:

> Augustine brought this work from the south over the salt sea to the island-dwellers, exactly as the Lord's champion, the pope of Rome, had previously set it out. The wise Gregory was well versed in many doctrines through his mind's intelligence, his hoard of ingenuity. Accordingly, he won over most of mankind to the guardian of the heavens, this greatest of Romans, most gifted of men, most celebrated for his glorious deeds.

It is time to turn to the northern world. Although this chapter on the sixth century began with a comparison of Clovis in France and Theoderic in Italy, it has had much to say about East–West relations. The next chapter on the seventh century will be to a considerable extent about North and South in the birth of Europe.

Chapter 3 . . . .

The Seventh Century: Cultural Watershed

The Conversion of the English to Christianity

Above a river in Eastern England people put beautiful things into a grave within a ship, and covered it with an earthen mound. Thirteen hundred years later what had survived in the acidic soil came to light in one of the great archaeological discoveries of the twentieth century, the Sutton Hoo ship burial. One can only admire the skill and care of the excavators who revealed the outline of the ship from variations in the soil where its timbers had completely decayed and lumps of limonite where its iron rivets had rusted away.[1] (See Figure 10.) Readers are advised to view the Sutton Hoo finds in print or electronic media at this point and, best of all, directly in the British Museum, should this be possible at some time in your lives. Perhaps the most aesthetically pleasing are a pair of golden shoulder clasps that would have joined together pieces of fabric which were sewn to them. They are decorated with little metal compartments, into many of which have been placed a bit of gold foil imprinted with a design topped by a piece of red garnet exactly cut to fit the compartment and into a few, a section of checkerboard blue and black millifiori glass. The millifiori technique entails fusing several different-coloured rods of glass together so as to make a pattern in cross-section, and the cross-sections must also fit their compartments. The technique of decorating by little compartments, often filled with enamel, is called cloisonné. Some application of lines of tiny gold beads, known as filigree, also contributes to the decoration of the shoulder clasps. The astonishing technical standard of such objects from Sutton Hoo is unparalleled on the Continent of Europe, similar to the superiority of metalwork in Celtic Britain before it became a Roman province, which hints at continuing traditions of craftwork in Britain underlying changes like the establishment of English kingdoms there.

While much about the Sutton Hoo ship burial can be debated (for an example see the next paragraph), a couple of conclusions are both historically certain and useful. Somehow the objects came to be buried together in eastern England, and represent cultural contact over a very wide area as we shall see; moreover,

Figure 10 In-situ photographs of the 'ship' as excavated at Sutton Hoo in England. Although its form and construction can be seen clearly, and excavators could even tell that it had been repaired, the original materials from which the ship was made have not survived. (© The Trustees of the British Museum)

they are material evidence of the elite society that the Christian missionaries were approaching. The helmet, shield and burial in a ship are evidence of a Swedish connection, which is all the more interesting because written sources do not speak of it although the greatest Old English poem, *Beowulf*, is about a Swedish king. The Sutton Hoo ship burial is pre-Viking, but attests to a long-standing pattern of cultural contact in the North out of which the Vikings eventually came. The sword and coins (but not the purse which held them) show contact with the Frankish world to the south. The burial obviously cannot predate the latest of the coins, struck in 625. An earlier example of English links with the Franks was the marriage of Bertha, daughter of a Frankish king, to King Æthelbert of Kent, to whom the missionaries were sent by Pope Gregory the Great. The wonderful hanging bowl, inside of which was fastened a fish on a swivel, its scales coated with tin so it would glisten as it swam through whatever the bowl held, was decorated with patterns that show the principles of Celtic art still operating in post-Roman Britain. The cultural background of several of these artefacts was complex: for example, the helmet, so Swedish in some respects, has other characteristics which indicate that it was of English manufacture. There were also exotic imports: a bowl from Coptic Egypt, fabric from Italy and the Levant, and Byzantine silver.

Illustrated here are the pair of silver spoons from Sutton Hoo (see Figure 11). The lower spoon, inscribed with the name PAULOS in Greek letters, is an apostle spoon from the eastern Mediterranean, where it is thought to have been made in or near Constantinople *c.*AD 600. The apostle Paul in the first century AD worked to establish and maintain Christian communities in the Mediterranean as far west as Rome; his letters to them form a major part of the Christian New Testament. His own conversion as recorded there in the Book of Acts was dramatic, and was later thought to have led to an immediate change of his original name, Saul, to Paul. The upper spoon in the illustration, like a number of Sutton Hoo finds including the aforementioned shoulder clasps, is unique: while other Paul spoons are known, it is the only one that is inscribed SAULOS. The two spoons are alike in form; it is the inscriptions that differ, not only in the name but in how the letters were made. Minute analysis of the SAULOS inscription suggests that it was done in the West not the East. An elaborate argument has been constructed on the evidence of these two spoons: that they were a baptismal gift to a particular Anglo-Saxon king (see below), with the names on spoons symbolising his conversion to Christianity, like Saul to Paul. This argument can be questioned in every aspect, not least because of the possibility that the first letter of SAULOS is just the Greek letter π mistakenly turned on its side! As one of my students once remarked, these are mysteries and likely to remain so, and as such are of limited historical significance. The real historical significance of the spoons lies in the presence of these exotic objects with undoubted Christian features (small crosses and apostolic names) in the kingdom of East Anglia in the early seventh century. The Christian features of the spoons, whether or not these were meaningful at the point of burial, are

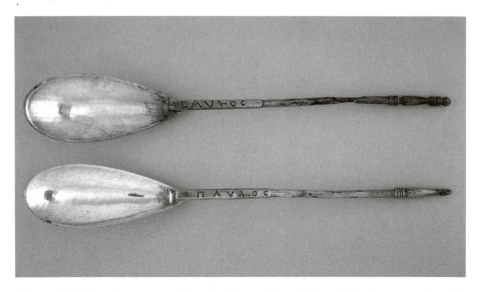

Figure 11 The silver spoons from the Sutton Hoo ship burial. As you read what the text has to say about them, ask yourself what contemporary Anglo-Saxons would have understood by these objects (© The Trustees of the British Museum)

just what would be expected in a region being missionised. The spread of Christianity was part of a wider process of cultural contact, and so were the reasons for its adoption.

To the early medieval rulers who chose the Christian religion for themselves and their people, conversion meant joining the club of civilised nations, not unlike the modern appeal of the European Community. This was not all that conversion meant, of course, and there were other sorts of conversion initiative besides royal, which were by no means exclusive of it or each other. Pastoral conversion initiative was that taken by priests and bishops to bring all of their flock into the Christian fold, and was very important in the conversion of the countryside. Papal was a special case of pastoral conversion initiative, and showed a developing sense of responsibility on the part of the pope for the universal welfare of souls. Monastic conversion initiative was a by-product of monasticism, in that monks would do their duty by pagans whom they came across when they withdrew to out-of-the-way places, or were deliberately established there for that very reason. Informal conversion initiative, operating through personal contact, should never be forgotten, for it was a factor even in the most harshly authoritarian of circumstances – not that authority within or outside of the family as in the case of lords and their followers was irrelevant to personal proselytising. Yet, before the end of the seventh century, every English kingdom had undergone a top-down conversion, where the king converted and brought his people to Christianity. We know about these matters from Bede, most respected of all early medieval historians, who wrote the *Ecclesiastical History of the English People* in the early eighth century from documents and oral testimony. For example, Aldwulf, king of East Anglia in Bede's lifetime, remembered seeing as a child the temple where a predecessor named Raedwald had one altar to Christ and another to the pagan gods. Sutton Hoo is in East Anglia and it is tempting to see the ship burial there as King Raedwald's grave, but we do not know.

The conversion of Bede's own kingdom of Northumbria in the first half of the seventh century involved complex cultural interchanges. In order that these can be understood, first some background is necessary on a part of Europe that has been little mentioned in previous chapters. In comparison to what had happened on the Continent, Britain was unusual in that some of the ex-Romano-British ruled themselves in kingdoms to the west and north rather than all being taken over by the Anglo-Saxons. The latter, that is the English, had established kingdoms in the east and south, as would be expected given their origins in coastal regions of the Continent on the other side of the North Sea.[2] There was also some Irish settlement, mainly in southwest Scotland. Map 3.1 shows how things stood by the early seventh century. The British, whose Christianity went back to Roman times, were true to their heritage and did not convert the pagan English barbarians to Christianity. Patrick's work among the Irish was an exception congruent with the pattern, as was pointed out in Chapter 1. The Irish themselves were to make a significant contribution to the spread of Christianity through monastic conversion initiative. By the sixth century an enthusiastic monastic movement was underway in Ireland. Some monks were moved to leave their native land altogether, in self-denying exile abroad to be further considered in the next section. In these circumstances the monastery of Iona was founded in the Irish colony in southwest Scotland. From Iona Christianity was spread to the Picts in northern Britain, and eventually to English Northumbria as we shall see. When Pope Gregory innovatively despatched his missionaries at the end of the sixth century, the English kingdoms were pagan, but Christianity was established in the rest of the British Isles.

The intricate nexus of conversion and culture in Northumbria can be seen by following the career of Abbess Hilda there, appropriately enough given that Bede's *Ecclesiastical History of the English People* has more space for women than any work of comparable scope before at least 1970. The account is best read with one eye on Map 3.1. Hilda was born into an English family with Northumbrian royal connections while her father was away in exile in a British kingdom (probably Elmet in the Midlands), where he was killed. She was baptised by Paulinus, whom Pope Gregory had also sent to Britain and who from 625 converted King Edwin of Northumbria and many others, until Edwin's defeat and death in battle all but undid his mission. Not long afterwards Oswald became king of Northumbria; he was already Christian, having been converted when in exile at the Irish monastery of Iona in southwest Scotland. Now he asked for monks to

Map 3.1 Britain in the early seventh century. Names of British (as opposed to English) kingdoms are italicised. The English kingdom of Northumbria comprised Bernicia and Deira

be sent from Iona to convert his kingdom, and ultimately Aidan and others came and accomplished this. Hilda was educated by these Irish, and in turn Bede credits her with having trained five future bishops in the double monastery of Whitby of which she was abbess. When trouble arose because the Irish differed in practices – but not in faith – from the Roman mission, a council was called to sort things out and met in Hilda's monastery: the Synod of Whitby in 664. She initially supported the Irish side, but accepted the council's decision that the Roman way was best. It is little wonder that the early Christian culture of Northumbria was so rich, given its hybrid vigour.

Civilisation Begins to Come Out of the North

The frontiers of the Roman Empire were zones of great cultural fertility, and the spread of Christianity in the British Isles bore remarkable fruit there and well beyond. At the beginning of the seventh century, the Irish monk Columbanus and his disciples went to northern Italy. There King Agilulf and Queen Theudelinda gave him land on which to found a monastery at Bobbio, where he died in 615. Within three years an Italian named Jonas became a monk at Bobbio, where he had access to those who had known Columbanus; later he spoke to others in France, and eventually wrote the *Life of Columbanus*. It offers a striking picture of Irish *peregrinatio*, self-denying perpetual pilgrimage, in terms which are neither vague nor all that conventional. In Ireland the young Columbanus, as a future monk, had a problem. As Jonas puts it, 'his fine figure, his splendid colour and his noble manliness' aroused 'the lust of lascivious maidens, especially of those whose fine figure and superficial beauty are wont to enkindle mad desires in the minds of wretched men' (actually Jonas says the devil did the arousing, of course). Columbanus was helped out of potential difficulty by an assertive Irish woman of a different kind, when 'he came to the dwelling of a holy and devout woman' who said this to him:

> I have gone forth to the strife as far as it lay in my power. Lo, twelve years have passed by, since I have been far from my home and have sought out this place of pilgrimage. With the aid of Christ, never since then have I engaged in secular matters; after putting my hand to the plough, I have not turned backward. And if the weakness of my sex had not prevented me, I would have crossed the sea and chosen a better place among strangers as my home. But you, glowing with the fire of youth, stay quietly on your native soil; out of weakness you lend your ear even against your own will, to the voice of the flesh, and think you can associate with the female sex without sin. But do you recall the wiles of Eve, Adam's fall, how Samson was deceived by Delilah, how David was led to injustice by the beauty of Bathsheba, how the wise Solomon was ensnared by the love of a woman? Away, O youth! away! flee from corruption into which, as you know, many have fallen. Forsake the path which leads to the gates of hell.

So Columbanus left his native province of Leinster in southeast Ireland, his home and family, literally over the body of his mother – she was alive but had thrown herself across the doorway to prevent him going – and went to study with a holy teacher named Sinilis and eventually joined the monastery of Bangor in northern Ireland. After many years as a monk and teacher there, Columbanus decided on the ultimate self-exile: to leave Ireland altogether. With his disciples he came via Brittany to the France of Gregory of Tours.

The contribution of people like Columbanus to the birth of Europe needs to be carefully assessed and kept in proportion. It has sometimes been claimed that the Irish saved Continental civilisation, but civilisation had not died out on the Continent, as we have seen. Columbanus was in correspondence with that prolific writer, Pope Gregory the Great, with whom the last chapter concluded. It is true that the Irish (and the English, see below) were a catalyst for monastic accomplishment including learning, which was mainly religious in content but stylistically in the tradition of Ancient grammar and rhetoric, and to which they brought a lively curiosity and ability to do a lot with what resources they had. Columbanus in particular made a real impression on the Continent. He was a religious revivalist, which in his time led to people joining monasteries. He founded three monasteries in France, of which Luxeuil is the best known, before his refusal to recognise the sons of one Frankish king as legitimate heirs made him *persona non grata* and he had to move on. The influence of Columbanus on Continental monasticism through his followers and the popularity of his monastic rule was wide. As for enthusiasm for learning, one can tell from what Jonas says about Columbanus that this was an important part of his tradition. The fine Latin that Columbanus himself wrote must have been the product of his Irish education, for which Jonas is a useful source. It was much better than the Latin of Jonas, who was writing his native language, which ultimately would turn into Italian, whereas Columbanus had learned his Latin well. By the end of the seventh century Bobbio had become an important cultural centre. True, the text of some older works was rubbed out as much as possible and then written over with new ones in what are called palimpsests, but this still shows attention to book learning. Monasteries like Bobbio and Luxeuil were cradles of European civilisation.

The British Isles had still more to offer, not least because the Irish inspired the English to monastic pilgrimage, conversion initiative and learning. There were cultural stimuli from the Mediterranean as well, to which the southern English monk and scholar Aldhelm referred as he posed this rhetorical question in the late seventh century:

> Why, I ask, is Ireland, whither assemble the thronging students by the fleet-load, exalted with a sort of ineffable privilege, as if here in the fertile soil of Britain, teachers who are citizens of Greece and Rome cannot be found, who are able to unlock themselves to the clever seekers of knowledge and unravel the dark difficulties of the heavenly books?

(To find out who the latter were, albeit in another context, see pp. 67–8 below.) Bede clearly states that significant numbers of the English went to Ireland 'either for the sake of religious studies or to live a more ascetic life'. The case of Egbert is most instructive. At a point of crisis, when he became seriously ill in an Irish monastery, he took a good look at his life and vowed that he would remain in permanent self-exile. Bede says that he got this information from a man to whom Egbert had spoken of it. Long afterwards Egbert, still in Ireland, decided to convert the heathen of Germany to Christianity. Of course the conversion of his own people, the English, was a precedent, and their kinship with the Continental Germans was recognised. There was precedent in Irish *peregrinatio*. Columbanus, before going to Italy, had had unsuccessful encounters with pagans in what is now Switzerland, whom his disciple named Gall was to convert. Bede clearly indicates that it was among the English in Ireland that the Anglo-Saxon mission to the Continent began before the end of the seventh century. Egbert's ship was wrecked before he could leave Ireland, but his disciple Willibrord established a successful bishopric among the Frisians, setting the pattern which notable men and women from England were to follow in the next century, as we shall see in the next chapter.

For the first time, civilisation would be seen to come out of the North. That this should be so to any extent whatsoever is a contradiction in terms from the viewpoint of the Ancient world, where the further one got from the Mediterranean the greater the barbarian darkness. It is one indication of great cultural change under way in the seventh century; and we are coming to the other. Here a point already made in the Introduction may be recalled. The contribution of the British Isles to the birth of Europe is illustrated by the print you are reading. The style of handwriting developed by the Irish and adopted by the English is known as Insular script. This, as was noted, was an important component of the reformed handwriting sponsored by Charlemagne in his Continental empire around AD 800, which Renaissance scholars imitated in their Humanist script (the basis of modern typeface) under the mistaken impression that it was Ancient writing. The early medieval origins of European civilisation traditionally have been overlooked. So has the role of non-European participants in defining Europe in the period, which we are about to examine.

The Rise of Islam

Far to the southeast, a little while before the Sutton Hoo ship was laid in the ground, a merchant from Mecca named Mohammed received religious under-standing. Mecca is situated in western Arabia, and despite the infertility of its district was prospering in the early seventh century from trade between southern Arabia, which was (and still is) the land of frankincense, and the Roman and Persian markets to the north; or, in early and modern terms, between Yemen on the one hand, and Syria and Iraq on the other. The contribution of significant cultural change on both the northwest and southeast frontiers of the old Roman world to the birth of Europe is the major theme of this chapter on the seventh century. Arabia was on the culturally fertile frontier of not only the Roman Empire but the Persian Empire as well. In the early seventh century these two empires were, not for the first time, locked in mortal combat with each other. From the Roman and Persian point of view, the Arabs were troublesome raiders, but manageable, and a useful source of troops. Once they were unified by the religion of Islam, they established in three generations an empire of their own that stretched from Spain to Afghanistan. (See Map 3.2.) These events are as dramatic as they are misunderstood. Many historically aware individuals think that the warriors of Islam gave the people they conquered the choice between conversion and death; however, forced conversion was rare. God specifically forbids it in the Quran, the Muslim holy book: 'let there be no compulsion in religion'. On the other hand, their conquests did spread Islam, of course, not least because it became thereby a religion of success. These matters will be discussed further below.

Islam began as a radical reform of existing religion. Allah was not a new god; objection was made to those who joined other gods to him in polytheism. Mohammed's first convert was his wife, Khadija, a businesswoman engaged in the typically Meccan pursuit of long-distance trade. Ibn Ishaq, who wrote the first biography of Mohammed and was a contemporary of Bede, had this to say about Khadija and Mohammed:

> So Khadija believed, and attested the truth of that which came to him from God and aided him in his undertaking. Thus was the Lord minded to lighten the burden of His Prophet; for whenever he heard anything that grieved him touching his rejection by the people, he would return to her and God would comfort him through her, for she reassured him and lightened his burden and declared her trust in him and made it easy for him to bear the scorn of men.

On the whole Mohammed's teaching was unwelcome in Mecca, which was already a pilgrimage centre with a considerable stake in the religious *status quo*. The move of Mohammed and his followers from Mecca to Medina, another trading town over 300 kilometres to the north, is the event with which the Muslim calendar begins (= AD 622[3]), for there Islam flourished. Soon Mohammed returned with an army which took Mecca, and its religious shrines were purified of idolatry. In the remainder of his life, the people of Arabia were unified by war and negotiation for the first time. When the prophet Mohammed died in 632, disintegration threatened, but instead under his successors, the caliphs, energies were directed outwards, as raiders from Arabia were successful beyond what one would think (and early Muslim historians did think; see below) had been their wildest dreams.

When the timing of the early Islamic conquests is considered, their historical significance becomes fully appreciated. To the north of Arabia the Roman Empire had apparently defeated the Persian Empire once and for all, with

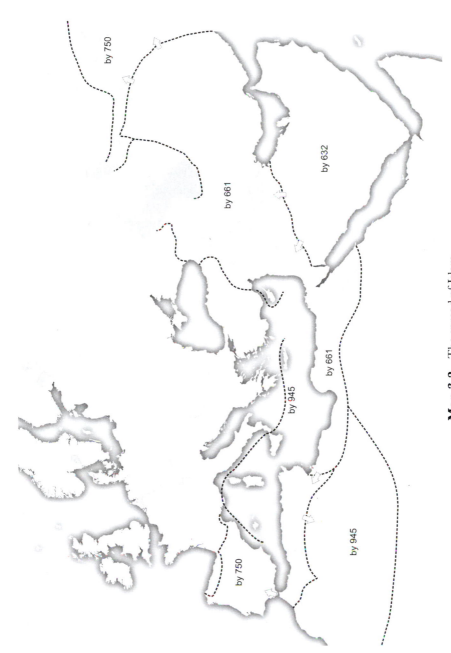

Map 3.2   The spread of Islam

by 750

by 632

by 661

by 661

by 945

by 945

by 750

Byzantine troops occupying Ctesiphon, the Persian capital. In 636, however, the Arab defeat of the Byzantines at the Battle of the Yarmuk River meant the end of the Roman Levant south from Antioch in which Malalas had written in the previous century. In 637 the Arab defeat of the Persians at Qadesiya ended the latter's empire forever, ensuring that when imperial power appeared again in the region, it would be changed beyond recognition into the caliphate of Baghdad, near Ctesiphon, as we shall see in the next chapter. Traditions of the Muslim conquest of Iraq celebrated the booty of the Persian capital, equivalent to at least 3 billion dirhams (silver coins) in one version. A later chronicler offers:

> An account of some amusing incidents that occurred at this time. One was that a certain Arab got hold of a leather sack of camphor. He brought it to his friends and they thought it was salt. They cooked food, put some camphor in it and perceived no taste to it. They did not know what it was. Then a man saw them, knew what was in it and bought it from them for an old shirt worth two dirhams. Another was that a desert Arab got a great jacinth worth a vast sum, but he did not know its value. One who knew its value saw him, and bought it from him for 1,000 dirhams. Later the desert Arab realised its value, and his friends blamed him, saying to him, 'Why did you not ask more than that for it?' He replied, 'Had I known that, after 1,000, there was a number bigger than 1,000, I would have asked it.' Another was that one of them took in his hand some gold, and said, 'Who will take this yellow (stuff) and give me white?' He thought that silver was more valuable than gold.[4]

The Arab conquest of Roman Egypt was achieved only a decade after the death of Mohammed and of Roman North Africa over to, but not including, Tunisia in five more years. Then it slowed, having reached the heartland of Byzantine Africa, well fortified and strongly defended; but North Africa was all taken by the end of the seventh century. These changes are impressive in their permanence.

The nature and impact of the Arab conquests, to which most of Spain was added early in the next century, must be carefully assessed. A key concept of Islam is the *umma*, or community of the faithful. As we have seen, there was a political and military dimension to the rise of Islam almost from the beginning. The Sunni/Shia schism in Islam originated as a dispute over whether the caliph had to be of the family of Mohammed, but instead it was companions of the Prophet and members of the ruling Meccan house of Umayya who gave rise to the Umayyad caliphate. Yet most people in the lands the caliphs conquered were at least nominally Christian, with a sprinkling of Jews, and both of these faiths have status in Islam as 'religions of the Book'. Judaism had more status under Islamic rule than the grudging toleration given to it in Christian lands. The penalty for apostasy was harsh in both *dar al-Islam*, 'the house of Islam', and under Christian rule as 'relapsed' converted Jews and heretics found at the cost of their lives. Polytheism, for example among the Berbers of North Africa, was not tolerated any more than its counterpart in Christian Europe. In the early

Middle Ages far more people were forced to convert to Christianity than to Islam. Under Muslim rule members of the *umma* were privileged while Christians and Jews were second-class inhabitants. There were tax incentives to convert to Islam. Also, Christians and Jews were not to advertise themselves: church bells were not to be rung, nor were new synagogues and churches to be built. What religious scholars thought should happen and what happened in reality were not necessarily the same; for example, church bells were heard in Muslim Spain. It is estimated that in the lands that the Crusaders attacked at the end of the eleventh century the majority of the population was Christian.

The establishment of the caliphate brought a new cultural dynamic to the Mediterranean and not only religion. Being both the language of the holy Quran ('Recitations') and of a spreading empire contributed immeasurably to the prestige of Arabic, which developed very quickly into a written language of learning and administration. Thus while early Islamic culture has Ancient Mediterranean roots, the result is different. This can be seen in one of the best known buildings in the world. Built in Jerusalem at the end of the seventh century, the Dome of the Rock renewed religious activity atop the mount where the Romans had destroyed the Jewish Temple in the first century, the desolation of which Eusebius in the fourth century had used to proclaim the victory of Christianity. The decoration and structural principles of the Dome of the Rock are late Antique, but this original, octagonal building was designed to accommodate pilgrims circling the second holiest shrine of Islam, after the Kaaba in Mecca itself. The culture of the caliphate also has important Persian roots, and here the continuity is more obvious, further distinguishing the Islamic from other Mediterranean regions. Economically the east, south and west of the Mediterranean became part of a vibrant commercial zone extending eastwards, reinforcing the eastern focus already detected in Malalas's *Chronicle*. To the north-west Europe, very much the 'Third World' of its day, was thrown back even more on its own resources, which were considerable. Politically the immense loss of Byzantine territory confined what remained of the Roman Empire to the north-east Mediterranean. Geographical advantages helped the Byzantines to hold these lands for the rest of the early Middle Ages, but this weakening of Byzantium had profound implications for Europe.

Evaluating the Pirenne Thesis

The historical significance of these vast changes for the birth of Europe will be brought out more by considering a monument of Western historiography, the Pirenne Thesis. Historiography is the writing of history, and of course the study which makes that writing possible; there are developments and fashions in it as in any human activity. At the beginning of the twentieth century the past was seen very much in terms of political developments, and the end of Antiquity and beginning of the Middle Ages seemed obviously to come with the fifth-century Germanic invasions. The early twentieth century was productive of great historical theories not least because historians were turning to new types of evidence and, indeed, new types of history. The Belgian historian Henri Pirenne, detained in Germany during the First World War, had a great deal of time to think about his field of early medieval history away from the normal responsibilities of a university teacher. The theory or thesis that he came up with would be fundamental for future study of the period, which would be transformed thereby from the wreckage at the end of the (Western) Roman Empire into a time when crucial developments occurred. Pirenne argued that the seventh-century Arab conquests not the fifth-century Germanic invasions brought about the end of Antiquity and the beginning of the Middle Ages.[5] In doing so Pirenne was innovative in two ways: his thesis is argued mainly from economic evidence and it proposes a non-European explanation for the origin of Europe. His thesis is otherwise Eurocentric; indeed it is Gallocentric, perceiving early European history mainly in terms of what was happening in Gaul or France, as tends to be the case in medieval historiography.

Henri Pirenne observed that despite the political change from Roman Empire to barbarian kingdoms, the Roman way of life – *romanitas* – continued in the West. The imported wines mentioned in the long passage quoted from Gregory of Tours in the last chapter would be an example. The barbarians admired *romanitas* and sought to imitate it: most gave up their own languages in favour of Latin and all adopted Christianity, eventually even Roman Catholicism (the Lombards abandoned Arianism for good in the later seventh century). The Mediterranean Sea continued to function as a unifying conduit for commerce and communication between regions with many similarities. Pirenne cites in support the presence in the West of not only Eastern wine but spices, olive oil, silk, papyrus from Egypt and gold acquired through commerce with the East. The Arabs, said Pirenne, broke this Mediterranean unity forever and thus ended the Ancient world; they brought about a three-way split into their caliphate, a much reduced Roman Empire and the European kingdoms which turned away from the Mediterranean to living off the land. This is the first part of the Pirenne Thesis. His economic arguments have since been challenged successfully from archaeological evidence, which in fairness was unknown to Pirenne. The decline of Mediterranean trade was a slow process not attributable to the Arab conquests. Fragmentation of the Mediterranean into regional economies can be seen already by the later sixth century, part of the ironic counter-productivity of Justinian's attempts at reconquest. Pirenne might have paid more attention to the role of Italy in connecting East and West. The North had resources and patterns of exchange of its own that Pirenne did not appreciate.

Read as a cultural thesis, following the current trend in historiography in which the present book participates, Pirenne's theory continues to provide valuable insight, however; and his major political conclusion, to be examined in a moment, is beyond dispute. First, an autobiographical reminiscence may shed a little light on how the study of history evolves. When I was beginning to teach in the later 1970s, I found an article written by Anne Riising just after 1950, which surveys what other scholars had said about the Pirenne Thesis, to be especially helpful. Most of the article surveyed economic studies, but there was also a short section on cultural investigations, of which Riising said there was need for more, that I found to be especially interesting. Cultural studies had yet to make its impact, but cultural approaches to history were in the air. At this point the cultural strengths of the Arabs outlined in the last paragraph of the preceding section should be recalled. With their own religion and language the Arabs offered a real alternative to entrenched Graeco-Roman cultural hegemony, and broke it with ease. The political weakness of Byzantium should also be recalled. In the other part of his thesis Pirenne related the Arab conquests to the phenomenal success of the Frankish ruler Charlemagne, who will be considered in the next two chapters. 'Without Mohammed, Charlemagne would have been inconceivable' is a neat but cryptic quotation,[6] for it leaves the key to the connection between them unstated: the weakening of what remained of the Roman Empire. The events about to be considered shed light on the place of Byzantium in early medieval history, linking the northern and southern regions with which this chapter has been concerned, and confirming the truth of Pirenne's statement just quoted.

In 662 Emperor Constans II came west, and in 663 campaigned unsuccessfully against Lombards encroaching on Byzantine territory in southern Italy. Constans was the last Roman emperor to visit Rome. When he was there in 664, he ordered the removal of all bronze decorations and sent them back to Constantinople. He went south to Sicily, where he was murdered in the autumn of 668. These events are unprecedented and it is assumed that Constans II's intention was to establish an Italian base for a Roman counterattack against the forces of Islam which were threatening the rest of North Africa. Also in 668, a newly consecrated archbishop of Canterbury, Theodore, originally from Tarsus in the Eastern Roman Empire which had been captured by the Arabs in 660, and the abbot Hadrian, originally from North Africa, travelled from the city of Rome north through France. Hadrian had been Pope Vitalian's first choice for archbishop, but had pleaded unworthiness and nominated Theodore instead. The pope insisted that Hadrian go with Theodore to England because Hadrian had been on missions in Gaul on two previous occasions and so knew the way. The pope's idea was that Hadrian would stop Theodore from introducing any dubious Greek customs once they had got to England. Hadrian was considerably delayed *en route*. By this time the weak Frankish kings had been eclipsed by strong nobles who held the office of mayor (greater one) of the palace, in this case Ebroin. To quote from the English historian Bede:

> Ebroin kept Hadrian because he suspected him of having some mission from the emperor to the kings of Britain, which might be directed against the kingdom over which at that time he held the chief charge. But when he discovered the truth, that Hadrian had never had any such mission at any time; he freed him and allowed him to go after Theodore.

(*Ecclesiastical History*, IV.1)

This chance reference in an ecclesiastical source gives a glimpse of a whole world of secular manoeuvring. The emperor whom Ebroin suspected of intriguing with the kings of Britain against the Frankish kingdom was Constans II, and the suspicions become less far-fetched when it is recalled that at the time he was in Italy, or more exactly Sicily. In the next century, faced with the Lombards' threat to unite all of Italy under their control and the papacy pleading for help against them, Byzantium was no longer in a position to do anything and the papacy turned to the Franks for assistance, with consequences to be examined in the next chapter.

Visigothic Spain

The remainder of this chapter will take a look at one seventh-century Western kingdom: Visigothic Spain. While the picture is incomplete, some of the elements that make it up are of considerable interest in themselves, and if carefully considered, have implications for the picture as a whole. We will start with a literary introduction:

> Of all lands which stretch from the West to India, you are the most beautiful, O Spain, sacred and ever-blessed mother of leaders and of nations. By right you are now queen of all the provinces, from whom not only the West but also the East obtains its light. You are the glory and ornament of the world, the most illustrious part of the earth, in which the glorious fecundity of the Getic [Gothic] people rejoices much and abundantly flourishes.

Thus Isidore of Seville begins his short *History of the Goths* with praise of Spain. By the early seventh century Isidore, whose family was mentioned in the last chapter, had become bishop of Seville and adviser of kings. He wrote another of the Great Books of the Middle Ages, the *Etymologies*, a sort of encyclopaedia constructed around the supposed derivations of words, drawing widely but rather indiscriminately on the Latin authors of the Ancient world. Isidore was asked to write this by the Visigothic king Sisibut, himself an educated man with a particular interest in the natural world. A poem on lunar eclipse written by Sisibut for Isidore survives, which opens with a reference to that king's law-giving and waging war that is no less interesting for being an echo of the greatest Latin poet Vergil on Augustus, the first Roman emperor. An early medieval author-bishop is no surprise, but a classically influenced poet-king is another matter. Sisibut's royal successor Suinthila in 624 defeated the last Byzantine forces in Spain and unified the peninsula under Visigothic rule for the first time, although its northern mountain peoples (the 'snowy Basque' and 'shaggy Cantabrian' in Sisibut's poetic language) continued to be troublesome.

The seventh century saw the culmination of efforts to build a unified Visigothic Spanish kingdom (see Map 3.3). Back in 589, King Recarred had converted to Catholic Christianity and insisted that his Arian subjects likewise

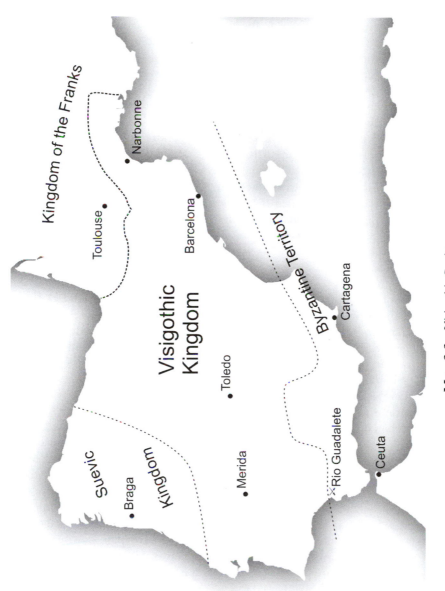

Map 3.3 Visigothic Spain

join the Catholic majority. From this point on, Visigothic kings associated them-selves as closely as possible with the Church, ruling with clerics like Isidore of Seville through a succession of royally summoned church councils. The decrees of these councils show how resolutely they supported the monarchy as an insti-tution, and include statements of the qualifications that a king should have; according to the Sixth Council of Toledo in 638, he had to be a Goth. The rela-tionship of Church and monarchy is visually expressed by the votive crown of King Reccesuinth, who reigned from 649–72. This golden crown, set with sapphires and pearls, was given by the king to hang in a church: hence it has suspending chains, a suspended cross in its centre and individual cloisonné letters dangling around its lower edge which read 'RECCESVINTHUS REX OFFERET'.[7] Rituals were developed to reinforce kingship. The ceremony of anointing a new king, first recorded in 672 but probably going back to the middle of the century, is a religious one which hitherto had been used to consecrate bish-ops, but the Visigoths found the biblical precedent of anointed kings in the Old Testament and applied it to their own rulers. Used for the line of Charlemagne from the mid-eighth century on, anointing became a standard part of European coronations, but the Visigoths had it first. Likewise swearing a sacred coronation oath was their innovation.

As was the case with the other early medieval kingdoms introduced in the first chapter, incoming barbarians had only constituted a very small part of the population of Visigothic Spain: something like two hundred thousand Goths to eight million Hispano-Romans. An inscription in Hebrew and Greek as well as Latin perhaps from the seventh century (see Figure 12) reflects further diversity to be expected in a Mediterranean land of the period. In the middle of the seventh century King Reccesuinth issued a relatively lengthy and sophisticated law code, the *Book of the Judges*, for all the people of his kingdom. This law code will be examined in the next paragraph, but the concern at present is with iden-tity. The extent to which Goths and Romans had previously lived under separate laws is debated, but in any case earlier codes were now superseded by Reccesuinth's law book. Goths and Romans had had separate administrative institutions, but the duke of the province and count of the city territory, origi-nally for Goths, came to suffice for everybody. Note that the units of government here were Roman; Roman too was the public post, a communication system that continued to function at least into the mid-seventh century. And overall people in Visigothic Spain spoke Latin turning into Spanish; the Gothic language died with Arianism if not before, and contributed few words to Spanish, which was to receive far more from Arabic. Nevertheless, the national identity that was evolv-ing for Spain was apparently the Gothic taken from its rulers, and was consid-ered such after most of Spain was added to the caliphate in the early eighth century.

The legal evidence for Visigothic Spain is extensive. Late Antiquity and the earlier Middle Ages are outstanding periods for the codification of law, which can be seen as an attempt to bring order to societies in need of it. Yet the nature and historical usefulness of the law codes produced in the post-Roman kingdoms

Figure 12 Trilingual inscription in Hebrew, Latin and Greek from Tortosa (Spain) on the River Ebro, not far from where it enters the Mediterranean Sea. (© Institut Amatller d'Art Hispànic)

of early medieval Europe have been debated. These show barbarian admiration for Roman law-giving and are an assertion of royal authority, but how much were they actually used: did judges have copies to consult when they heard cases? Well, the aforementioned Visigothic *Book of the Judges* sets an upper limit to its own price, and while this is high – 'it shall not be legal for a vendor to sell a copy of this book for more than four hundred *solidi* [gold coins]' – some distribution and practical use of the law code are implied thereby. In contrast to the contemporary Lombard law code known as *Rothair's Edict*, which jumps straight into plot and murder, the Visigothic code begins with two books on jurisprudence before passing on to a third concerning marriage, about which something may be said here. Considerable attention is given to the payment of money which, indeed, is said to be a prerequisite to a written contract of marriage; however, it is the reverse dowry, the payment from the man not the woman who is marrying that is meant. A law issued by Reccesuinth's predecessor King Chindasuinth specifies that this amount cannot be more than a tenth part of the man's property. Thus Visigothic law illustrates points made at the end of Chapter 1 about the relatively better access of women to wealth in late Antiquity and the early Middle Ages. Likewise the Visigoths continued late Roman practice of equal inheritance of sisters and brothers and, indeed, gender was a negligible factor in Visigothic inheritance.

Visigothic Spain had its problems. Like every other early medieval kingdom, its kings were subject to challenge from the aristocracy because the sources of their power were so similar. After Roman taxation faded away, the wealth of kings, like that of nobles, came primarily from their lands. Disputes over royal succession were frequent and dynasties could not get established: King Reccesuinth, the successful son of a royal father, was quite exceptional in the seventh century. Spain was especially characterised by localism. Perhaps its cities and regions had got used to going their own way, surviving as best they could on their own resources, during the decades of power vacuum when Spain had been little more than a sphere of influence for the Visigoths, before the latter's defeat by the Franks in 507 had forced the relocation of the Visigothic kingdom from southwest France to Spain. On the other hand, some people wanted to take the religious unity of Visigothic Spain still further. Isidore criticised King Sisibut for trying to convert the Jews by force rather than persuasion, and in the second half of the seventh century there was increasingly restrictive legislation against them. This harmed the Jews and the kingdom. Early medieval kingdoms needed all the resources, including people, that they could get, and usually early medieval rulers realised it; the social disorganisation of the period also was not conducive to persecution. In Spain these measures against the Jews contrast with their toleration under Arian and some Catholic rulers. The capacity for both remarkable tolerance and intolerance that characterises Spanish history was already present in the Visigothic kingdom.

The main difficulty at the end of the Visigothic kingdom was, of course, one about which nothing could have been done: geography. Spain was always liable to be affected by wider developments in the Mediterranean, and was especially linked to what happened south of the Mediterranean. In 711 a raiding force of Arabs and Berbers from newly conquered North Africa, under the command of Tariq ibn Ziyad, defeated the Visigothic king Roderic in Spain. As was the case in the Muslim conquests of Syria and Iraq (and would be in the Norman Conquest of England centuries later) a decisive battle made all the difference. The only part of Spain that remained under Christian rule was the mountainous far north, the part least affected by Rome and the Visigoths. From what has been said earlier in this chapter, it will not be surprising that the earliest Christian source for the conquest of Spain, the *Chronicle of 754* written in Muslim Spain,

Figure 13   Interior of the church of San Juan de Baños in northern Spain (dedicated in 661), with its horseshoe arches. (© Institut Amatller d'Art Hispànic)

does not present it in terms of the spread of a religion but rather as the invasion of a people called Saracens, an old ethnic name for the Arabs that predates the rise of Islam. One image will fittingly conclude this examination of Visigothic Spain: the horseshoe arch. Usually thought to have been introduced by the Arabs, it is in fact a feature of Visigothic architecture, as can be seen in the church shown in Figure 13, dedicated by King Reccesuinth in 661. Its origins lay in the provincial architecture of Roman Spain. There is continuity, but it would be transformed almost beyond recognition in the vibrant culture of Muslim Spain.

The seventh century was the great cultural watershed in the birth of Europe. The rise of Islam involved many people, the phenomenon of civilisation coming out of the North very few, but they were an important few, and their activity intensified in the eighth century and will be considered at the beginning of the next chapter.

The Eighth Century: Formation of the Core of Europe

Boniface and the English Mission to the Continent

At the beginning of the eighth century a complete copy of the Bible was made in northern England. The quality of its text of Jerome's Latin biblical translation, known as the Vulgate and the oldest to survive, is still well regarded. Its frontispiece shows an early stage of biblical production by the Hebrew priest Ezra, surrounded with the paraphernalia of a scribe. This illustration and its presumed sixth-century Italian manuscript model celebrated the writing of sacred scripture, which was now done in northern as well as southern Europe. In 716 Abbot Ceolfrid of the linked monasteries of Wearmouth and Jarrow took this Bible south as a gift to Pope Gregory II in Rome. Although the abbot died *en route* his gift reached its destination, but subsequently turned up at the monastery of San Salvatore on Monte Amiata in Tuscany and now, known as the Codex Amiatinus, is in Florence. In the same year a middle-aged monk from England named Wynfrith also travelled south, with the aim of converting the Frisians, a people living on the marshy coast of the North Sea.[1] Things didn't look too promising for missionary work at that point and Wynfrith returned to England, but two years later he set out again. This time, bearing a letter of introduction from his bishop, Daniel of Winchester, he went straight to Pope Gregory II in Rome to get papal backing for his mission. This he received together with a new name, Boniface, and was sent to work in Germany. There he was successful, and in 722 was consecrated bishop by Pope Gregory. At the pope's request, Charles Martel, Frankish mayor of the palace, extended to Boniface the protection that missionaries always need.

Still in the early stages of his mission, Boniface received a letter from Bishop Daniel of Winchester with the following advice on how to convert pagans. It gives rare insight into how people like this were thinking at the time.

And so, moved by affection and good will, I am taking the liberty of making a few suggestions, in order to show you how, in my opinion, you may overcome with the least possible trouble the resistance of this barbarous people.

Do not begin by arguing with them about the genealogies of their false gods. Accept their statement that they were begotten by other gods through the intercourse of male and female and then you will be able to prove that, as these gods and goddesses did not exist before, and were born like men, they must be men and not gods. When they have been forced to admit that their gods had a beginning, since they were begotten by others, they should be asked whether the world had a beginning or was always in existence. There is no doubt that before the universe was created there was no place in which these created gods could have subsisted or dwelt. And by 'universe' I mean not merely heaven and earth which we see with our eyes but the whole extent of space which even the heathens can grasp in their imagination. If they maintain that the universe had no beginning, try to refute their arguments and bring forward convincing proofs; and if they persist in arguing, ask them, 'Who ruled it? How did the gods bring under their sway a universe that existed before them? Whence or by whom or when was the first god or goddess begotten? Do they believe that gods and goddesses still beget other gods and goddesses? If they do not, when did they cease and why? If they do, the number of gods must be infinite. In such a case, who is the most powerful among these different gods? Surely no mortal man can know. Yet man must take care not to offend this god who is more powerful than the rest. Do they think the gods should be worshipped for the sake of temporal and transitory benefits or for eternal and future reward? If for temporal benefit let them say in what respect the heathens are better off than the Christians. What do the heathen gods gain from the sacrifices if they already possess everything? Or why do the gods leave it to the whim of their subjects to decide what kind of tribute shall be paid? If they need such sacrifices, why do they not choose more suitable ones? If they do not need them, then the people are wrong in thinking that they can placate the gods with such offerings and victims.

These and similar questions, and many others that it would be tedious to mention, should be put to them, not in an offensive and irritating way but calmly and with great moderation. From time to time their superstitions should be compared with our Christian dogmas and touched upon indirectly, so that the heathens, more out of confusion than exasperation, may be ashamed of their absurd opinions and may recognise that their disgusting rites and legends have not escaped our notice.

This conclusion also must be drawn: If the gods are omnipotent, beneficent and just, they must reward their devotees and punish those who despise them. Why then, if they act thus in temporal affairs, do they spare the Christians who cast down their idols and turn away from their worship the inhabitants of practically the entire globe?[2] And whilst the Christians are allowed to possess the countries that are rich in oil and wine and other commodities, why have they left to the heathens the frozen lands of the north, where the gods, banished from the rest of the world, are falsely supposed to dwell?

The heathens are frequently to be reminded of the supremacy of the Christian world and of the fact that they who still cling to outworn beliefs are in a very small minority.

If they boast that the gods have held undisputed sway over these people from the beginning, point out to them that formerly the whole world was given over to the worship of idols until, by the grace of Christ and through the knowledge of one God, its Almighty Creator and Ruler, it was enlightened, vivified and reconciled to God. For what does the baptising of the children of Christian parents signify if not the purification of each one from the unclean-ness of the guilt of heathenism in which the entire human race was involved?

Recalling the previous chapter or looking at Map 4.1 here will show how wildly inaccurate and amazingly bold were the claims made in this letter even for the known world of its day. Across the south stretched the Muslim-ruled caliphate, albeit with its mainly Christian population, and east of the area in which Boniface worked it was pagans all the way to the ocean. Yet Europe would be almost entirely Christian by the end of the Middle Ages, and to this extent the confidence of the letter was not misplaced and, indeed, was instrumental in bringing about that very result. Clearly, early medieval mission involved a lot of talking. Even in the most top-down conversions the leaders had to be convinced, and so too did their followers whose counsel they habitually sought. Moreover, although there was frequently an element of compulsion in medieval conversion, the capacity of authorities to control people was limited, especially by inade-quate communication, leaving plenty of need for persuasive preaching and argu-ment by missionaries. Of particular interest in Daniel's advice to Boniface is the emphasis on getting the pagans to 'think big' about the whole universe and the whole earth, creating religious needs that only Christianity could meet in contrast to their locally based faith. Above all, the identification of Christianity with civilisation and success, interestingly expressed in Mediterranean terms of olive oil and wine, comes through loud and clear. Boniface was himself part of the wider world that came to the pagans, altering their worldview in ways that made them receptive to the universal religion of Christianity. So were the Frankish soldiers who, among other things, protected him. The kingdom of the Franks was expanding and consolidating control over the region, known from Ancient times as Germany, in which he worked.

Boniface is one of the most important people in European history, for he was instrumental in forming the core of Europe. This statement requires a lot of explanation and background, and what is meant by the core of Europe will become clearer as the chapter progresses. First a little more consideration will be given to Boniface himself and the English mission on the Continent, with an excursion further afield. Boniface's life and even his death were pre-eminently successful according to the medieval way of thinking. After many years spent in

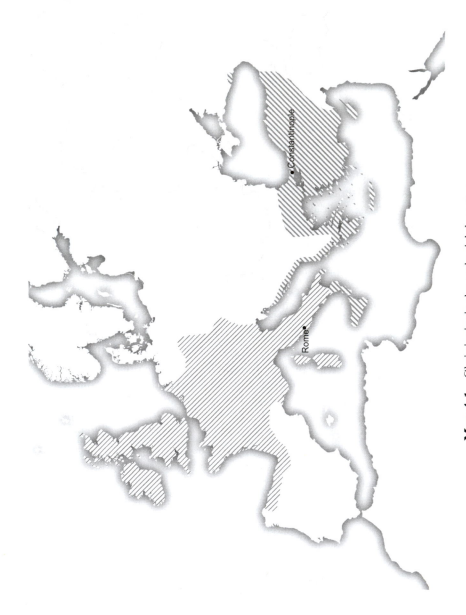

Map 4.1 Christianity in the early eighth century

establishing the Church in Germany and reforming the Frankish Church, Boniface decided to try again to convert the Frisians. The result was that they martyred him in 754. The book which he is said to have used as a shield against his attackers (shown here in Figure 14) survives at the important monastery of Fulda which he founded. Boniface was one of a number of English monks and nuns who worked to establish and advance Christianity on the Continent in the eighth century. For example, Boniface consecrated Willibald as bishop of Eichstätt in Bavaria in 741. An account of Willibald's travels (discussed below) was written by the English nun Huneberc at Heidenheim in Germany. Heidenheim was a double monastery for men and women, then under the joint control of Bishop Willibald's own brother and sister, Wynbald and Waldburg, who like him had come from England to the Continent.[3] Boniface still received support from within England. In a letter he requests Abbess Eadburga there to add to the books and ecclesiastical clothing which she has already sent 'by copying out for me in letters of gold the epistles of my lord, St Peter, that a reverence and love of the Holy Scriptures may be impressed on the carnally minded to whom I preach . . .', in other words those people who have their minds on earthly rather than spiritual treasure. Boniface understood the value of impressing the people he was trying to convert, most notably when he cut down the oak tree at Geismar which was sacred to the pagans, and built a chapel of St Peter out of its wood.

These English abroad could be very enterprising. As a young man the above mentioned Willibald went as far as the Holy Land. Huneberc's account of his travels[4] is a particularly interesting source that offers valuable evidence of continuing contacts between West and East in the eighth century and reinforces what was said in the last chapter about lands conquered by the forces of Islam. When Willibald and his fellow travellers ran into difficulty with the Saracens in Syria, it was as strangers of unknown origin who were suspected of being spies. They were assisted on this occasion by several people. An elderly, wealthy man, after questioning them, said, '"I have often seen men coming from those parts of the world; fellow countrymen of theirs, they cause no mischief and are merely anxious to fulfil their law"', a respectful reference to Christian pilgrimage. A merchant, failing to buy their release from prison, saw to it that they were fed, had a bath twice a week, and took them to church on Sunday. A man from Spain, his brother who was the chamberlain of the Muslim ruler, and the captain of the ship which had brought Willibald and his companions from Cyprus ('which lies between the Greeks and the Saracens' then as now) finally managed to obtain their release. Later, in Jerusalem, Willibald pushed his luck when:

> he bought himself some balsam [medicine, whence the word 'balm'] and filled a calabash with it; then he took a hollow reed which had a bottom to it and filled it with petroleum and put it inside the calabash. Afterwards he cut the reed equal in length to the calabash so that the surfaces of both were even and then closed the mouth of the calabash. When they reached the city of Tyre the citizens arrested them, put them in chains and examined all their baggage to find out if they had hidden any contraband. If they had found

Figure 14 Ragyndrudis Codex, late seventh or early eighth century, preserved at Fulda in Germany. It is of interest not only because of its traditional association with the martyrdom of Boniface, Ragyndrudis was the laywoman who commissioned the manuscript. It contains a work, the *Synonyma* by Isidore of Seville, which was of particular interest to lay people as a guide to Christian life and also suited a missionary context. (Fotodesign Erich Gutberlet)

anything they would certainly have punished them and put them to death. But when they had thoroughly scrutinized everything and could find nothing but one calabash which Willibald had, they opened it and snuffed at it to find out what was inside. And when they smelt petroleum, which was inside the reed at the top, they did not find the balsam which was inside the calabash underneath the petroleum, and so let them go.

Readers, note: according to Huneberc, Willibald was curious about the world. So was she.

While the English mission to the Continent was, as pointed out in the last chapter, Irish-inspired, its results differed somewhat from the impact of Irish activity there. What Huneberc says about Willibald and, indeed, what (a different) Willibald says about Boniface describes their motivation to leave England in the familiar terms of Irish pilgrimage: forsaking kin and country. Huneberc adds that Willibald 'was eager to go on pilgrimage and travel to distant foreign lands and find out all about them'. He only joined Boniface after years of travel and as a monk at Monte Cassino in Italy when the pope told him that Boniface wanted his help. Like the Irish, these English on the Continent were a catalyst working to overcome residual reluctance to convert pagan barbarians there. Much of the initial Christian conversion in the areas where Boniface worked had been carried out by the Irish and their Continental disciples. Boniface often had to deal with incomplete Christianisation, where the efforts of others had not been followed up. He was a great organiser, and the four popes for whom he worked welcomed his initiative. For example, Bavaria had only one bishop until Boniface created three more and divided Bavaria into four dioceses. One of these was Eichstätt, of which Willibald was consecrated bishop by Boniface. In a letter to Boniface approving these arrangements, Pope Gregory III wrote:

> You have no permission, brother, to remain in one district once your work there has been completed. Strengthen the minds of your brethren and the faithful who are scattered throughout the West and continue to preach wherever God grants you opportunity to save souls. When the need arises consecrate bishops according to canon law in your capacity as our representative, and instruct them to observe apostolic and Catholic doctrine.

The English had a special contribution to make on the Continent, moreover: their marked orientation to the papacy, which reflected the way many of their ancestors had been converted by the mission of Pope Gregory the Great, was an influential contrast to earlier Frankish isolation from the bishops of Rome.

Frankish–Papal Relations

The development of relations between the Franks and the papacy is enormously important in the history of the early Middle Ages, and a key component in forming the core of Europe. At the beginning of the eighth century these relations were negligible, with the papacy paying more attention to the English than the Franks, while at the end of the century they could not have been more significant, with the pope about to crown Charlemagne Roman emperor. In the process royal, papal, pastoral and monastic conversion initiative (for definitions of these categories see p. 56 above) all fused into what would remain the standard pattern of Christianising the eastern frontier of Western Europe. For the eighth-century Frankish rulers, conversion and establishment of Church institutions was a vital part of consolidating their control over long-claimed lands and extending it over new ones. The organisation of the German Church was carried out under the auspices of the papacy through its primary agent Boniface, who was made archbishop in 732 and papal legate (envoy) in 738. This was his status in the letter cited in the previous section, in which the pope refers to the role of the Frankish ruler Charles Martel as well as Boniface in converting the Germans, and to the approval of Boniface's diocesan reorganisation by the duke and nobles of Bavaria. Then in the 740s, working with the mayor of the palace Carloman, who was Charles Martel's son, and still with papal backing, Boniface led a reform of the Frankish Church itself. Through all this activity he helped to connect Frankish leaders with the papacy. In 747 Carloman became a monk, leaving his brother Pepin sole mayor of the palace. To appreciate what happened next, both the Franks and the papacy in the eighth century must be examined against the background of their earlier history.

The Franks are the great success story of early medieval Europe. Of the Continental kingdoms which emerged from the crumbling Roman West theirs was the only one to survive to the end of the eighth century. France had certain strengths and also lacked certain problems that beset other kingdoms. It was never attacked in Justinian's campaigns of the sixth century, which ended the Vandal and Ostrogothic kingdoms. An army from Muslim Spain got as far as the Tours/Poitiers area, where it was defeated in 732/3 by the forces of Charles Martel. This is sometimes dismissed as just a raid, but raiding is what made the caliphate. The Franks tended to win. In this case they had logistic and strategic advantages over long-distance raiders, but the pattern of Frankish victory extended over a variety of circumstances. That extensive eastern frontier may have contributed to their military success in particular, for there the Franks could campaign, collect booty and levy tribute including a supply of fierce warriors to fight for rather than against them. From the beginning the great strength of the kingdom of the Franks was the integration of its people, especially within Catholic Christianity, as was pointed out in Chapter 2. By the eighth century the amazingly complex ethnicity of early France had coalesced into identification along territorial lines, but the kingdom was not unified and its regional identities reflected this: Frankish in the north, in the southeast Burgundian and southwest Aquitanian from the old Roman province(s) of Aquitaine (see Map 4.2).

Dynastic stability might have been strength, but was not. There was only one ruling family, yet the entitlement of all of a Frankish king's sons to rule a share of the kingdom led to civil war and regionalism, and the power of these

Map 4.2 France and Italy in the eighth century

kings, like their counterparts elsewhere, was liable to aristocratic challenge. The descendents of Clovis, called Merovingians after an earlier ancestor Meroveus, reigned long after they had lost their power to the mayors of the palace. Latin *maior palatii* means 'the greater one of the palace' and designated the top palace official. Ebroin, mentioned in the previous chapter, was mayor of the palace of Neustria, the 'new' region, the western of the two portions into which northern France had split. It was in Austrasia, the 'eastern' region where the original Franks came from, that the ancestors of Charles Martel, Carloman and Pepin rose to power in the seventh century. Now, in the eighth century, the family was going from strength to strength. Charles the Hammer (= *martellus*) united Neustria to Austrasia at the outset of his rule, but the southern regions of France had gone their own way for many years and were conquered with difficulty: Burgundy by Charles and Aquitaine by his son Pepin. Yet, in the first half of the eighth century when these mayors of the palace were ruling, there were still Merovingian kings. In a society where revenues from land were by far the greatest source of power, the last Merovingians were said to have had only one estate and to have functioned as ceremonial heads of state, similar in the latter respect to modern European monarchs. Pepin wanted to be king, and asked the pope to authorise his usurpation.

The bishops of Rome began the eighth century within the Roman Empire ruled from Constantinople, also known as Byzantium. Every new pope had to be approved by the emperor, and papal documents were dated by imperial reigns. This is the case with the papal letter to Boniface quoted above, which was written in the joint reign of Emperors Leo III and Constantine V. Rome was part of the central Italian strip of Byzantine territory, the Exarchate of Ravenna, which divided the Lombard kingdom in the north from the Lombard duchies in the south (see Map 4.2). On the other hand, the popes had long assumed *de facto* rule over the region around Rome, which itself had been transformed into the city of the Church. As the eighth century proceeded the old links with the Byzantine Empire became more frayed. The Iconoclast Controversy, a dispute about the use of icons, painted religious images, in Christian worship, set anti-image emperors against pro-image popes. The above mentioned Emperor Leo III was the great protagonist of iconoclasm and antagonist of the papacy. In the early 730s he punished papal disobedience about icons, and resistance to increased imperial taxation besides, by confiscating papal estates in southern Italy and Sicily as well as transferring ecclesiastical control over these regions together with the southern Balkans and Crete from the pope to the rival patriarch of Constantinople. Moreover, the Byzantine Empire, with its heartland in Asia Minor under attack by the Arabs and its northern frontier by the Bulgars, could not protect its interests in central Italy. The Lombards were on their way to joining north and south and ruling a united Italy including Rome, and the papacy wanted help to prevent this. Again it must be emphasised how much a part of the Mediterranean world these popes were. Of the four with whom the long-lived Boniface dealt, Gregory III was a Syrian and Zacharius was a Greek. Boniface encouraged such men to look north.

What was wrong with the Lombards, that the popes did not want to be ruled by them? They were not only Christian but Catholic. Before Justinian's Reconquest of Italy the papacy had lived for decades under Arian rule without problems until the last years of Theoderic's reign. The point is that not only the Roman emperor functioned as the head of the Church – Leo III is exceptional only in the degree of religious change that he sought to bring about – all conscientious Catholic early medieval rulers considered that they had responsibility for right religion in the lands they ruled. They normally summoned Church councils and appointed bishops. There were variations: the Visigothic kings as seen in the last chapter had developed a strong identification with the Church, whereas the Lombards' ideology of the ruler was more secular and that of the earlier Franks nowhere near as religious as it was about to become. In any case rulers, conscientious or otherwise, utilised the Church in their lands as a concentration of wealth and opportunity for patronage. At the beginning of the sixth century so august a bishop as Remigius of Reims did not argue with Clovis over an ecclesiastical appointment that the king wanted (see p. 00). For the pope, at least the emperor was far away in Constantinople. A Catholic ruler of Italy would certainly have dominated the papacy, which had developed a taste for independence since the crumbling of the Roman Empire in the West. As well, the Lombards had intruded on Italy when it had just been reconquered by the East Romans in the sixth century. The eighth-century bishops of Rome were heirs to many years of effort in maintaining the Roman Empire in Italy against the Lombards, which for the region around Rome had, to a considerable extent, been that of papal effort as early as the time of Gregory the Great. Imperial interest had become papal interest.

The dates in what follows show how remarkably Frankish and papal interests dovetailed to produce a historical result. In 739 Pope Gregory III innovatively but unsuccessfully asked the Franks for help. With the Lombards encroaching on the Exarchate, even to the extent of occupying its capital Ravenna from time to time, although royal control over the southern duchies was their aim at this stage, more than appeals to the Byzantine Empire was needed. Pope Zacharias used diplomacy to good effect: at one point (742) in a novel move, he left Rome and went to speak to the Lombard king in person and secured the return of what the Lombards had taken as a donation to St Peter, first bishop of Rome.[5] The empire was becoming irrelevant. In 745 Boniface advised Zacharias to seek help from the Franks. 749 saw a new Lombard king, Aistulf, who would try to take over central Italy and fail. In 750 Pepin, the Frankish mayor of the palace, put his problem about the kingship to the pope as an authority, and Zacharias replied that the person with the power should have the royal title. Eighth-century sources record that Pepin was chosen king according to Frankish custom and anointed by bishop(s) – the *Royal Frankish Annals*, not the earliest source, says that this was done by Boniface himself – which was new in France. The fate of the last of the Merovingians was to be sent to a monastery, the long hair which had distinguished the line of Clovis replaced by the tonsure. These things happened in 751; in the same year in Italy, King Aistulf captured

Ravenna and by 752 he was demanding the submission of Rome and its region. The new pope Stephen II appealed to Byzantium for assistance, negotiated fruitlessly with the Lombard king, and when 'in particular he saw that no help would come his way from the imperial power' as the contemporary entry in the *Book of the Popes* explicitly states, he asked King Pepin of the Franks for help against the Lombards. Not surprisingly, Frankish envoys arrived with a positive response; what is surprising is that, when subsequently they accompanied the pope to the Lombard court, King Aistulf allowed the party to pass on to France. Pope Stephen's journey into France in 753–54 was unprecedented.

This is the decisive turning of the papacy from the Byzantines to the Franks, motivated by the need for protection. Pepin agreed to undertake a military campaign in Italy. Stephen anointed not only Pepin but his queen Bertrada and his two sons Charles (known to history as Charlemagne, from Latin *Carolus magnus*, i.e., Charles the Great; ruled 768–814) and Carloman (ruled 768–71), legitimising the new dynasty of Frankish kings, which is called Carolingian from its notable eighth-century rulers named Charles. The pope also added to the title of 'king of the Franks' that of 'patrician of the Romans'; hitherto the patriciate had been an imperially bestowed rank. This will not be the only indication that the papacy was perpetuating the Roman Empire on its own terms. It took three years of Frankish campaigning to bring the Lombards into line, and in the meantime envoys from the Byzantine Empire arrived and were said in the *Book of the Popes* to be 'unhappy' at what the Franks were doing. Well might they be, because central Italy was forever lost to the Empire. In 756 Pepin gave the cities taken back from the Lombards to St Peter in what is called the Donation of Pepin. From this point on the pope has been recognised as an independent territorial ruler. It could only have happened in the power vacuum that was Italy. Indeed, the formation of this Frankish–papal axis, about which there is more to say, could only have occurred in the wider power vacuum in which Europe was taking shape. Here the Pirenne Thesis, examined in the previous chapter, is quite correct. The weakening of what remained of the Roman Empire by the Islamic conquests ensured that the lands of the Franks and beyond would not remain merely the hinterland of Ancient Mediterranean civilisation.

Thus there was a double *coup* in the middle of the eighth century with the Carolingian usurpation of the Frankish kingship and the papal usurpation of the right to rule central Italy. Both were justified by the religious authority of the successors of St Peter, whom Christ referred to as the 'rock' (which is what 'Peter' means) on which he would found the Church and who was buried in Rome, and both were achieved by the success of the Carolingian rulers. And there was a third, unrelated *coup* at the same time: far to the east, the Abbasid dynasty of caliphs took power from the Umayyad dynasty. Only Spain remained under Umayyad rule, so the unity of the caliphate was itself broken. As may be recalled, the Umayyads had their roots in the aristocracy of Mecca and their right to rule was acknowledged by the Sunni, but not the Shia sect of Islam. The Abbasids ruled as descendents of Mohammed's family (Abbas was his uncle) and were initially supported by the Shia. Much of their backing came from Persian families that had converted to Islam, and the rise of the Abbasids has been seen as a claim of such *mawali* ('clients' of the Arab conquerors) to a full share in the power dynamics of the caliphate. Its capital was moved from Damascus to Baghdad, drawing the focus of the Islamic world further east and enhancing the cultural divide in the Mediterranean. It was to Baghdad in the later eighth century that a visitor from India brought a mathematical text employing the numerals that the Arabs would eventually pass on to Europe, including the number zero essential for calculations today. The system of numbering that appears on the pages of the book you are reading was not adopted in Europe until after the period it is about, however. Learning began to flourish under the caliphs of Baghdad at the same time as the revival of learning was undertaken under Charlemagne, which will be considered at the end of this chapter. Such historical coincidences as outlined in this paragraph can be useful in providing chronological pegs on which to hang an understanding of the early medieval past.

Back in Italy, the days of the Lombard kingdom were numbered. Its last phase can be usefully glimpsed by focusing on Abbess Ansilperga and the institution of which she was the head. The monastery of San Salvatore in Brescia was the most technologically sophisticated place of which we are aware in the Lombard kingdom. It had an aqueduct, lead piping, a filtered cistern and, apparently, baths, and possessed overshot, geared, vertical, even synchronised watermills. Its church had iron doors. San Salvatore was founded and richly endowed by Ansilperga's parents Ansa and Desiderius, who went on to become king and queen of the Lombards in 757. What we know about it suggests that Lombard elite culture, including literacy, should not be underestimated. The existence of prominent royal monasteries for women in the early Middle Ages is notable, too. The strategic marriages of Ansilperga's three sisters reflect the political situation of the Lombard kingdom: to the ruler of a southern Lombard duchy which Desiderius aimed to take over; to Tassilo, duke of Bavaria, a perennial thorn in the side of the Franks as we shall see; and to Charlemagne, king of the Franks, although he soon ended the marriage, probably because the death of his younger brother and rival King Carloman left him in sole power and with no need for a Lombard alliance.[6] When King Desiderius attempted to conquer the papal territory in central Italy, Pope Hadrian called on the Franks for help, and this time they conquered the Lombard kingdom. In 774 Charlemagne became king of the Lombards as well as of the Franks, having solemnly recognised the boundaries of the papal territory in central Italy. He was also patrician of the Romans, but went on to provide more than the protection that the pope wanted. After Hadrian had endorsed a compromise by an Eastern Church council to end the Iconoclast Controversy, Charlemagne called the Synod of Frankfurt in 794 which found that the pope was wrong and insisted that he change his position. Papal fears of being dominated by secular rulers were well founded.

The Frankish Kingdom

Considerable attention has been given here to the formation of the Frankish–papal axis, and more will be said about it at the beginning of the next chapter; however, Frankish historical annals written at the time are mainly a catalogue of military campaigns and treasure. The consolidation of Frankish control and its extension to new lands, especially in the origins of what would become Germany, are also important in forming the core of Europe. These developments are well illustrated by Bavaria and Saxony (see Map 4.2). Long claimed by the Franks, Bavaria was incorporated into their kingdom with great difficulty in the second half of the eighth century, for its duke, Tassilo, had other ideas. Tassilo was given the duchy as a child in the 740s by his uncle Pepin, the Frankish mayor of the palace, and as an adolescent in the 750s he became Pepin's vassal. (It shows how far this term of dependency and the social arrangement it represented had risen on the social scale that a duke could become the vassal of a king, as Pepin now was.) Yet in the 760s, Tassilo departed with his forces from a campaign that Pepin was conducting in Aquitaine, rendering him open to accusation of what the Franks called *herisliz*, 'army splitting', and married Liutperga, one of the above mentioned daughters of the king of the Lombards. The beautiful chalice shown here (see Figure 15), of

Figure 15 Chalice, *c*.780, given by Duke Tassilo and his wife Liutperga to his monastic foundation at Kremsmünster, where it is preserved. Gold and silver, the latter inlaid with niello, a black, sulphur alloy. (Stift Kremsmünster)

English workmanship, is inscribed with their names, expresses their patronage of the Church, and is an unmistakable sign of their ambition when read in the context of other evidence. The alliance of the duchy of Bavaria with the kingdom of the Lombards was calculated to advance the interests of both against the Franks. For years Duke Tassilo pursued an independent course, but in the 780s the Franks required his submission (Charlemagne at one point sent three armies against Bavaria) and ultimately deposed him.

The conquest of Saxony took a long time, although the decade of the 780s, which saw Charlemagne's success in Bavaria, was crucial here too. Whereas the Bavarians, among whom, it will be recalled, Boniface and Willibald had worked, were nominally Christian, paganism was still strong among the Saxons, including in their leadership. In 785 the Saxon leader named Widukind submitted to Charlemagne and was baptised. An ornamented box for holy relics, made of oak overlaid with gold, silver, cloisonné enamel, pearls and semi-precious stones including reused Classical engraved gems, is said to have been the king's baptismal gift to Widukind, who in turn gave it to the Saxon monastery which he founded. Notice the immediate participation of an elite convert in church patronage. There is some evidence about the pagan practices of Saxons among whom Christianity had come. One was rubbing pieces of wood together to make sacrilegious *nodfyr* or *niedfyr*, 'need-fire', a practice otherwise attested in Northern Europe. Also sacrilegious to the Christians were funeral practices like keening over the dead. Eighth-century reference to *spurcalia*, 'pagan rites', in February, which is still referred to as *Sporkelmonat* in modern German dialect, indicates that such customs were deeply entrenched. Charlemagne's legislation for Saxony in 782 was draconic, prescribing the death penalty for everything from human sacrifice to what we would call 'closet paganism'. The extent of forced conversion in Saxony drew a protest from Alcuin, the Englishman who was Charlemagne's chief advisor: 'a man can be coerced into baptism, but he cannot be coerced into faith.' This was a minority view in the Middle Ages. To Einhard, whose biography of Charlemagne was written early in the next century, conversion was the means by which the Saxons 'were to be united with the Franks and become one people with them'. And so it happened: the nation of Germany began as the eastern part of the Frankish kingdom.

The Franks did not always win: in 778 there was a famous defeat. Extending his activities into new territory, Charlemagne campaigned at the request of one Muslim ruler against another in northeast Spain. On the way back, as is related in the *Revised Frankish Annals* (but not the original version), Charlemagne

> moved into the pass across the Pyrenees. At the highest point of this the Basques lay in ambush; they attacked the rearguard and threw the whole army into great commotion and disorder. And although the Franks were manifestly superior to the Basques in both weapons and courage, yet they were rendered their inferiors by the steepness of the terrain and the character of the battle, which was not fought fairly. A great number of palace dignitaries whom the king had appointed to command the troops were killed

in this action. The baggage was plundered and the enemy promptly melted away in all directions, thanks to his knowledge of the country. The sorrow of this wound which he received overshadowed in the king's heart much of what had been successfully accomplished in Spain.

This is the historical kernel of the *Song of Roland*, an epic poem first written down *c*.1100 in a manuscript which survives. One cannot help thinking that of such circumstances, including the initial cover-up, great literature is made. More than 60 years after the event, the names of the dead on this occasion had not been forgotten. 'Since their names are widely known, I have neglected to give them,' wrote the anonymous biographer of Charlemagne's son Louis. Their legend was presumably taking shape.

The Carolingians' engagement with Spain continued in the late eighth century, although it was only in 801 that the capture of Barcelona anchored the Spanish March (= border region) in the northeast of the peninsula (see the map of the Carolingian Empire in the next chapter). Charlemagne himself did not go again to Spain, but eventually sent his son Louis, to whom he had given the rule of Aquitaine in southwest France, on campaign beyond the Pyrenees Mountains. People from Muslim as well as Christian Spain came to both of these rulers. The Visigoth Theodulf, scholar and poet, joined Charlemagne's court after 778, and participated in the educational reforms discussed at the end of this chapter. At the end of the eighth century Charlemagne received a visit from Sadun, the Muslim governor of Barcelona who submitted himself and his city, but not for long, and Abd-Allah, a disaffected member of the ruling family of Muslim Spain, the Umayyad emirs of Cordoba. The similarity of the parti-coloured arches of Charlemagne's palace chapel at Aachen, built at this time, and of the great mosque of Cordoba, begun slightly earlier, will be observed in the illustrations and suggests cultural contact (see Figures 16 and 17). As well, envoys arrived from Alfonso II of the Christian kingdom of the Asturias in northwest Spain, bearing what the *Royal Frankish Annals* record as 'an extraordinarily beautiful pavilion-tent' and 'coats of mail, mules and Moorish prisoners as tokens of his victory' at Lisbon. It was well to advertise such success to the powerful Franks. All of this is part of the visual display that marked the court of a really great early medieval ruler, in receipt of contacts from all over the known world, as will be further shown for Charlemagne at the beginning of the next chapter. Not only because of the Spanish March but also because of the overall power and prestige of the neighbour to the north, the Frankish way of doing things would be highly influential in Christian Spain.

Indeed, the exercise of power by, and under, the Carolingian rulers would be widely influential in Europe, and must be carefully examined. Carolingian France looks different from the earlier society portrayed by Gregory of Tours that was considered back in Chapter 2. Partly this is the result of its greater distance in time from the Roman Empire. Also, the Carolingians, who as successful rulers set the practice and expectations of their followers and even their opponents, were an Austrasian family, from the original Frankish heartland in the northeast, including the least Romanised part of Gaul. Theirs was a

Figure 16   Interior of Charlemagne's palace chapel at Aachen. (© Domkapital Aachen [photo: Ann Münchow])

Figure 17 Interior of the Great Mosque at Cordoba, Spain, begun 785. (© Institut Amatller d'Art Hispànic)

profoundly rural world of manors and monasteries. Moreover, they were an aristocratic family that had risen to rule over many years, and as rulers they continued to use the means to power that had got them where they were. These means to power can be well grasped by analysing the following description of an aristocrat named Dodo from a mid-eighth-century saint's life:

> Dodo was the *domesticus* of Prince Pippin and he had many estates and many armed men in his following.

It is short, but even so is most useful if analysed in sections. The first part is about public power. A *domesticus* was a palace official, which is what Pepin himself was technically too, being mayor of the palace. 'Prince' (*princeps* = 'the first person') was a useful title in the circumstances, and it is not surprising that the writer applied it to one who was not Pepin the father of Charlemagne, but Pepin of Heristal, the father of Charles Martel. Such public offices, of which the most common were countships (see below), were referred to as 'honours' (*honores*) and were a means to power not only for those who held them, but for those who bestowed them in patronage. In this respect there was continuity from earlier France, but also change.

The rest of Dodo's power was private, and its sources were the same as for the Carolingian rulers. The middle part of the description refers to his landed wealth, which could be of more than one type and have a variety of origins. He may have inherited, bought, been given or taken outright ownership of lands. Such an estate was referred to as an 'allod' and its possession as 'allodial tenure'. Or he may have acquired use but not outright possession of lands through an arrangement with a church or his prince, known as *precarium* or *beneficium*, holding it in precarial tenure, as a benefice or benefit, land let on favourable terms. In any case Dodo received revenues from the lands which consisted of a small surplus scraped off the production of subsistence peasants who generally came with the land. Land meant people in the Middle Ages. Pile enough little surpluses together and you have a great lord like Dodo: a landlord of peasants. What has just been written is so important in understanding the basis of (not just early) medieval power that readers are encouraged to reread it once or twice. Lordship over peasants and how these primary producers lived will be examined in the next chapter, based on detailed source material that becomes available in the early ninth century. Dodo was also a lord of fighting men. The last part of the description is about the private power of lordship over a military retinue. The Latin word used for his followers is *pueri*, his 'boys', which by the eighth century had become equivalent to *vassi*, 'vassals'. (For a discussion of these terms see p. 25 near the end of Chapter 1.) Again, Carolingian rulers were, like Dodo, landlords of peasants and lords of fighting men; moreover, even their distribution of public office was reinforced by vassalage.

Carolingian governance rested on the bases outlined above. As kings, Pepin and his successors appointed palace officials, although, not surprisingly, they did not have mayors of the palace. The Carolingians like their Merovingian predecessors continued to rule through public officials called counts, who represented them in the old city territories that (not without change) went back to Roman times. Originally county boundaries may have been determined by who collected the tax, but in the eighth century public taxation was no more. There were still tolls and dues, for the collection of which the counts were responsible. They also had military responsibilities but, in contrast to the episode reproduced from Gregory of Tours's *Histories* on p. 43, no more public garrisons; counts produced private armies of supporters for the Carolingian kings. The judicial function of these counts was of particular importance, and the count's court, Latin *mallus*, was the primary setting for their role as public officials. Carolingian organisation was brought to bear on the office of count, and some old anomalies were regularised; for example, the governor/bishops of Chur in what is now Switzerland, whose office was a sub-Roman survival of provincial government there, were replaced by counts under Charlemagne. In his *Capitulary* [edict, law] *concerning the Regions of Saxony* of 782 he established the counts' authority in this newly conquered region. Of particular importance in this is his delegation to the counts of authority to impose the *bannus*, a fine for major or minor offences, in their jurisdictions. Of course the ultimate public authority was the king's over his subjects, which he could delegate to counts, dukes and other officials. So important were the private power relationships in Carolingian society, however, that the public ones could almost be eclipsed.

Carolingian rule comprised to a considerable extent the sorts of private lordship described in connection with the aristocrat Dodo. Its mainstay was revenues from the royal estates, as these rulers did not tax. The taxation system inherited by early medieval kings from the Roman emperors had withered away everywhere before the eighth century. So kings were also landlords of peasants. The supply of royal land was limited, as the Carolingians had reason to know. True, booty from frequent military campaigns provided a valuable supplement to royal resources. The most spectacular example was the treasure of the Avars, themselves accomplished looters, that was won in campaigns on the Danube river and handed on to Charlemagne, who gave the lion's share to the papacy and distributed much among his supporters. The best gifts were of land, however. Carolingian rulers were also lords of fighting men. The Carolingian rulers utilised vassalage in a number of respects. It could set a tricky relationship on what was hoped would be the right course. Duke Tassilo of Bavaria, as mentioned earlier in this chapter,

> commended himself with his hands to vassalage. He swore many, innumerable oaths, placing his hands upon the relics of the saints. He promised fidelity to King Pepin and to his sons mentioned above, the lord Charles and Carloman, as a vassal, with right mind and firm devotion, ought in justice to do to his lords.

Vassalage was vital in raising private armies, which was all there were. It reinforced administration. Counts were royal vassals. It would be fair to say that the lifeblood of Carolingian rule was not bureaucracy but vassalage. In employing it in their governance the Carolingians institutionalised what was essentially private patronage, a most important development that will be reinforced by what is said in the next chapter.

Carolingian governance should not be underestimated. The rulers knew that they should be organised, and could be surprisingly so. Charlemagne planned for the supply of his armies, in contrast to the usual medieval circumstances where armies lived off the surrounding countryside, doing harm to friends as well as foes. The most spectacular example is when he decided to take on the Avars on the Danube in 791:

> To this end he assembled a most exceptionally powerful force from throughout his entire realm and accumulated provisions; then, dividing his army into two corps, he embarked on the campaign. He ordered count Theoderic and

Meginfrid, his chamberlain, to whom he entrusted one corps, to march along the northern bank of the Danube, while he himself, with the other corps, which he kept with him, took the southern bank of the same river in heading for Pannonia, and the Bavarians, with the army's supplies, which were transported by boat, were ordered to proceed downstream on the Danube.

(Revised Frankish Annals)

According to the original version, the Avars saw this coming and ran; they soon accepted Christianity, but had to give up their treasure as mentioned previously. One of the reasons why the Carolingians had so much time for the Church was the usefulness of its organisation, particularly monastic organisation. Monasteries even helped him in organising for war, being important sources of men and material for military campaigns. The most notable achievement of Charlemagne, however, was his educational reform. It is rightly dealt with in a discussion of Carolingian governance, for it was quite recognisably government policy. In two capitularies of the late eighth century, *On the Cultivation of Learning* and Section 72 of the *General Admonition*, Charlemagne expressed concern over low standards in ecclesiastical literacy, lest 'there being too little skill in writing, there might also be far too little wisdom in understanding the holy Scriptures' and, even more basically, 'they pray badly because of the incorrect books'. Of course another reason why the Carolingians had so much time for the Church is that they were believers, to whom monasteries were spiritual powerhouses of those 'fighting for us with their holy and pious prayers'.

The Carolingian revival of learning was directed at those in the Church, but was not confined to them. To improve education Charlemagne made use of some foreign experts. From Italy he brought in Paul the Deacon, whose *History of the Lombards* was quoted in the previous chapter, and Peter of Pisa. Theodulf was one of several scholars who came north from Spain. Alcuin was from England, although Charlemagne contacted him in Italy. His teacher at the cathedral school of York had been a pupil of Bede. Alcuin was the foremost advisor of Charlemagne and is an important example of civilisation coming out of the North. Carolingian learning was focused on the basics, and aimed at correct religious texts and indeed music, which was sought in Rome. Theodulf, who became bishop of Orleans at the end of the eighth century, might have personifications of the seven liberal arts painted on the wall of his episcopal palace, but most attention was given to the first three, grammar, rhetoric and logic, especially grammar. Alcuin wrote textbooks on these subjects, and on spelling. The improved handwriting known as Caroline script was developed in this period. This is the beginning of what modern scholars call the Carolingian Renaissance, applying this term from a much later Italy back to a period that Renaissance humanists did not realise had transmitted to them the Latin texts which they loved. The label is justified, however, by what Alcuin wrote to Charlemagne in 799: 'but your noble efforts have now brought about a re-birth of civilised standards in every kind of knowledge and of useful erudition', for 're-birth' is what 'Renaissance' means. In the same letter Alcuin also wrote, 'I can only wish that your authority may stimulate the education of the children at the palace; they should reproduce in their best style the lucid words by which you convey your thought so that, wherever the king's writ runs, it should display the nobleness of the king's wisdom.' The Carolingian court continued to school young people in the wisdom of the world, as it had done in Charlemagne's youth, but the definition of worldly wisdom was broadening to include book-learning.

Charlemagne was the most successful ruler in early medieval Europe, and rightly will figure in more than one chapter of this book. Looking back from our perspective, we can see that the eighth century indeed saw the formation of the core of Europe with the Frankish–papal axis, origins of Germany and northern focus. The last needs explanation. The Carolingian powerbase was in Austrasia, the northeastern part of the Frankish kingdom. There Charlemagne established his capital at Aachen/Aix-la-Chapelle at the end of the century. What this place had to recommend it was Roman baths. Einhard, the educated, lay, Frankish advisor and biographer of Charlemagne, is clear on this when he writes:

> He took delight in the steam-baths at the thermal springs, and loved to exercise himself in the water whenever he could. He was an extremely strong swimmer and in this sport no one could surpass him. It was for this reason that he built his palace at Aachen and remained continuously in residence there during the last years of his life and indeed until the moment of his death. He would invite not only his sons to bathe with him, but his nobles and friends as well, and occasionally even a crowd of his attendants and bodyguards, so that sometimes a hundred men or more would be in the water together.

Aachen was also located in the region where Carolingian family lands and those of their supporters (doubtless including magnates to whom Einhard was referring) were concentrated. For the inspiration of his palace chapel there (illustrated in Figure 16) – 'now is the time for prayers in the royal palace, where a fine building rises with its wonderful dome', wrote Theodulf – Charlemagne's architects could look south to the church of San Vitale in Ravenna if not further east. The model for his palace hall was nearer to hand: the basilica of the Roman Emperor Constantine at Trier (now in Germany), which in the fourth century had been one of four capitals scattered around the Roman Empire. The eighth-century Franks ruled from the north.

Yet sometime around the second half of the eighth century someone writing in the interests probably of the papacy, possibly of the Franks or maybe of both together looked back over the preceding centuries and forged a document known as the Donation of Constantine. In this false charter the Roman emperor Constantine in the early fourth century, grateful to Pope Sylvester for his conversion and his cure from leprosy (according to fifth-century papal myth), supposedly gave the West to the pope and took himself off to Constantinople to rule the East from there. Were this true, little of what this book has been about so far would have happened. It is false, but shows how older, Mediterranean, imperial ideas persisted.

The Ninth Century:
Expanding the Boundaries

The Carolingian Empire

On Christmas Day of AD 800 in St Peter's church at Rome before the shrine of the saint amid splendours of silver and gold, silk and jewels that gleamed under many lights, Charlemagne was crowned by Pope Leo III and acclaimed by the people present as Roman emperor. Then, continues the account in the *Royal Frankish Annals*, Charlemagne 'was adored by the apostolic one [i.e., the pope] in the way the emperors of old were'. Acclamation was indeed the way Roman emperors were made. Popes had had no role in designating the emperors of old, but the patriarchs of Constantinople had crowned Eastern emperors after, not before, their acclamation since the second half of the fifth century. Papal coronation of a Roman emperor nevertheless would not have been a problem in the fantasy world of the Donation of Constantine, the forged document mentioned at the end of the previous chapter, according to which Emperor Constantine in the fourth century had given his imperial diadem to the pope, who had not put it on but was not said to have given it back either. In reality Pope Leo was very much in Charlemagne's debt at that point. He had sought his help after being physically attacked by local enemies in Rome and had been allowed to clear himself of charges brought against him by swearing to his own innocence. 'From that moment on,' wrote the disapproving contemporary Byzantine chronicler Theophanes, 'Rome has stood under the power of the Franks.' He said that the pope crowned Charlemagne in repayment, and the *Book of the Popes* does not contradict this, declaring that Charles deserved the acclamation as emperor for his defence and love of the Church and bishop of Rome. The writer of the *Annals of Lorsch* (a Frankish monastery) gave reasons why the imperial coronation of Charlemagne was appropriate: essentially there was no emperor at the time, for in the East a woman ruled (see below), and Charlemagne held the former imperial seats of Rome and elsewhere in the West in his power.

With a great deal of hindsight, modern historians usually have explained and interpreted this extraordinary event as follows. The papacy had succeeded in avoiding inclusion in a Lombard kingdom of all Italy, but now the Franks were active there. Charlemagne had added the Lombard kingdom in northern Italy to his own, and his forces were engaging with southern Lombards when he was in Rome assisting the pope. This was Charlemagne at the height of his powers, which were far greater than any Lombard ruler had possessed. Was the papacy going to end up in an empire of the Franks? Only on my terms, said Pope Leo, and surprised him with an imperial coronation in the middle of a church service. In other words, the coronation was an attempt by the papacy to assert its control over the Franks and maintain its independence in the papal territory. Historians cite in support the later statement by Charlemagne's biographer Einhard that Charlemagne 'made it clear that he would not have entered the cathedral that day at all, although it was the greatest of all the festivals of the Church, if he had known in advance what the Pope was planning to do'. This is itself interpreted to mean that Charlemagne realised and regretted that he had been outmanoeuvred ceremonially to the extent that he owed this grand new title and whatever authority that went with it to the pope. In fact what Einhard goes on to say is that the imperial coronation resulted in prolonged dispute with the Byzantines, who were most displeased by it. There is also the fact that near the end of his life Charlemagne had his one surviving son Louis crown himself emperor at Aachen, which could be taken as a ceremonial declaration of imperial independence from the papacy, although Louis the Pious was subsequently crowned by the pope when the latter visited France and the imperial title was thenceforth regarded as in the pope's gift. Whatever the reasons for the imperial coronation of Charlemagne, an institution was created thereby that was to endure in one form or another in Europe until 1806, although it was not called the Holy Roman Empire in the early Middle Ages.[1]

Charlemagne's diplomatic contacts about this time are fascinating. A year after his imperial coronation he unsuccessfully proposed marriage to Irene, the first woman to rule the Roman (Byzantine) Empire in her own right. (She is not the best of feminist icons, having blinded her own son to gain power.) This is one of the great 'what ifs' of history and as such is apt to be lightly dismissed, but note that our source for it, the above mentioned Byzantine historian Theophanes, states that the marriage was intended to 'unite east and west' and that Irene was willing but an adviser, the eunuch Aetios, intervened, and in any case Irene was soon overthrown. And then the elephant arrived in the kingdom of the Franks. A few years previously Charlemagne had sent three envoys to Caliph Harun al-Raschid; to be precise the date was 1197, the year that Charlemagne had received a visit from a disaffected relative of the Umayyad emirs of Spain, whose mortal enemy was the Abbasid caliph, which is interesting. The Abbasids, it will be recalled, ruled from Baghdad. Two of the envoys died, but Isaac the Jew returned to Charlemagne with magnificent gifts from one great and distant ruler to another, including an elephant that bore the name of the first caliph of the dynasty, Abul Abaz. Delivered to Charlemagne at his capital Aachen, the elephant lived eight more years until it died when being taken on campaign against the Danes. Finally, there were the problems with the pre-existing Roman Empire to sort out, not only Byzantine resentment over Charlemagne having been made emperor, to which Einhard referred, but also direct confrontation between Franks and Byzantines in southern Italy and the Adriatic. Negotiations with the Byzantines eventually resulted in their recognition of Charlemagne's imperial title, but they had no doubts that it was they who were the Romans.

After becoming emperor Charlemagne had an equestrian statue of King Theoderic the Ostrogoth brought from Ravenna in Italy to his new capital at Aachen. Here may be an indication of how Charlemagne saw himself: as a Germanic king with Roman trappings, like Theoderic. The statue of Theoderic does not survive, but an equestrian figure of Charlemagne, or possibly his grandson Charles the Bald, is illustrated in Figure 18. Such sculptures had a Roman prototype. Charlemagne would have also encountered Theoderic in Germanic

Figure 18 Equestrian statue of Charlemagne or Charles the Bald. The figure of (either) Charles is ninth century, but the horse is a fifteenth-century replacement. (© Photo RMN – Jean-Gilles Berizzi)

legend. Charlemagne's biographer Einhard wrote that 'he directed that the age-old narrative poems, barbarous enough, it is true, in which were celebrated the warlike deeds of the kings of ancient times, should be written out and so preserved' (they have not been, in this form). Like Theoderic, Charlemagne was to be celebrated in song, with the best known of the many legends of Charlemagne and the 12 peers, supposedly his leading noblemen, being the *Song of Roland*, which as mentioned in the previous chapter was based on a disastrous event of the late eighth century and preserved in a manuscript written *c.*1100. Yet already in the late ninth century history morphed into legend in the *Deeds of Charles* (the Great), compiled to entertain his descendant Charles the Fat when the glory days of the Carolingian empire were long in the past, by an author who was a monk at the monastery of St Gall and is very likely to be identified as Notker the Stammerer. Charlemagne and his army had come to Italy to attack the Lombards. From a tower at Pavia, the Lombard capital, King Desiderius and a Frankish exile watched the enemy approach: baggage, army, royal escort, clergy and finally the ruler himself.

> Then came in sight that man of iron, Charlemagne, topped with his iron helm, his fists in iron gloves, his iron chest and his Platonic shoulders clad in an iron cuirass. An iron spear raised high against the sky he gripped in his left hand, while in his right he held his still unconquered sword. For greater ease of riding other men keep their thighs bare of armour; Charlemagne's were bound in plates of iron. As for his greaves, like those of all his army, they, too, were made of iron. His shield was all of iron. His horse gleamed iron-coloured and its very mettle was as if of iron. All those who rode before him, those who kept him company on either flank, those who followed after, wore the same armour, and their gear was as close a copy of his own as it is possible to imagine. Iron filled the fields and all the open spaces. The rays of the sun were thrown back by this battle-line of iron. This race of men harder than iron did homage to the very hardness of iron. The pallid face of the man in the condemned cell grew paler at the bright gleam of iron. 'Oh! The iron! Alas for the iron!' Such was the confused clamour of the citizens of Pavia. The strong walls shook at the touch of iron. The resolution of the young grew feeble before the iron of these older men. When therefore Otker, who had foreseen the truth, with one swift glance observed all this, which I, a toothless man with stammering speech, have tried to describe, not as I ought, but slowly and with labyrinthine phrase, he said to Desiderius: 'That is Charlemagne, whom you have sought so long.' As he spoke he fell half-conscious to the ground.

The situation is reminiscent of Charlemagne's well-planned approach to the Avars (see pp. 94–5 of the previous chapter), the truth of which there is no reason to doubt. Indeed the author quoted above gives his source for Charlemagne's wars in what he was told as a child by Adalbert, a very old

Frankish warrior who had fought against the Avars and others on the eastern frontier. It was not hard to make the real Charlemagne larger than life.

Charlemagne seems to have felt a heightened responsibility as emperor and was particularly engaged in the Roman activities of codifying old laws and making new ones. For example, a revised version of the Salic Law of the Franks, originally codified under Clovis, was issued by Charlemagne in about 802. It survives in over 50 Carolingian manuscripts, which is a great many for an early medieval text, especially a secular one, and suggests that it was actually used by judges. His care for administration is reflected in surviving written orders addressed to counts by royal agents known as *missi dominici*. The *missi* were literally 'those sent' by the ruler (*dominus*, 'lord'), in this case to check up on whether the counts were carrying out royal commands and their judicial duties. The counts are assumed to be literate in the document. It can be very frank:

> Next, take the greatest care that neither you yourself nor, insofar as you can control the matter, anyone in your county become caught up in the evil strat-agem of saying: 'Let us keep quiet until these *missi* have moved on and judge our cases among ourselves afterwards!', and that those cases do not remain unjudged or at least suffer delay in consequence. Strive rather to ensure that they are judged before we come to you.

The counts were the king emperor's regional representatives; note the passing reference to the limit of their control. About governance at a lower level, a directive from a capitulary (as Carolingian laws are known), dated 810, 'Concerning the common people, that everyone compel their subordinates to obey better and better and consent to the imperial commands and orders' is most instructive, for it shows Charlemagne ruling through private authority. If Carolingian society was more coherently organised than that in the world of Gregory of Tours, it was along simple lines of lordship and dependency, grounded in sheer practicality and reinforced by values of honour and shame. From this perspective the rule of the Carolingian king emperors, and even more of their Ottonian and Salian successors in tenth- and eleventh-century Germany considered in the remaining chapters of this book, can appear to be a superstructure that rises to dizzying heights.

There was very little of Christian Continental Western Europe that was not in the Carolingian Empire of Charlemagne's one surviving son Louis the Pious (ruled 814–40)[2]: only the southern Lombard duchies, Byzantine Italy and the little kingdom of the Asturias in northern Spain (see Map 5.1). What is proposed here is to look at what being in this empire meant for ordinary people, about whom we have some details for the first time. To begin with, readers are reminded of what such people meant to the Carolingian Empire: they were its sustenance. Consider any elite individual (as we did with Dodo in the previous chapter), institution (as in the case below) or even object (such as the Coronation Gospels featured on the frontispiece of the book you are reading) and reflect that

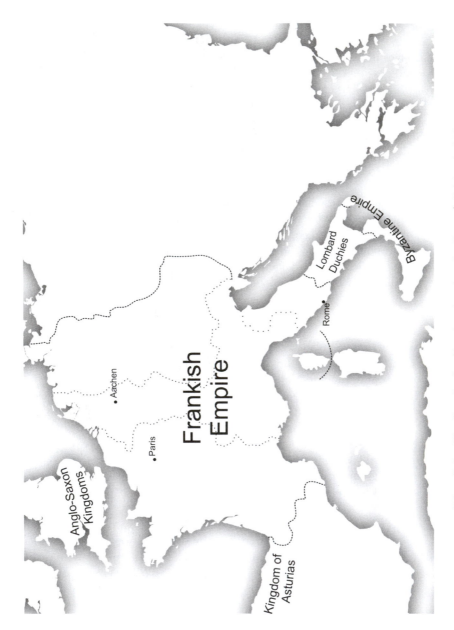

Map 5.1 The Carolingian Empire, showing also lines of division in 843

the existence of each and every one was made possible by the labour of peasants. As Theodulf of Orleans admonished the Carolingian elite:

> Their sweat and their toil made you rich. The rich get their riches because of the poor. But nature submits you to the same laws. In birth and in death you are alike. The same holy water blesses you; you are anointed with the same oils; the flesh and blood of the lamb [Christ, in the ceremony of the Mass] nourishes you all together.

His intended audience might not have cared to think overmuch along these lines, but they knew well enough where their wealth came from; otherwise we would not have sources like the following. The Polyptyque (a fancy word for 'book') of Abbot Irminon is a record of the landed estates and people of the monastery of St Germain-des-Prés near Paris made in 825–29. Thanks to a mode of production in which power was based on wealth drawn directly from estates and to the Carolingian push for organisation on the part of rulers and the monasteries that they patronised, precise data from literally the grassroots level have been preserved, in a limited sample. The vast proportion of the inhabitants of the Carolingian Empire, even allowing for greater urbanisation in its southern parts, were subsistence peasants. They did not necessarily live like the people who are about to be introduced. These are the ones who can be seen.

Here is an example of a peasant family, the basic unit of agricultural production of those surpluses by which the Carolingian elite, in this case a great monastery, was supported:

> Actard, villein (*colonus*), and his wife, also a villein (*colona*), named Eligilde, 'men' of St Germain, have with them six children called Aget, Teudo, Simeon, Adalside, Dieudonnée, Electard. They hold a free manse containing five bonniers of arable land and two ansanges, four arpents of vineyard, $4^{1}/_{2}$ arpents of meadow. They provide four silver sous for military service and the other year two sous for the livery of meat, and the third year, for the livery of fodder, a ewe with a lamb. Two muids of wine for the right of pannage, four deniers for the right of wood; for cartage a measure of wood, and 50 shingles. They plough four perches for the winter grain and two perches for the spring. Manual and animal services, as much as is required of them. Three hens, 15 eggs. They enclose four perches of meadow.

Bonniers, arpents, muids and perches are measurements of various kinds. Much else that is unfamiliar in this passage from the Polyptyque of Abbot Irminon will be explained in the course of considering what being in the Carolingian Empire meant for these people. *Coloni* (to give the Latin plural) were free tenants, in this case living on a free manse or working farm. As a free man, Actard might have been required to swear allegiance to his emperor. Actard does not fight for him, however, but instead of (which is what 'for' means in the passage) military service and supply (livery), the family pays (sous are coins). It is part of their rent to the monastery of St Germain-des-Prés, which has the obligation to provide soldiers and supplies for the army. The family pays in goods and coin for two extras: pannage, which is running pigs in the forest, and collecting wood from it. The rest of what they owe is labour services, working for the landlord (the monastery), although the carrying service (cartage) has been commuted to payment in raw and finished material. Some agricultural work is specified; however, 'manual and animal services, as much as is required of them' has just that open-ended arbitrary quality that goes with servitude, and is virtually indistinguishable from 'manual service where they are ordered' owed by a slave family settled on a free manse in the same estate.

In other words, the free/unfree distinction, which went back to Roman government and taxation, was breaking down; this is just one of the overall observations that can be made from the passage, but it especially relates to what being in the Carolingian Empire meant, or did not mean, for these peasants. The Carolingians, as may be recalled, did not tax. What the peasants paid, they paid to their landlord, for whom they also worked. The practices of giving slaves their own dwelling and land which could be passed on in their family, and of requiring labour services from free tenants as in the example cited, made the distinction between them nominal. Originally the status of land and people would have been the same, but generations of intermarriage and land transfer meant that it often was not, as in the case briefly referred to at the end of the previous paragraph. All of the peasants, regardless of their technical status (or gender), were 'men of St Germain'; the monastery, not the empire, was the authority in their lives. Thus the labels applied to people in the Polyptyque testify to a transition from public to private authority. True, the monastery was supposed to mediate imperial directives to its dependants and compel their compliance, but it had interests of its own: fostering and protecting the network of estates with which it had been endowed, and on which every man, woman and child was an asset. Notice above the typically medieval ascription of ownership/lordship to the saintly founder, Germanus of Paris (d.576), whose rights had to be upheld by all possible means, including the compilation of the Polyptyque of Abbot Irminon. All of this is not to say that the Carolingian Empire had no effect on these peasants. Carolingian rule had brought them a century of peace and prosperity. There had been no fighting in the Paris area since Charles Martel established his rule over Neustria at the beginning of his reign. Unfortunately, that was to change as the ninth century went on.

In one important respect Carolingian success rested on luck. With the exception of a few years, there was only one overall ruler per generation: Charles Martel (719–41), Pepin (741–68), Charlemagne (768–814) and Louis the Pious (814–40). Yet the Carolingians like their Merovingian predecessors considered that sons should share in rule, even when they were still mayors of the palace. Long before Louis' death his four sons were causing problems, and after it the Carolingian Empire broke apart in continuing civil war. In the last years of Louis' reign a letter was written from the monk, Lupus of Ferrières, to the layman Einhard, royal adviser and biographer of Charlemagne, that may be surveyed as a fitting conclusion to this section on the Carolingian Empire. It represents the hope of the Carolingian Renaissance. These two men met on the plane of scholarship, Lupus the younger disciple putting questions to Einhard the elderly master. Lupus begins by consoling Einhard over the death of his wife, whose name was Imma and for whom he offers prayers. He recommends that Einhard read what Augustine of Hippo wrote about sorrow in a particular chapter of the *City of God* in the early fifth century. Lupus discusses his plans to visit Einhard, referring in passing to two abbots on imperial business. Then he asks his questions, first about passages from the textbook *On Arithmetic* written by Boethius in the sixth century. One is a verbal description of a cube, which Lupus quotes and says, 'I do not understand the shape of this intricate thing, and I am in desperate need of your help to grasp the meaning of it.' He also wants to study another arithmetical text, the *Calculus* probably written by Victorius of Aquitaine in the fifth century, with Einhard's guidance. Carolingian scholarship did extend to the higher liberal arts. Another enquiry is about Latin pronunciation, which the Carolingians worked out anew from Latin poetry that scanned according to the sound of words. Lupus asks Einhard to send him a copy of letters of the alphabet in uncial script (see the frontispiece of this book) drawn by a royal scribe 'with the painter, whenever he returns'. A promise to return a book of secular Latin poetry by Aulus Gellius and other books to Einhard when Lupus visits him, and a reference to other enquiries about Greek words, conclude the letter. Einhard died a few months before Louis the Pious did. He would not have liked what happened next when Carolingian luck ran out.

Nithard and Dhuoda

Two lay writers of the Carolingian Renaissance, Nithard and Dhuoda, provide particularly useful evidence for the period of the civil wars that would eventually see the end of the Carolingian Empire. Since both in their own way address the same situation, that situation must be properly introduced. When Louis the Pious became emperor in 814 he had three sons: Lothair, Pippin and Louis, later known as 'the German'. He soon made provision for them to share in his rule: Lothair the eldest as emperor (and eventual successor); Pippin as king of Aquitaine, which is what his father had been when Charlemagne died; and Louis as king of Bavaria. There was also another sub-king left over from the reign of Charlemagne: Bernard, who had succeeded his deceased father, the brother of Louis the Pious, to rule in Italy. Worried by the aforementioned arrangements that Louis made for his sons, Bernard revolted, was blinded by order of his uncle Louis and died. It was only the first revolt against Louis the Pious. When Louis' wife Irmengard, mother of his three sons, died, Louis married Judith of that most durable of all European families, the Welfs, and in 823 they had a son, Charles, eventually called 'the Bald'. The subsequent revolts were about giving this youngest son a share of rule, which his mother and father insisted upon. The last of the repeated divisions of the Carolingian Empire between these sons, made shortly before Emperor Louis died in 840, is revealing. His son Louis the German still had Bavaria (after trying for much more), Lothair had the rest of the eastern part of the Empire plus Italy (and the imperial title), and Charles had the western part of the Empire. The other son Pippin had died, but his own son, also called Pippin, claimed the kingship of Aquitaine by inheritance from his father. Midway through the reign of Louis the Pious the emperor acquired the services of Bernard, duke of Septimania where France meets Spain, whose apparently inexplicable influence over Louis the Pious led to accusations of a sexual liaison with Empress Judith and witchcraft. Nithard does not make them, but says that Bernard did the empire no good. Bernard was Dhuoda's husband.

Nithard was the son of Angilbert, adviser and poet at the court of Charlemagne, and Bertha, Charlemagne's daughter. Theirs was not a marriage. Nithard wrote a short historical text, which begins with a background summary of the reign of Louis the Pious, and then focuses on the continuing power struggle between Louis' sons (and others) after the old emperor's death. This author participated in the events that he chronicled:

> While I was writing this at the Loire near St. Cloud, an eclipse of the sun occurred in Scorpio in the first hour of October 18, a Tuesday [841, four months after the events he was writing about]. After breaking off these negotiations Louis and Charles rose at dawn, occupied the peak of a mountain near Lothair's camp with about one-third of their army, and waited for Lothair's arrival and the striking of the second hour, as their men had sworn. When both had come, they fought a violent battle on the brook of the Burgundians. Louis and Lothair were engaged in heavy fighting in a place called Brittas; there Lothair was overcome and fled. The troops which Charles confronted at a place called Fagit immediately took flight. But the part of our army which attacked Adalhard and others at Solemnat, and to which I gave vigorous assistance with God's help, fought bitterly. There the fight was a draw, but in the end all of Lothair's party fled.

You may, if you like, picture Nithard as one of the contemporary Carolingian soldiers on the cover of this book. Nithard's lord, at whose request his *Histories* was written, was Charles the Bald, youngest son of Louis the Pious by his second wife Judith. On an earlier occasion Charles sent Nithard as one of two envoys to Lothair, the eldest son to whom the imperial title (which was not divided) had passed. Lothair 'deprived Charles' emissaries of the benefices which his father had given them because they did not want to break their fealty and join him'. In other words Nithard lost some lands because he wouldn't switch sides in the conflict. In the fierce competition of rulers for supporters, private lordship flourished anew. For example, after various reversals Lothair, anxious to keep up the numbers of his supporters, 'distributed public property for private use', Nithard wrote. Long afterwards, under Charles the Bald, countships would become hereditary, making public office a family possession.

At the same time as Nithard was compiling his *Histories*, in her home at Uzès in southern France Dhuoda was writing a manual of advice for her son William, whose lord, like Nithard's, was King Charles. In fact, Nithard says that as a consequence of the battle, on which he is quoted above, William was sent by his father, Duke Bernard of Septimania, to do the king homage – to become his 'man' (= Latin *homo*) in high-level dependency in contrast to the low-level dependency of peasant 'men of St Germain' – provided that certain lands were given by Charles, of course. Dhuoda calls her son a hostage. Their statements are compatible in the circumstances, which include a suggestive series of dates. Her husband Bernard had been the controversial top official of Louis the Pious, who died on 20 June 840. Nine months later on 22 March 841, Dhuoda gave birth to their second child, who was taken before baptism from his mother to his father in Aquitaine by the local bishop and Bernard's men; she does not know her own child's name. She says she has not seen her older son William since he was 14, his age when he became Charles's vassal. Bernard told her to stay in Uzès, where she was useful to him. Toward the end of the manual she writes to her son:

> I acknowledge that, to defend the interests of my lord and master Bernard, and so that my service to him might not weaken in the March and elsewhere – so that he may not abandon you and me, as some men do – know that I have gone greatly into debt. To respond to great necessities, I have frequently borrowed great sums, no only from Christians but also from Jews. To the extent that I have been able, I have repaid them. To the extent that I can in the future, I will always do so. But if there is still something to pay after I die, I ask and I beg you to take care in seeking out my creditors. When you find them, make sure that everything is paid off either from my own resources, if any remain, or from your assets – what you have now or in what you eventually acquire through just means, with God's help.

Dhuoda represents the high and the low in early medieval womanhood: subjugated to the family interest and yet active in that interest. Her resources were real. It would have been a woman of well-off family who was married to Bernard in the palace at Aachen, as she tells us, and this was the era when the reverse dowry from man to woman was the main payment in a marriage and women inherited property. Few modern women could write a manual as relatively learned as Dhuoda's, with its trendy etymology (derivation of words) and numerology (number symbolism).

Dhuoda wrote to her son about values. Most are religious, and provide valuable evidence of Carolingian lay piety. Love of chastity, justice and the poor were deemed appropriate to stress in this advice to a young aristocrat, which is not to say that it was heeded. William is to pray seven times a day, as the monks do. He is to read books for spiritual improvement, including the Bible. In the latter Dhuoda emphasises the Beatitudes, the blessings spoken by Christ in the Sermon on the Mount, and the psalms of the Old Testament. The secular values are of particular interest because of their redressing the balance of so many early medieval sources which have to do with the Church. Book 3 of her Manual advises William on how to deal with various people in the world: his father Bernard, his lord Charles, his lord's family, noble magnates, great and lesser men and priests. Loyalty to one's lord is stressed:

> May the madness of treachery never, not once, make you offer an angry insult. May it never give rise in your heart to the idea of being disloyal to your lord.

Charles's royal status is mentioned, but the language of lordship prevails over that of kingship. Indeed, it appears in family relations, for William is especially urged to be loyal to his father, and Dhuoda writes of her *servitium*, as of a vassal to a lord, to Bernard in the passage quoted previously. Dhuoda gives particular attention to counsel, which was owed to lords as well as military service. The good counsellors whom she recommended to William should have included people like Nithard, with his sense of public government undermined (we would say 'white-anted' in Australia, with reference to termites eating away a structure from within) by private concerns.

Nithard's *Histories* shows us the society about which Dhuoda's advice was given as he writes of royal vassals, homage, sworn fealty (Latin *fidelitas*, 'faithfulness') and what Nithard and Dhuoda saw as its opposite: the transfer of allegiance from one to another of the contending sons of Louis the Pious. Nithard does not mention Dhuoda but he does give us Hildegard, the sister of Charles the Bald. When Charles learned that Hildegard was holding captive one of his counts, Adalgar (who had accompanied Nithard on the diplomatic mission referred to above), in the city of Laon, where she was abbess of a monastery, he rode there overnight with his forces. Hildegard speedily agreed to release Adalgar, but Charles's men wanted to burn the town to the ground. Charles succeeded in calling them off, and Hildegard did him homage. Laon was in the contested region of northeast France between the Rivers Seine and Meuse, which Louis the Pious had granted to Charles the Bald but Lothair claimed after his father's death. It was a family quarrel and Hildegard was included. Her authority came not only from her royal lineage but also as abbess of a monastery which was a significant institution in the city of Laon. The incident gave Nithard an opportunity to say something positive about his lord King Charles the Bald, for whom he wrote the *Histories*. By the end of the work he implies that Charles was unwise to seek the continuing assistance (by marrying into the family) of the seneschal (palace official) Adalhard, who had ill advised Louis the Pious to give public assets to private individuals in order to gain their support. On the whole Nithard's content is far more secular than Dhuoda's – he could enjoy well-organised, staged combat between Saxons, Gascons (Basques), Austrasians and Bretons when the armies of Charles the Bald and Louis the German had joined forces against Lothair – but his political morality is informed by his religious faith.

Neither Nithard nor Dhuoda were optimistic about the future, and with good cause. They wrote just before the 843 Treaty of Verdun by which Louis the Pious's surviving three sons, Lothair, Louis the German and Charles the Bald, divided Europe into France, Germany and a strip of often contentious lands in between, setting problems for the future (Lorraine, long disputed between Germany and France, derives from Lotharingia named for Louis' eldest son). The divisions are indicated on Map 5.1. Civil war continued and was joined by other problems to which we are about to turn. More immediately, Charles the Bald executed Bernard of Septimania, Dhuoda's husband, after which their son William, acting on a family obligation that Dhuoda never mentions, tried to avenge his father's death but was killed instead of King Charles.[3] We seem to have returned to the France of Gregory of Tours, where Merovingian kings after Clovis were always arguing over their share of the kingdom, only now the fragmentation was to go much further. Clearly royal vassalage was an unsustainable basis for effective government if the Carolingian rulers were contending for supporters. Nithard registers something significant when he has Charles say that 'it seemed not a bit fair to him that he should surrender to Lothair the kingdom from the Meuse to the Seine which his father had given him, especially, since so many of the nobility in these areas now supported him.' There was always the potential in Carolingian governance for building such power bases. In this case of course it suited the ruler very well. Yet his successors as kings of France could not prevent the process occurring at levels below them. Royal authority (*bannum*) devolved onto hereditary counts and dukes, and ultimately any noble with a castle and soldiers, as will be explained at the end of the next chapter. The future kings of Germany, on the other hand, would control their officials and make Carolingian government work until almost the end of the period of this book, as will be explained in its remaining two chapters.

Nithard and Dhuoda were by no means the last products of the Carolingian Renaissance, which went on for decades in the disintegrating empire. Charles the Bald reigned as king of the western Franks and finally as emperor until 877 and was associated with many other texts besides Nithard's *Histories*. The aforementioned Lupus of Ferrières, who lived until 862, wrote a letter of advice to Charles the Bald, which is all platitudes until the last sentence: 'You will crush and defeat the rebels, having God, as we believe, fighting on your side, and after a hard temporal reign you will gain a kingdom which is eternal and truly peaceful.' Charles had a library that included *On Arithmetic* by Boethius, one of the texts in the letter by Lupus cited at the end of the previous section of this chapter. Some of the most beautiful manuscripts of the Carolingian Renaissance were made for Charles the Bald. The most extraordinary of those who benefited from his patronage was the following. One of a number of Irish scholars on the Continent was John Scotus Eriugena (= John the Scot born in Ireland), the only original theologian of the early Middle Ages. His translation of the writings of the sixth-century philosopher Pseudo-Dionysius from Greek to Latin was inspected and approved by Anastasius, the papal librarian, in a letter written to Charles the Bald in 860:

It is a wonderful thing how that barbarian, living at the ends of the earth, who might be supposed to be as far removed from the knowledge of this other language as he is from the familiar use of it, has been able to comprehend such ideas and translate them into another tongue. I refer to John Scotigena, whom I have learned by report to be in all things a holy man.

Civilisation still came out of the north, but so did the Vikings, the Northmen.

The Vikings

According to surviving written evidence, the Vikings appeared suddenly in the last years of the eighth century. Charlemagne's adviser Alcuin, who was from northern England, reacted thus to news of the attack on the island monastery of Lindisfarne there in 793:

> It is some 350 years that we and our forefathers have inhabited this lovely land, and never before in Britain has such a terror appeared as this we have now suffered at the hands of the heathen. Nor was it thought possible that such an inroad from the sea could be made.

After this the Vikings attacked repeatedly: from the Irish Sea by 795, from the Bay of Biscay by 799, throughout the ninth century and beyond. Alcuin's words convey a double shock: at the surprise of the attack and the paganism of the attackers. His last statement as quoted is very interesting in showing the practical perception at the time, although we do not know on what this was based. In the days before radar, of course, an enemy out at sea was virtually undetectable, whereas at least word would spread of one moving by land. In general at this time, organised Christian Europe was impinging on its pagan neighbours by conquest and conversion. Heathens were not expected to appear out of nowhere, attacking its most sacred institutions. Monasteries, which had become repositories of movable wealth, were the Vikings' favourite targets; the situation of some on islands, meant to emphasise monastic separateness from ordinary society, of course put those monasteries in harm's way from seaborne raiders. They came to Iona, the important monastic foundation of St Columba, in 795, 802 and 806; a new monastery of St Columba away from the coast at Kells in Ireland was built in 807. Whether the most beautiful manuscript known as the Book of Kells dates from the eighth or beginning of the ninth century and was produced at Iona, Kells or even elsewhere, it represents the apex of northern Christian culture in the lands the Vikings attacked.

A page of another manuscript, the Codex Aureus ('Golden Book'), has a story to tell about English and Vikings in the ninth century. Its splendid appearance would not be apparent from a black-and-white photograph, but may be imagined from the following description. On it are framed words about the birth of Christ from the Gospel of St Matthew in alternating lines in which either the letters of the words or the background of the words are illuminated with gold foil. In the latter case the letters are brightly painted. This and further ornament of the text combines Insular and Continental motifs, as one would expect from a manuscript from southeastern England. Yet it is the plain text added above and below the words of the Gospel on this page that is of especial interest to us here:

> In the name of our lord Jesus Christ. I Alderman Aelfred and Werburg my wife have acquired this book from a heathen army with our true money, that is, with pure gold, and this we have done for the love of God and for the good of our souls, and because we were not willing that this holy book should remain any longer in heathen hands.

It goes on to record the couple's gift of the Gospels to Christ Church at Canterbury, to be used by the religious community there, and specifically to be read from each month for the souls of Aelfred, Werburg and Alhthryth. Their names also appear evenly spaced down the right-hand margin of the orna-mented Gospel text, with an indication that Alhthryth is the couple's daughter. The Gospel readings are to continue and the book is to remain in the church as long as there is baptism there. The last phrase, which renders the sense of two slightly different statements in the text, can be taken as an assertion of Christianity itself in hard times. As for the Vikings, they liked shiny bright valu-able things and were prepared to use violence to get them; they were also not averse to non-violent transactions. Both are illustrated by this case of a looted Gospel Book redeemed by a pious couple.

The quintessential Viking activity was piracy, mainly in the older sense of attacking places from the sea or up rivers or overland if necessary, but they were also engaged in agriculture, stock-raising, hunting and gathering at home, settlement elsewhere, development of towns, trade, tribute-collecting, merce-nary service, formation of kingdoms and exploration. Most of these will be illustrated in this or later chapters, for the Viking Age persisted throughout all but the end of the period remaining to be covered in this book; some require elaboration and/or for the links between them to be explained. Coastal raid-ing has already been considered through the example of Lindisfarne. Dorestad, a Frisian trading post on the Rhine delta, was easily accessible and repeatedly attacked in the ninth century. On the other hand, the city of Trier, which the Vikings reached in the late ninth century, was far inland, not only up the Rhine but also up its tributary the Moselle. Trier, as mentioned in the previous chapter, had been one of the late Roman imperial capitals, and it is thought that the Roman street plan there survived until, but not after, the Viking sack. Fearsome as Viking hit-and-run raids were, what was worse was when they established year-round bases, typically at the mouth of rivers, in lands they were attacking. This happened for the first time on the Continent in 843, the year that the Carolingian Empire was divided between the three sons of Louis the Pious, when the Vikings appropriated the formerly monastic island of Noirmoutier off the mouth of the Loire river in western France. In Ireland these bases became its first towns. Ninth-century Scandinavia had its own trading posts (see pp. 127–8 below for Kaupang) and towns like Hedeby in

Denmark and Birka in Sweden. At home the Vikings lived off the land and its produce, which of course varied widely from Denmark to middle-northern Norway, supplemented by tribute if there were neighbours who could be strong-armed into paying it, as are also illustrated later in this chapter. Viking settlers carried their lifestyle abroad, but readily adapted to the culture of the lands in which they lived unless these were unsettled, as was the case with Vikings who ventured into the North Atlantic to the Faroe Islands and Iceland in the wake of Irish monks (who didn't remain).

Now that the Vikings have been properly introduced, they need to be viewed against a broad historical background. The Vikings should be understood in the context of ongoing northern seas exchange which they extended, but did not originate; the Scandinavian links of the early-seventh-century Sutton Hoo ship burial should be recalled here. On the other hand, the importation of walrus ivory, a product of the far north, into England, where it was to prove a welcome alternative to hard-to-get elephant ivory, came only in the Viking Age. We will see an enterprising Northman displaying these wares there later in this chapter. Lands even further north than the Carolingian Empire and the British Isles came to participate in the birth of Europe, they did so in a largely new way, and the initiative came from the Northerners. The reasons why the Vikings moved in on organised Christian Europe are imperfectly understood, although the view that they came out of rising prosperity rather than severe destitution has much to recommend it. Eighth-century development of beautifully designed sailing ships made their voyages possible. The Gokstad warship is a surviving example from the mid-ninth century. It is shown here together with the slightly earlier, ornamented Oseberg ship (c.800), also from Norway, in which a queen was buried (see Figures 19 and 20). The latter vessel would be suitable only for coastal waters, and can remind us of the long evolution of Scandinavian ships to the point where they could be sailed straight across the open sea. Finally, people did not live north of organised Christian Europe, the wealth of the British Isles, the wealth, power, and overall success of the Carolingian realms, where Charlemagne was going from strength to strength just before the Viking Age began, without there being some effect. Formerly, Scandinavian participation in the fifth-century invasions of the Roman Empire had been relatively small. By the ninth century the (Carolingian) Empire was closer and readily accessible to Scandinavia.

The Vikings should also be understood in the context of attacks on Europe by Saracens and Magyars as well (see Map 5.2). Like the Vikings, the Muslim Saracens were now sea-borne raiders, although they too could venture into the interior of Europe. The Abbasid Caliphate was disintegrating, and the Aghlabid rulers of Ifriqiyah (Africa, designating roughly modern Tunisia) went their own way. In the ninth century almost all of Sicily was taken over by Muslim forces from North Africa, and there was extensive Saracen raiding in the Mediterranean. St Peter's church outside Rome was itself pillaged by the Saracens in 846; in the consequent fortification of the area around it lie the origins of the Vatican City. The Magyars, on the other hand, raided overland

Figure 19 The Gokstad ship (*c*.850) could have carried Viking warriors overseas. (© Museum of Cultural History – University of Oslo, Norway; photo: Eirik Irgens Johnsen)

from eastern into western Europe from the end of the ninth century on. They were one of several groups who are usually referred to as 'steppe nomads', that is, people from the grasslands where Europe meets Asia. The Avars were another such group, whom the Magyars replaced in power after the former were defeated by Charlemagne as mentioned in the previous chapter. Like the Huns, with whom they and the Avars are incorrectly identified (which is not to say that their identity was not taken on by the descendants of Huns, Avars and other people besides), the Magyars raided very fast over immense distances and reached Italy and France.[4] The disintegrating Carolingian Empire suffered attacks from all three, Vikings, Saracens and Magyars, as did its unfortunate

113

Figure 20 The prow of the Oseberg ship (*c.*800) *in situ* as excavated. The discovery of these ships in Norway in the late ninteenth century was fundamental to our understanding of the Viking Age. (© Museum of Cultural History – University of Oslo, Norway; photo: O. Væring 1904)

monastery of Luxeuil in particular, sacked by Saracens after 860, Vikings in 888 and Magyars after 917. These were the last invaders of Western Europe, which would henceforth impinge on the rest of the world. Eastern Europe, however, would suffer further invasions.

The geographical scale of Viking activity is amazing: by the 860s this extended from Iceland to Constantinople. While their best known theatre of action was the terrible shunting of Viking armies back and forth between

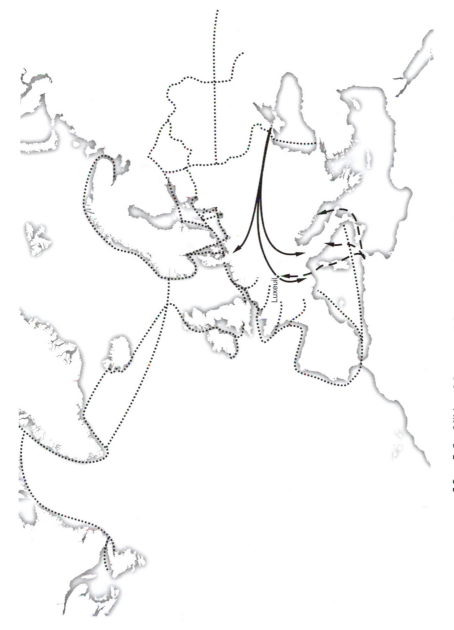

Luxeuil

Map 5.2 Viking, Magyar and Saracen activity in the last invasions

England and France depending on which one of the latter was mounting the least effective defence against them in the ninth century, what will be focused on here are their activities in the east and the south. Before turning to these, please note the following. It is often stated that the Swedes went east to Russia and beyond and that the Norwegians and Danes went west. This generalisation is too neat; for example, the first to go to Iceland is said to have been a Swede, Gardar Svarvarsson. Of course some Swedes tended to look east, where the lands across the Baltic Sea were ripe for tribute and Muslim silver coins were obtainable from much further afar. In the ninth century come two references to people called Rus, from whom the name Russia derives, both of which are testimony to the extent of Viking activity. The first takes us back to the court of Louis the Pious in 839:

> There also came envoys from the Greeks sent by the Emperor Theophilus. They were Theodosius, metropolitan bishop of Chalcedon, and Theophanus the Spatharius and they brought gifts worthy for an emperor, and a letter. The Emperor received them with due ceremony on 18 May at Ingelheim. The purpose of their mission was to confirm the treaty of peace and perpetual friendship and love between the two emperors and their subjects. They also brought congratulations and exultation in the Lord on the victories that our Emperor had gained with heaven's help in his wars against foreign peoples. Theophilus in friendly fashion urged the Emperor and his subjects to offer up thanks to God for all these victories. He also sent with the envoys some men who said they – meaning their whole people – were called Russians (*Rus*) and had been sent to him by their king whose name was the Khagan for the sake of friendship, so they claimed. Theophilus requested in his letter that the Emperor in his goodness might grant them safe conducts to travel through his empire and any help or practical assistance they needed to return home, for the route by which they had reached Constantinople had taken them through primitive tribes that were very fierce and savage and Theophilus did not wish them to return that way in case some disaster befell them. When the Emperor investigated more closely the reason for their coming here, he discovered that they belonged to the people of the Swedes. He suspected that they had really been sent as spies to this kingdom of ours rather than as seekers of our friendship, so he decided to keep them with him until he could find out for certain whether or not they had come in good faith. He lost no time in sending a letter to Theophilus through the same envoys to tell him all this, and to add that he had received them willingly for the sake of his friendship for Theophilus and that if they were found to be genuine, he would supply them with the means to return to their own fatherland without any risk of danger and send them home with every assistance, but if not, he would send them with envoys of ours back to Theophilus for him to deal with as he might think fit.
>
> (*Annals of St-Bertin*)

Vikings were attacking Louis' kingdom; he knew them when he saw them. Likewise the Arab geographer al-Yaqubi at the end of the century identified the Rus with the Vikings, who had earlier raided Muslim Spain in circumstances to be considered presently.

The role of the Rus in the origins of Russia has been hotly debated in modern times, for reasons which, on the one hand, have far more to do with Slavic nationalism than with Soviet communism and, on the other, include a Western European perspective that tends to ignore Eastern Europeans. When the *Russian Primary Chronicle* was compiled at the end of the period covered by the book you are reading, the rulers of Kiev were happy to trace the origins of their principality back to outsiders from further west. The Varangians came from overseas and imposed tribute on the Slavs. The Slavs succeeded in expelling the Varangians, but fought each other. The Slavs then went overseas to particular Varangians called Rus and requested leadership to restore law and order. Rus settlement and rule from Novgorod by Prince Rurik in northern Russia was the result. This had an offshoot further south at Kiev, which Prince Oleg, the next ruler after Rurik, soon took over and made the centre of his principality in the later ninth century.[5] The archaeological record is very Slavic, but with significant intrusive Scandinavian elements. It indicates contact of Scandinavian with Muslim lands via the Russian rivers that began well before the Vikings came south from Kiev in an unsuccessful attempt to take Constantinople *c*.860, the event on which the (inaccurate) chronology of the *Chronicle* is pegged. The activity of the Vikings in Russia intensified in the second half of the ninth century and much more so in the next century until the Muslim silver, which had funded their trade in human and animal produce, above all furs, ran out with the exhaustion of the Central Asian mines. A key to solving the aforementioned debate lies in the ability of the Vikings to assimilate readily into the power structures of foreign lands. Here it may be relevant that, in the long passage quoted above, the Rus at the court of Louis the Pious called their king Khagan, which was the standard title of rulers on the eastern border of Europe (see the next note). The personal names of the Russian rulers would in a century change from Norse (like Rurik and Oleg) to Slavic.

As already mentioned, the Vikings encountered the Muslim world by western as well as eastern routes. Two major forays in the ninth century warrant examination, in part for what these reveal of the way the Vikings operated. They did not waste time. In 844 they struck south from Noirmoutier (see p. 111 above) down the Atlantic coasts of France and Spain. Estuaries were a great opportunity for Vikings, and they raided up the Garonne. Then they attacked Christian Spain. 'At the same time the people of the Northmen, a pagan and extremely cruel people previously unknown to us, arrived in our region with their naval forces,' says the ninth-century *Chronicle of Alfonso III*, and goes on to record the successful defence by King Ramiro I of the Asturias. On the Atlantic coast of Muslim Spain, however, the Vikings sacked Lisbon and other towns before going up the estuary of the Guadalquivir for the sack of Seville, to which the aforementioned Muslim geographer al-Yaqubi refers, as does the *Chronicle of Alfonso*

III. After further weeks of raiding from this base, they were utterly defeated by the forces of the Umayyad ruler Abd al-Rahman II, who hanged many of the prisoners from trees in the city. Whatever those who got back to Noirmoutier said, another large fleet, this time of 62 ships, sailed from there again for Spain in 859, led by Hastein and Bjorn Ironsides. Proceeding through the Straits of Gibraltar, these Vikings attacked the Mediterranean coasts of North Africa, Spain, France, Italy and probably other lands as well. When the Vikings came to the Balearic Islands of Majorca and Minorca, 'they depopulated them with the sword', according to the *Chronicle of Alfonso III.* Typically, the Vikings overwintered at the Rhone river-mouth on the island of Camargue, and then attacked upriver. Around the coast in Italy, they came to the town of Luni, which had been a centre of Roman marble production but was by now unimpressive, and are said to have thought that it was Rome itself. A year later, they were defeated by the Muslims in a naval battle on the Atlantic side of the Straits of Gibraltar. Despite a final *coup* of holding King García of Pamplona for ransom, the venture was not an unqualified success, for two-thirds of the Viking fleet had been lost. The pickings were easier further north.

In the early ninth century the Vikings did not trouble Carolingian Europe very much. Charlemagne's measures against them were successful, including naval defence. These were continued in the reign of Louis the Pious. It was not the time, however, to be indulging in civil war, which became and remained the main focus of attention of the Carolingian rulers as the ninth century went on. In the last years of the reign of Louis the Pious raiders came down from Denmark onto the Frisian coast. Then in the intensifying civil war after the death of Louis the Pious in 840, the Vikings caused real problems. They come into the last years of Nithard's *Histories*, and he died fighting them in 845. In the same year King Charles the Bald paid the Vikings 7000 pounds of silver to go away from Paris, which they had sacked on Easter Day. Spare a thought for the descendants of the peasants in the Paris area, who were discussed above, on this occasion and even more during the Viking siege of Paris in 885–86. (The latter is illustrated in Figure 21 as it was imagined in the nineteenth century before people knew what Viking ships looked like.) Armies must eat and these were living off the land. The destruction of the monastery of St Germain-des-Prés presumably brought relief from dues and services for people like those surveyed in the Polyptyque, but one wonders how many peasants got through the winter. Thus there was devastation to much more than monasteries, although it was unusual for any of those to escape attack by someone. Here there was also a human cost of course. When Archbishop Rimbert of Hamburg-Bremen was in the Danish trading town of Hedeby, he saw chained slaves who protested that they were Christians, including one woman who demonstrated that she had been a nun by singing psalms. The shocked cleric bought her freedom with his horse.

Even the Vikings as raiders have sometimes been given a positive economic role of increasing circulation of wealth, but this needs to be carefully assessed and weighed against their destructive effect. There is one commodity which, or rather whom, raiders must often have put on the market. Whereas a Viking

Figure 21 This nineteenth-century artist's reconstruction of Norsemen besieging Paris in 885–86 is notable for its misrepresentation of Viking ships before the discoveries of the real thing at Gokstad and Oseberg in Norway. (The Bridgeman Art Library)

could stow coins in a chest, or wear or wrap up a fine Frankish sword, captives if they were not soon ransomed or required to serve their captors would have been expensive to maintain and could be sold for profit. As in the previous example, the slave trade prospered from a ready supply of captives, and found plenty of demand in Scandinavian societies, the British Isles and the more distant Byzantine and Saracen markets. Viking Dublin was one of the principal centres of the slave trade. The Viking expedition to the Mediterranean which has just been described is specifically stated in an Irish source to have brought enslaved Moors to Ireland, where they were referred to as 'blue men'. Also a great deal of silver changed hands in pay-offs like the one mentioned in the previous paragraph. The prohibition in 864 by King Charles the Bald against selling weapons and horses to the Vikings shows that they were consumers, and that there were opportunists among his subjects. For payment some of the silver that this king had three years previously paid the Vikings to go away – they didn't – would have done nicely. His grant in 873 of a market for the Viking island base – pirate nest would not be too strong a term – in the River Loire can be seen at least in part as an attempt to regularise its supplies, especially food. It too became a centre for the slave trade. Both cases show that the presence of raiders could stimulate trade. The presence of balances and weights in Viking graves has been seen as signifying Viking trading as well as raiding; however, what was weighed was not necessarily acquired by trade: witness a Frankish tribute to Vikings in 866 of 4000 pounds of silver 'according to their scales'.

People will not put up with disorder forever. Around 880 things got completely out of hand after a large Viking army had come across to the Continent from England following the successful defence by King Alfred the Great there. The Carolingian kings were still contending among themselves and with a rebel from Provence; any royal victories over the Vikings were insufficient. Thus we see Archbishop Hincmar of Reims, another long-lived product of the Carolingian Renaissance, recording the last *Annals of St-Bertin*: how even the Carolingian capital of Aachen was in the hands of the Vikings, where according to another source they used Charlemagne's palace chapel as a stable for their horses, and how he himself escaped from Reims with the body of the patron saint Remigius and the church treasures. At the conclusion to the aforementioned siege of Paris in 885–86, after the city had been bravely defended by its count, Odo, another Charles, the Fat, the first to rule the whole Empire since his grandfather Louis the Pious, paid off the Vikings in silver. The Franks then deposed Charles the Fat for incompetence and chose Odo to be king. It was not the end of the Carolingians, as the French crown went back and forth between them and Odo's family, who ultimately became the Capetian royal dynasty, well into the next century. Its significance is that in the appalling violence of the later ninth century on the Continent what worked, if anything, was local defence. There are a few disapproving notices of groups of ordinary people banding together in sworn associations of mutual self-help against enemies, but overwhelmingly the solution was lordship. The English experience of dealing with the Vikings was rather different, and will be examined in the last part of this chapter. Before that we will consider instructive events in later ninth-century Eastern Europe: the top-down conversion of Bulgaria to Christianity.

Khan Boris of Bulgaria

The Bulgars, like the Magyars, were nomads from the grasslands where Europe meets Asia who had come west to settle among and rule over Slavs; only they did so much earlier than the Magyars. They were mentioned in passing, along with the Slavs themselves and the Avars, as a threat to the Byzantine Empire in Chapter 2 on the sixth century. Among the Byzantine disasters of the seventh century, the Slavs took over most of Greece and the Bulgars (see Figure 22) extended their authority below the Danube, the old boundary of the Roman

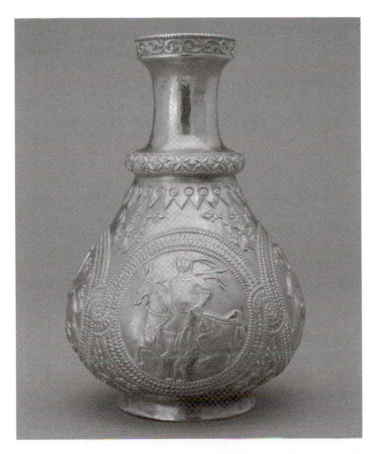

Figure 22 Mounted warrior with prisoner decorating one of the golden objects in the Nagyszentmiklós treasure found in the area ruled by the Bulgars in the ninth century. Note the severed head hanging from his saddle. (Kunsthistorisches Museum, Vienna)

Empire. The eighth-century account of the travels of the English pilgrim Willibald discussed in Chapter 4 refers to southern Greece as Sclavinia; Byzantine control was restored there in the ninth century. Here the same observations on identity apply as were made in Chapter 1: namely that it was determined by the group ruling over ethnically mixed populations. In Bulgaria the Christian minority ruled over by the Bulgars almost certainly included some descendents of the Visigoths for whom Ulfila had translated the Bible into Gothic, people who had not trekked west with the Visigoths with whom this book began, although they may no longer have been ethnically distinct. The ninth-century Carolingian writer Walahfrid Strabo was told that a German liturgy was in use on the west coast of the Black Sea. Map 5.3 shows Bulgaria and its neighbours in the ninth century. The Bulgars had begun the ninth century with a spectacular defeat of Byzantine forces, after which their khan[6] Krum was seen drinking out of Emperor Nicephorus's skull. Charlemagne's earlier defeat of the Avars, mentioned in Chapter 4, had extended the territory tributary to him over to where the territory tributary to the Bulgar khan began. Thus the Bulgar khanate lay between the empires of the Byzantines and the Franks. In the eastern shadow of the Frankish Empire, as it disintegrated, grew up the Czech kingdom of Great Moravia. All of this is to set the background for Khan Boris and the conversion of Bulgaria.

In 862 Khan Boris of Bulgaria approached the more distant Franks with a request for alliance including an offer of conversion to Christianity. His Byzantine southern neighbours forestalled this by sending an army, with the result that Boris agreed to accept Christianity from them. He was baptized in 864 or 865, and the top-down conversion of Bulgaria followed. Boris realised immediately the political implications of Christian conversion. His insistence on an independent Bulgarian Church saw him change religious allegiance from Constantinople to Rome and back again. Also, Boris used Christian conversion to unite his ruling Bulgar and subject Slav populations. These events, about which we are relatively well informed by surviving communication from the patriarch of Constantinople and the pope of Rome to Boris, are very significant. The Byzantine Empire did not want a strong Bulgaria or increased Frankish influence on their northern border. What had happened in Italy was bad enough. There was also religious competition for Eastern Europe. In a letter Pope John VIII warned Khan Boris not to get his Christianity from the Byzantines, who 500 years earlier had consecrated a heretical bishop for the Visigoths. (This is apparently a reference to Ulfila; such early medieval uses of the past are interesting in themselves.) Khan Boris cleverly played off all sides to reap the benefits of conversion, which were nothing less than the Christian Roman template of rule. Top-down conversion always gave rulers a great new opportunity to tell their subjects what to do. Organisation of the Church meant organisation of the kingdom. Patriarch Photius held up Emperor Constantine the Great himself to Boris as a role model. Pope Nicholas I sent him a law code. Bulgaria was joining the club of civilised nations. It was not an easy process, not least because of the difficulty in knowing where to draw the line between religion

Map 5.3 Bulgaria and its neighbours

and society. Replying to a query from Boris, Pope Nicholas assured him that it was all right for his converted people to continue to wear trousers. All was not just cultural cringe to superior Christian civilisation, however.

The last years of Boris's reign saw a cultural development which had profound implications for the history of Eastern Europe. Its background is as follows. By Boris's lifetime, the Slavic kingdom of Moravia lay between the Bulgar khanate and the east Frankish kingdom. The foreign relations of Moravia were the mirror image of those of Boris's realm. Back in 862, the same year that Boris made his initial approach to the Franks, Rastislav the ruler of Moravia asked the more distant Byzantines for missionaries to his people, countering the Frankish influence among them. Byzantium was happy to oblige. A great scholar, Constantine, later called Cyril, and his brother Methodius were sent. An alphabet was devised to write the Slavic language, the Bible was translated into it and a Slavic liturgy was created for worship. When later in the century Frankish pressure led to the expulsion from Moravia of this mission, disciples of Cyril and Methodius were welcomed in Bulgaria. From 885 on, with the enthusiastic patronage of Boris, they set about training a native clergy and cultivating Slavic literacy. The so-called Cyrillic alphabet was developed at the end of the century to replace the less satisfactory one originally created by Cyril and Methodius, known as Glagolitic. Many translations from Greek into Slavic were made, including in the next century the secular history by John Malalas examined in Chapter 2. The elevation of Slavic into a sacred and written language, subsequently spreading with the conversion of Serbia and Russia, was of immense cultural significance, for it buttressed Slavic culture in the areas most to be affected by the later Mongol and Turkish invasions The ninth century is crucial in the development of Eastern Europe. In some contrast to the aggressive conversion policy of the Franks, Byzantium in the essentially defensive tradition of late Roman foreign policy employed conversion to create a Christian northern buffer zone of on-side barbarian kingdoms, the Byzantine commonwealth. As for Khan Boris, he lived out the century in voluntary retirement in a monastery; political cunning need not be incompatible with real religious belief.

Alfred the Great

Far to the west, another extraordinary ruler, a younger contemporary of Khan Boris, was struggling with Vikings. Alfred, known as 'the Great' only after the Middle Ages, in 871 came to the throne of Wessex, which fast became the only kingdom in England that was not controlled by the Vikings (see Map 5.4). Alfred almost lost his kingdom to them, hiding out in the winter of 878 in the western marshes of Somerset while his subjects began to make accommodations with the Danes. Yet he rallied forces in the spring and won a great victory at the battle of Edington, after which the Danish army under Guthrum made peace, became Christian and settled in the part of eastern England subsequently known as the Danelaw because of the presence of these and other Vikings. A further result of

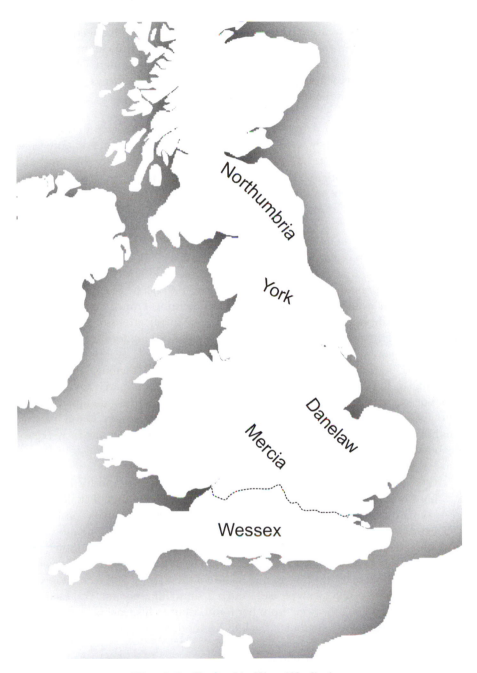

Map 5.4   England in King Alfred's time

Alfred's success in 878 was that another Viking invasion force crossed instead to the Continent, with the catastrophic results chronicled by Archbishop Hincmar of Reims as referred to above. Alfred proceeded to develop an effective defence against the Vikings in southern England. A network of fortifications known as burhs provided points from which defence could be mounted where it was needed, and arrangements were made for defenders to be always on hand. He also attempted to beat them in their element:

> Then King Alfred ordered 'long-ships' to be built with which to oppose the Viking warships. They were almost twice as long as the others. Some had sixty oars, some more. They were both swifter and more stable, and also higher, than the others. They were built neither on the Frisian nor on the Danish pattern but as it seemed to Alfred himself that they would be most useful.
>
> (*Anglo-Saxon Chronicle* for 896)

Intriguing as this passage is, the point to take in all of this is the extent of royal central planning. And it worked: Alfred's kingdom became the nucleus for a reconquered England that was united as it never had been, which was achieved after his death in 899. The contrast with fragmenting France could hardly be greater. Yet Alfred may have been inspired by the fortifications of King Charles the Bald in France, and Wessex was a much smaller kingdom to defend than France.

Alfred did more, however: he sought to restore book-learning. A debt to the Carolingian Renaissance is quite possible. As a child Alfred had even visited the court of Charles the Bald, where his father married Charles's daughter Judith, who then lived in England for several years. Yet it is a story about Alfred's English mother Osburh that his biographer Asser tells to show his early regard for books:

> One day, therefore, when his mother was showing him and his brothers a book of English poetry which she held in her hand, she said: 'I shall give this book to whichever one of you can learn it the fastest.' Spurred on by these words, or rather by divine inspiration, and attracted by the beauty of the initial letter in the book, Alfred spoke as follows in reply to his mother, fore-stalling his brothers (ahead in years, not in ability): 'Will you really give this book to the one of us who can understand it the soonest and recite it to you?' Whereupon, smiling with pleasure she reassured him, saying: 'Yes, I will.' He immediately took the book from her hand, went to his teacher and learnt it. When it was learnt, he took it back to his mother and recited it.

This passage should give us pause. No reputation for learning has attached to King Aethelwulf of Wessex, Alfred's father, or his entourage, whereas King Charles the Bald of France was an educated patron of texts and art (see p. 109), whose court could be praised for its scholarship. Nevertheless, a decorated book is here seen to be part of the life of the royal family in Wessex. The poetry was in their old native tradition, but textual literacy, introduced with Christianity, has become part of their culture. And it is interesting to see a mother educating her children in this way. Much later, maintaining Wessex and more under his control, King Alfred became actively involved in book production. Like Charlemagne, he had a programme of education and assembled scholars (from England, Wales and the Continent); however, unlike Charlemagne, he translated texts from Latin to his own language.

As King Alfred explains in the preface to one of these, he considered how learned and well run England had been in the past 'before everything was ransacked and burned' and conceived the plan 'that we should turn into the language that we can all understand certain books which are the most necessary for all men to know'. This description certainly applied to the text so prefaced: Pope Gregory the Great's *Book of Pastoral Rule*, known in English as the *Shepherd-book*, which has already been mentioned in connection with its author at the end of Chapter 2. It was written for bishops and Alfred sent a copy to every bishop in his kingdom. Somewhat as in the story of his childhood quoted above, Alfred 'learnt it' from his teachers, his clerical advisors, and then translated. He also rendered into English more freely Boethius's *Consolation of Philosophy*, even more freely Augustine's *Soliloquies* or *On Seeing God*, and literally the first 50 psalms. Others in his learned circle translated Gregory the Great's *Dialogues* and Orosius's *History against the Pagans*. Note that all of these authors (except the psalmist) fall within the centuries covered in this book that you are reading. This cultural evidence from Alfred's court is unusual. The Christianisation of Germany, in which English missionaries participated as will be recalled, resulted in a limited amount of translation from Latin to German in the ninth and tenth centuries. As was mentioned in the previous section of this chapter, there was a great deal of translation from Greek to Slavic in Bulgaria beginning at the same time as the English translations we are examining here were made, but again the context was conversion and the formation of an original Christian culture in Bulgaria. By the end of the ninth century Christianity was long established in England, but was under threat. To ignore learning, King Alfred may have felt, was to be like the barbarians who were all around.

To the geographical section of Orosius's *History against the Pagans* wonderful additions were made, extending his knowledge further north and east. The first of these is reported statements of a Viking trader at King Alfred's court named Ohthere, or Ottar to the Scandinavians. He was a well-off farmer at home, which was atypically far north in Norway so most of his livestock were reindeer. He obtained northern products by hunting and collecting tribute from the Lapps; he brought tusks of walrus ivory to King Alfred. Violence is implied by the tribute and stated in endemic raiding between Scandinavian peoples. Ohthere was an explorer who had sailed around the North Cape of Norway because he 'wished to find out how far the land extended due north, or whether anyone lived to the north of the unpopulated area'. He was a man who lived by his knowledge of sailing directions, and he traded down to the seasonal depot of

Sciringesheal (Kaupang) on the south coast of Norway and Hedeby at the bottom of Denmark (where Rimbert freed the nun, p. 118) – and obviously over to England. The account calls Alfred Ohthere's lord, and perfectly complements these statements about Alfred from Asser's biography:

> He similarly applied himself attentively to charity and distribution of alms to the native population and to foreign visitors of all races, showing immense and incomparable kindness and generosity to all men, as well as to the investigation of things unknown. Wherefore many Franks, Frisians, Gauls, Vikings, Welshmen, Irishmen and Bretons subjected themselves willingly to his lordship, nobles and commoners alike, and, as befitted his royal status, he ruled, loved, honoured and enriched them all with wealth and authority, just as he did his own people.

The second addition to Orosius's geography is an account by Wulfstan, an English merchant, of his voyage in the Baltic Sea. It begins where Ohthere leaves off, at Hedeby, and gives sailing directions as far as the mouth of the Vistula river, by present-day Gdansk in Poland, formerly part of East Prussia. The original Prussians spoke a Baltic language akin to Latvian and Lithuanian. Wulfstan reports briefly on their lifestyle – 'There is a great deal of honey and fishing' – and at length on their custom of exposing their dead.

To us the writings of King Alfred the Great are particularly precious because they express the point of view of someone who, however religious, was a layman not a professional churchman. The great virtue, secular and religious at the same time, which comes through loud and clear from what he writes is wisdom. In an especially free part of his translation of Boethius's *Consolation of Philosophy*), presented as a dialogue between Wisdom and Mind, Alfred speaks directly and practically of his role as king and is worth quoting at length:

> Look, Wisdom, you know that desire for and possession of earthly power never pleased me overmuch, and that I did not unduly desire this earthly rule, but that nevertheless I wished for tools and resources for the task that I was commanded to accomplish, which was that I should virtuously and worthily guide and direct the authority which was entrusted to me. You know of course that no one can make known any skill, nor direct and guide any authority, without tools and resources; a man cannot work on any enterprise without resources. In the case of the king, the resources and tools with which to rule are that he have his land fully manned: he must have praying men, fighting men and working men.[7] You know also that without these tools no king may make his ability known. Another aspect of his resources is that he must have the means of support for his tools, the three classes of men. These, then, are their means of support: land to live on, gifts, weapons, food, ale, clothing, and whatever else is necessary for each of the three classes of men. Without these things he cannot maintain the tools, nor without the tools can he accomplish any of the things he was commanded to do.

Accordingly, I sought the resources with which to exercise the authority, in order that my skills and power would not be forgotten and concealed: because every skill and every authority is soon obsolete and passed over, if it is without wisdom; because no man may bring to bear any skill without wisdom. For whatever is done unthinkingly, cannot be reckoned a skill. To speak briefly: I desired to live worthily as long as I lived, and to leave after my life, to the men who should come after me, the memory of me in good works.

The Vikings as raiders – and it has been established that this was by no means their only activity – killed, injured and abducted people and destroyed some of the things they had made at a time when everything was in short supply in the early medieval economy except land. Alfred's words reflect that reality and also the human capacity to cope with it.

Figure 23 'Some can see, some hear, some feel, some smell.' The Fuller Brooch, English, ninth century, silver inlaid with niello, depicting the five senses in its central panels, belonging to the same thought-world as Wisdom's analysis of the means of perception in King Alfred's translation of Boethius's *Consolation of Philosophy* (41.5). Wisdom, talking about immobile creatures in the sentence just quoted, missed out taste (upper left on the brooch). (© The Trustees of the British Museum)

The Nadir of Europe

King Alfred is a bright spot at the end of a century in which Europe's fortunes were approaching their nadir, that is, their low point. Precisely because of the extent of disorder, on the other hand, the opportunities for women to access wealth and power were approaching their apex. The following protests against their intrusion into even public power:

> It is astonishing that certain women, against both divine and human law, with bare-faced impudence, act in general pleas and with abandon exhibit a burning passion for public meetings, and they disrupt, rather than assist, the business of the kingdom and the good of the commonweal. It is indecent and reprehensible, even among barbarians, for women to discuss the cases of men. Those who should be discussing their woollen work and weaving with the residents of the women's quarters, should not usurp the authority of senators in public meetings just as if they were residents of the court.

This is a canon of the episcopal synod of Nantes at the mouth of the River Loire in western France in 895, and the context is grim. Back in 843, Nantes had suffered a sack of frightful brutality by Vikings, who, it may be recalled, had just established a base on the island of Noirmoutier off the coast there. In 850 the defences of Nantes were destroyed by Bretons (see below). One can practically see Pope Hadrian II in 868 shaking his head in dismay as he writes of what a hard time the bishop of Nantes has, caught between Vikings and Bretons, and yields to Breton pressure in granting him the status of archbishop (seen as necessary for Breton independence) against right order in the Church and the pope's better judgement. Early in the next century Viking control of the region was accepted by the kings of France, but ultimately not by the Bretons. These were just the sort of conditions in which women could do better, or much worse, than in more organised society which entailed male domination.

The circumstances of Brittany in the ninth century are also very revealing of the effect on Europe of the Carolingian Empire. Brittany, the northwest peninsula of present-day France, only became part of the Empire in the time of Louis the Pious. We see him in 818 telling the abbot of the Breton monastery of Landévennec to change the customs there and adopt the Rule of St Benedict. The monks conformed: the near-monopoly which the Benedictine Rule came to have in early medieval Western Europe owes much to Carolingian policy. Louis made a Breton called Nomenoë imperial *missus* (agent) for Brittany. After Louis' death Nomenoë did not remain faithful to Louis' son Charles the Bald, but took over the counties of Rennes and Nantes, which had not been part of Brittany. He laid the foundations for an independent Breton kingdom that arose in the time of his son. An important part of these foundations was Carolingian administration. Nomenoë's use of the Church – he favoured church reform and sought independence from the Archbishop of Tours – and vassalage in building up his powerbase was also Carolingian. Even in its dissolution the Carolingian Empire made a difference. Likewise, in Germany, becoming part of the Carolingian kingdom and empire meant participating in success, a heady experience for those counts, dukes, bishops, abbots and *missi*, who became royal vassals and served the rulers and their own interests. In the course of the ninth century the foundations were laid for the emergence of a relatively strong kingdom out of what had been East Francia. The success of Germany in the tenth century and the Norman conquests of the eleventh century would ensure that the Frankish way of doing things, including dealing with disorder, would affect the whole of Europe. Yet at the end of the ninth century Germany was only in embryo and Normandy did not yet exist.

The area covered by this chapter has expanded to range from Iceland to Russia, which constitute the limits of Europe today. The earlier Carolingian conquests were of fundamental significance in the consolidation of organised Christian Europe. Yet in the ninth century the main role in expanding the boundaries of Europe was played by the people on its fringes, who included themselves in the birth of Europe.

Chapter 6 . . . .

The Tenth Century:
Nadir to Take-Off

A Tale of Three Cities

About the year 900, Bishop Theodolach of Worms wisely provided for the maintenance of the walls of his city. Among possible enemies, the Magyars were especially threatening, for in the early tenth century they destroyed the Eastern European kingdom of Moravia, repeatedly defeated Frankish armies and raided well to the west of Worms. Worms lay in the eastern Frankish kingdom, identified as Germany after the old Roman usage. After the deposition of Emperor Charles the Fat in 887, the line of Carolingian rulers there thinned to two illegitimate sons and a child, and then ran out. The times could hardly have been less secure, the urbanised Roman Empire (in which Worms originated) was far in the past, and so urban life in Europe was at its lowest point; however, towns existed, and Worms is an example. It will be compared in this first section of the chapter with two other examples of tenth-century towns of different sorts: Lucca in Tuscany (northern Italy) and York in the Viking kingdom of the same name (northern England). Our three cities represent the zones of early medieval urbanisation. Around the Mediterranean towns were deeply rooted. To the north they were an inheritance of Romanisation; this was the origin of Tours, examined back in Chapter 2 and of Le Mans, which will be considered in the next chapter as an example of the rise of towns in eleventh-century Europe and may be compared with the three cities here. Beyond what had been the boundaries of the old Roman Empire, cathedrals, fortresses and associated mercantile settlements existed which could knit together into towns in future. In the case of English cities like York, which are on the sites of Romano-British ones, the discontinuity is so great that they are placed in the third zone. Certainly Viking York belongs to a recognisable type of northern town that has been archaeologically excavated from Dublin to Novgorod. The three cities are also a nice contrast in the evidence that we have for them.

Bishop Theodolach left a record of his arrangements, the *Description of the City of Worms*, which has survived embedded in a later city chronicle (consult the

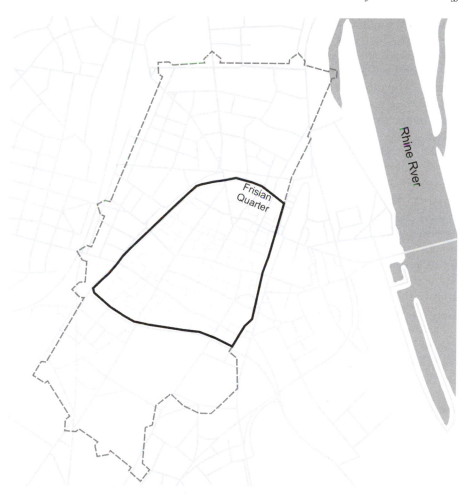

Map 6.1 Plan of Worms

plan in Map 6.1). Basically the walls of Worms were divided into sections and each was to be looked after by a different group of people. In the northern part of the city was the Frisian Quarter, and the Frisians themselves were to take care of restoring the wall up there as far as the River Rhine. The Frisians, from the marshy lowlands along the North Sea, were particularly associated with being merchants. Now turning south the first part of the wall along the Rhine was in the care of eight named settlements in the countryside north of Worms. Rebuilding one gate on this side of the city was the responsibility of a monastery, and the section down to another gate, the Pfauenpforte, was to be looked after by the city folk with rights of common, perhaps formed into an association. More settlements outside of Worms had to provide for maintenance of the wall down to its southern angle, and so on around it in a clockwise direction back to the Frisian Quarter. Finally the inhabitants of an area northwest of Worms as well as everyone else were to furnish all the defences that the city needed.

Worms was a fortification, a place where the bishop's cathedral was, and also a place where commerce was carried out. It was one of several towns on the great river Rhine where Frisian traders were based. The Vikings hit the Frisian commerce hard; as we have seen, some of the first raids were on the coast of Frisia. Worms was further up the Rhine than the Vikings raided, even in the terrible decade of the 880s. The market at Worms was confirmed by royal grant in 947, in which connection the Frisians were mentioned. Worms had a mint at the end of the century, by which time the Frisian Quarter had become the Jewish Quarter. Yet note the presence of these specialised commercial groups, the Frisians and the Jews, suggesting that trade was not a regular part of people's activity in the area. Most of the population seems to have been in the country-side. Worms lay in the middle region of Europe to which the Romans had brought urbanisation, but it had become a profoundly rural place. In Christian Mediterranean lands, towns shrank but remained the centres of the surrounding countryside (whereas further north there were other centres, as will be seen). The walls of Worms made a significant difference to people in the area, however. Cities were almost always proof against the Magyars, who preferred to raid country districts. Imma, daughter of a count from southern Germany, was led away captive by the Magyars after they took her father's fortress. When they reached the region of Worms and were raiding round about, she was offered for sale as a slave, and was redeemed by a man from Worms, in whose household she remained. These were hard times; nevertheless, after its sack by the Huns in the fifth century, an event remembered in Germanic literature, Worms went safely through the Middle Ages and the subsequent Wars of Religion until its capture by French troops with artillery in the seventeenth century permanently reduced its importance as a German city. The necessity for urban fortification in Europe existed from late Roman through early modern times, a great historical phase that cuts across traditional periods.

For the Italian city of Lucca we have a whole archive of early medieval documents, those of its archbishops, which enable life there in the tenth century to be reconstructed. Typically for Italy, it retained its Roman street plan, which is very well preserved. Whereas Worms occupied more than half of the area it had done in Roman times, extending from the Roman boundary on the west over to the Rhine, Roman Lucca was all there, if dilapidated. Certainly the latter would have been the case with the amphitheatre, whose function had fallen from favour with the coming of Christianity. There is mention in the later tenth century of vaults which had underlain the Roman amphitheatre at Lucca; these were probably for storage, but the shape of that amphitheatre can still be traced from the houses built upon its foundations. Evidence, especially of the establishment and maintenance of its many churches, indicates not only that early medieval Lucca occupied the whole area enclosed by its Roman walls, but also that it extended beyond them. The amphitheatre site was outside the walls, as were the palace of the duke of Tuscany and several churches. Lucca had suburbs. This is cause for reflection. Lucca is situated in northern Tuscany beside the river Serchio, which in the early Middle Ages was a tributary of the river Arno. The cities of Pisa on the Arno and Fiesole further up its valley were sacked by the Vikings on their ninth-century Mediterranean raid described in the previous chapter. The episcopal diocese of Lucca shared a boundary with that of Luni, the place which those same Vikings were said to have mistaken for Rome. Lucca was on the road to Pavia, the one city which the Magyars sacked in the early tenth century. Saracen raiders were not impossible, for they had a base at Le Freinet in Provence and frequented the islands of the Western Mediterranean. Even at this time of maximum threat, people did not perpetually cower behind walls, although these were there if needed.

Streetscape and buildings can be glimpsed. As mentioned, early medieval Lucca was a city of churches, of which there is evidence for over 50 before the tenth century began, by which time foundation and endowment of churches had dropped off. A few like the suburban church of S. Pietro Somaldi bear the name of the patron founder (Sumuald) as well as the patron saint (Peter). Small, unprepossessing buildings, which could be beautifully decorated inside, the sound of bells, perhaps a whiff of incense made their presence felt; note that church services were not confined to Sunday mornings in our period. Houses could be concentrated together, but many were set among gardens, suggesting that Lucca and its suburbs had a decidedly 'leafy' appearance, as modern real estate agents might put it. In tenth-century Lucca one would see houses of stone, brick or wood, occasionally of two stories, and the odd tower. The trendy place to live may have been near the cathedral. There were three palaces: of the king, the duke (see the next paragraph) and the bishop. At the beginning of the tenth century there is mention of the bishop's palace having a loggia, that is, an arcaded gallery open to the outside, probably on an upper floor. The royal palace, originally Lombard, then Carolingian, was within the city walls near the Roman forum; the ducal palace was outside the western gate of the city. The latter had a heated room where judicial proceedings were held. King Louis III, a late Carolingian ruler in Italy at the beginning of the tenth century, expressed envy at the court of the duke, with whom he was staying. A quarter of a century later, King Hugh took the ducal palace for himself. Lucca had a mint, also near the forum. The site of the latter is marked by the church of S. Michele in Foro; whether the forum served as a marketplace, as tended to happen in early medieval Italian cities, is not clear. The population of Lucca included merchants, craft workers, professional people, not least those in the Church, and aristocratic landholders.

The relation of Lucca to the surrounding countryside is of great importance. It was in all ways the centre of a rural hinterland, as Ancient cities had been. All over early medieval Europe, cities were the seat of bishops, as Worms was. Lucca was also the seat of secular authority, which requires some explanation. Tuscany is another example of the difference that Carolingian administration meant even as the Carolingian Empire broke up, a subject discussed at the end of the previous chapter. In these circumstances the counts of Lucca assumed responsibility for the March (border region) of Tuscany as its dukes or marquises (rulers of a march). As the administrative centre of the March of Tuscany, Lucca was a more important place than it had been in the Roman Empire or the Lombard Kingdom. As mentioned at the end of the preceding paragraph, the aristocracy tended to reside in the city, close to the sources of power both secular and ecclesiastical. Even lesser ambitious folk in the countryside cultivated an association with the archbishop of Lucca, their local power strategies oriented to those of the city. Even though the archbishops increasingly bestowed lands on aristocrats in an attempt to gain their support toward the end of the tenth century, what did not develop in the region around Lucca were private lordships that were alternatives to the city, as occurred all over Europe north of the Alps. There networks of rural manors of kings, dukes, counts and other lords, bishops and monasteries were other sources of power set beside, and to some extent sidelining, urban settlements, though bishops were always based in cities and cities were everywhere valued as concentrations of wealth and prizes in war. Leaving Lucca to live off the wheat of its plains, the fish of its river and the bounty of extensive wetlands in the south of its region, we turn to our third city, a Viking town.

Whereas the documentary evidence for Worms offered one overall view *c*.AD 900, and that for Lucca offers views of bits of the city, the evidence for tenth-century York in northern England is the archaeological equivalent of the latter. The main excavation was carried out, in modern terms, at numbers 16–22 Coppergate, that is, several lots along one street the name of which, typically for old York, includes the Norse word for 'street', *gata*, as befits its Viking past. A number of minor excavations at other sites in York have produced evidence which, taken together with that from Coppergate, gives a picture which is consistent but of necessity very patchy. When using archaeological evidence in historical (or any other) study, the question must always be asked: what area precisely has been dug and/or surveyed? Much of the evidence from Viking York consists of 'small things forgotten', in James Deetz's beautiful phrase, but is no less extraordinarily informative and compelling for that.[1] The historical context for this evidence is reasonably clear, and the evidence fits it reasonably well. York originated as the Romano-British city of *Eboracum*. When Pope Gregory the Great sent his missionaries to convert the English to Christianity at the end of the sixth century, he planned for Britain to have archbishops at London and York because these had been the principal cities of Roman Britain, which is an interesting early medieval use of the past. English *Eoforwic* saw (archi)episcopal and royal activity on the Roman site, but there is very little evidence of anything like a town. In 866 the Danes captured the place and a Viking kingdom came to be centred on *Jórvík*; however, the archbishops remained there. In the tenth century the English regained control of it from 927–39, 944–48 and from 954 on; otherwise it was in the hands of Danish or Norwegian kings of York, the latter with strong links to Dublin in Ireland.

The beginning of early medieval activity on the Coppergate site that was excavated can be correlated with the coming of the Vikings to York. Then, in the early tenth century, house/workshops were built and their rectangular yards laid out along the street. The materials used for buildings and fences were flexible wooden branches woven around wooden posts and perhaps coated with clay. Later in the century the buildings were replaced with timber ones partly sunk into the earth. Those who lived there carried on commercial manufacturing: woodworking, metalworking including minting, glassmaking, weaving, leather-working, and the creation of jewellery from amber (fossilised resin imported from the Baltic) and jet (a particular form of coal that can be carved and polished, obtainable in England). There were other imports: jewellery from the Celtic, or rather Hiberno-Norse West; soapstone from Norway, which along with the amber marks the connection of York to the Viking world; Frankish pottery and querns for grinding grain from the Continent; silk from the Byzantine Empire; a cowrie shell from the sea off Arabia; and a fake *dirham* coin all the way from Samarkand. These do not constitute the main interest of the archaeological evidence from *Jórvík*, however. The Coppergate site, situated on land between the rivers Ouse and Foss, was damp and therefore organic remains were preserved there. Thus, as well as stone spindle-whorls and pottery loom weights to show that spinning and weaving were done, the textiles themselves have some-times survived, as have leather goods. A much fuller picture of everyday life is possible. There are prosaic aspects like a tenth-century woollen sock, knitted in a particular way that has not died out in Scandinavia, and subsequently mended. Utterly down to earth are the microscopic round-worm eggs still preserved in the cess-pits, showing that the Vikings had their little problems. They also had their fun: among the evidence thereof are the wooden bridge of a lyre (compare the earlier instrument illustrated in Figure 5) and wooden panpipes that can still be played. Whereas we do not know what notes lyre-strings were tuned to play, the pipes produce the notes from A to E, with the C sharpened. To leap from the particular to the general in conclusion, tenth-century York was a wooden town with similarities to excavated counterparts from Dublin to Novgorod. If the population estimate of about 10,000 at the end of the century is correct, it was a big city.

Odo of Cluny, Gerald of Aurillac and Charles the Simple

In 910 Duke William of Aquitaine founded the monastery of Cluny (see Map 6.2), a much more significant place than Worms, Lucca or York in early medieval history. William may have been Dhuoda's grandson,[2] but in any case her writing shows the background of Carolingian lay piety from which he emerged. The raids of the Vikings and others had hit monasteries hard in the ninth and early tenth centuries. Their need for lay protectors or 'advocates' was very real. Yet they had another set of problems of which the advocates were part. Monasteries were concentrations of wealth on the landscape in an economy of scarcity; where as stated previously everything was in short supply except land.

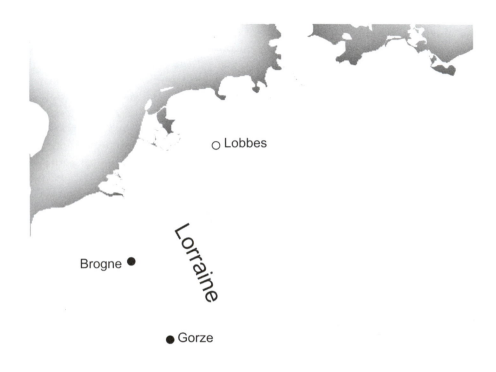

Map 6.2   Centres of monastic reform

Monasteries had a great deal of land, and Cluny in particular was about to get a lot more, as the result of pious donations; land of course meant revenues from the workers who came with it, as we saw in the previous chapter. Rulers, nobles, bishops and even heads of other monasteries were eager to share in the fortunes (in more ways than one) of a monastery. Cluny was intended to be an autonomous establishment for monks free from lay or local church interference; to this end it was placed in the immediate care of the pope, which was not unprecedented. Its monks followed the Benedictine Rule according to Carolingian standards which emphasised liturgy, that is, communal worship. This meant that their lives were spent to a very unusual extent in song. Cluny was part of a trend of monastic restoration, with counterparts further north in Lorraine. For example, Odo, abbot of Cluny from 927–42, was called upon to reform other monasteries in France, Spain and Italy. This monastic reform movement displayed little interest in improving the lot of women in religious life (but see the statement attributed to Odo of Cluny below; there is much male inconsistency in women's history). Male reformers intent on restoring right order in the Church tended to focus on men and to see women as threats to their virtue. The number of monasteries for women that were destroyed in raids and later refounded as monasteries for men was not small.

In his *Life of St Odo*, John of Salerno details the monastic practices at Baume, over 40 miles from Cluny, under Abbot Berno, who became the abbot of Cluny as well when that monastery was founded. These were the origins of Cluniac practices, which would be elaborated as the century went on. At one point John refers to the custom of his own monastery, assumed to be at Salerno in southern Italy. Readers are warned that they are about to be bored – as even John himself recognises at the end of the passage – but the activity of a small but influential minority of people in the period under study is most directly comprehended from material like this:

> They observed especially the custom of silence. At unsuitable times no one might speak or consort with another of the brethren in the cloister of the monastery, and on days when a twelve-lesson Office was celebrated no one might speak in the cloister before chapter on the following day. Within the octaves of Christmas and Easter there was strict silence day and night. This short silence, they said, signified the eternal silence. When there was necessity to ask for anything they made various signs to each other, which grammarians I suppose would call the language of the fingers and eyes. This usage had developed to such an extent among them that, if they were without the use of their tongues, the signs, I think, would suffice to indicate everything necessary. But on ferial days and in the other octaves of the saints there was this arrangement. On ferial days in the day and night Office together they sang one hundred and thirty-eight psalms, from which we subtract fourteen for the sake of the weaker brethren. But against this must be put the special prayers which our brethren say which are seen to exceed the psalter and also the two Masses and the litanies. At each of the canonical hours they knelt

twice. During the other octaves which were mentioned, they sang seventy-five psalms only in the day and night Offices together, and they knelt once and rested twice. There are many other points which I think may be omitted lest they should weary the reader.

There are many unfamiliar terms in the passage, but suffice it to say that the subject is the daily monastic routine of silence and communal prayer and psalm-singing at three-hourly intervals, and how this related to the ordinary days and festival days of the Church year. By the late tenth century the monks were singing at least 175 psalms a day at Cluny.

If this was the cutting edge in tenth-century Europe, some explanation is required. Such preoccupations can be explained by religious belief joined to the conviction that the monastic lifestyle was the best to which people could aspire, as close to the angels as people could get. Monasteries were conducive to the salvation of the people within them and of those outside (not least their founders and donors) for whom monastic prayers were said; moreover, they were conducive to the expression of the power of God in the world. Monasteries were, in modern terms, spiritual powerhouses tapping the overwhelmingly greatest energy source. This was done by focusing on God, and the surest means thereto, in the early medieval view, was liturgy, worship by the monastic community. Monasteries had been devastated by raiders, to whom John of Salerno refers on occasion; monastic communities needed to be restored: John of Salerno wrote to inspire monks, who could be far from the angels, however. The passage quoted above is bracketed by clear references to child sexual abuse and how to avoid it. Before he became abbot of Cluny, Odo was the master of the monastic school at Baume. There it was the custom, John explains, for the schoolmaster never to be alone with a boy without another boy present, and at night not to be so without a lantern. When one night a boy had to go to the toilet Odo complied with the rule by waking another boy as well, but accompanied them without a candle because the toilet (which John unfortunately does not describe) was adequately lit from within the dormitory. The next day Odo was accused in chapter (the formal gathering of the monks to consider the business of the monastery) of breaking the rule. John presents the incident as an illustration of Odo's patience in humbly begging forgiveness of Abbot Berno and does so with a matter-of-factness that modern readers can find startling if not shocking. John tells us that he spent under two years in Odo's company. Note that Salerno is south of Naples, a long way from Cluny in Burgundy; the network of communication that would arise from such connections was an important part of Cluniac influence in Europe.

Odo of Cluny himself wrote within the years 924–26 the *Life of St Gerald of Aurillac* which is very edifying for historians, especially as it is about a layman. At the point of using the evidence of two saints' Lives in a row, some consideration of this type of writing is called for. Hagiography (writing about holy people, saints) is not biography in any normal sense. The Lives of saints are instead a sub-genre of Ancient panegyric, works of praise. A balanced view or even token criticism is not to be expected in saints' Lives; miracles are, but it is not necessary to pass judgement on their truth or otherwise to use hagiography in the study of history. Indeed, experienced users of saints' Lives tend not to accept any particular episode, miraculous or otherwise, as necessarily true unless it is corroborated by other evidence. For one thing, these texts are like sponges, sucking up any good stories, including those of other saints, that can be used in praise of the subject and spiritual edification of the reader/hearer. If the Life is reasonably contemporary with its subject, and especially if the author knew him or her as John of Salerno did Odo of Cluny or spoke with people who had known the saint as Odo did with acquaintances of Gerald of Aurillac, this does make a difference, for at least the author will get the context right. What is praised in that context can be very revealing. Count Gerald of Aurillac, who lived in south-western France in the late ninth and early tenth centuries, was praised by Odo of Cluny for reasons which included the following:

1. He was pious, chaste, went several times on pilgrimage to Rome and founded a monastery.
2. He obeyed the biblical commandments, including the injunction: 'Woe to you that join house to house and lay field to field' (Isaiah 5.8).
3. He maintained his earthly position (property, role as count; Gerald's abilities in this respect are seen by his biographer as God's favour on a just man) and got on well with everybody.

How far Gerald was typical of the spirit of his age may be considered point by point, with comparative material included where appropriate. The first, of course, very much reflects the monastic agenda of the author, Odo, who is presented by his own biographer, John of Salerno, in one episode as wishing that each and every woman in the region would become a nun. Odo was concerned not with the survival of the human race but its salvation. At one point his hero Gerald was sexually tempted by the sight of a beautiful girl:

> Overcome at length, he sent word to the mother of the girl that he would come by night. He followed the messenger, violently hastened to the death of his soul. Meanwhile, as captives in chains remember with groans their former liberty, with sighs Gerald remembered the familiar sweetness of the divine love. And though but weakly, he asked God that he should not be entirely swallowed up by this temptation. Gerald came to the agreed place, and the girl entered the room; because he was cold he stood at the hearth facing her; divine grace looked on him, and this same girl appeared to him so deformed that he did not believe it was she whom he saw, until her father assented that it was so.

Gerald left, and subsequently 'ordered the father forthwith to give the girl in marriage, presented her with her liberty, and granted her a small holding'. The *droit de seigneur* to a woman on her marriage is a myth, but the ability of a lord to have a young woman he fancied would be a reality known to Odo, who came from the same social background and grew up not in a monastery, but at the court of Duke William of Aquitaine. The significance of lay piety at this time should be emphasised. Duke William is an example of it as already stated, and so are the myriad donors of land to the monastery of Cluny which he had founded. According to John of Salerno, who says he had it direct from Odo, Odo's father was an educated man who participated in prayers throughout the night before church festivals; one is reminded of how the laywoman Dhuoda advised her son to keep the canonical hours of prayer. Saints' Lives of pious laymen are not common and if Odo was going out of his way to cultivate lay piety by writing the *Life of Gerald,* it was because there was material for him to work with.

The second point shows Count Gerald of Aurillac at his most atypical, for joining house to house and laying field to field perfectly expresses the bit-by-bit acquisitiveness characteristic of the period. Two case studies illustrate this feature at contrasting social levels and in different environments. To the north, throughout the tenth century, the counts of Anjou assembled their regional power base, culminating in the countship of Fulk Nerra (987–1040). By purchase, marriage or force they acquired more and more territory, which by the end of the tenth century was fortified with a dozen castles. Their reputation for success in war and pious attention to the Church (especially at Tours, the next city east of their county town of Angers) grew over time. The result was an enlarged county of Anjou which took in the former county of Tours and more besides. To the south late in the century a well-off peasant family near Barcelona began to accumulate property which would enable it to rise to local eminence in three generations. In a situation reminiscent of Lucca – which we examined in the previous section, and not least because of the survival of documents – they cultivated relationships with the cathedral clergy of Barcelona. The many small purchases of one of the members of this family, a man named Vivas, were normally of property which bordered on his own. Joining house to house and laying field to field is exactly what Vivas did. Even the care with which details of donations to Cluny were recorded there reflects this mentality, although the generosity of the donors was seen as its opposite and a help to their salvation. The dangers of institutional acquisitiveness were unrecognised. As for Gerald of Aurillac, 'He himself never bought land, except one small field which happened to be surrounded by one of his properties,' says Odo in a perceptive choice of terms in which to praise his exceptional subject.

Nevertheless (the third point), Odo presents Gerald as a fully functioning count and lord and the picture that he draws fits in with and extends what we know from other sources. It is unclear what Gerald is count of. The public office of count had become rather murky with the disintegration of the Carolingian Empire, the title inherited or claimed and the county, going back ultimately to an old Roman city territory, losing definition. The above mentioned case of Anjou is an example. Yet as count, Gerald was a royal vassal according to old Carolingian practice, and in him the public office of count is still recognisable.

We see him presiding in the *mallus*, the count's law court. Of course, being Gerald, he is extraordinarily merciful, avoiding capital punishment. He commands soldiers – also being Gerald, he bids them not to use the sharp edges of their weapons – and has vassals. Odo of Cluny, who again knows the context well, reveals the complexities of Gerald's position. Despite being pressured to do so, Gerald would not commend himself to Duke William of Aquitaine instead of the king of France, nor to another count. Praise of Gerald in this respect high-lights how fragmented and privatised power had become in tenth-century France. About this time the word 'fief' (of Germanic origin ultimately Latinised as *feodum* or *feudum*) begins to be applied in documents to a grant of land in return for service (earlier known as *precarium* or *beneficium*, usages which continued). One looks in vain for this sort of thing where Gerald is concerned, however. His lands were inherited from his parents and owned outright, and his vassals were main-tained by other means. These extensive allodial properties came with a depen-dent population over which Gerald's authority is presented as being limited only by his self-restraint, of which we have already seen an example.

Two more episodes in the *Life of St Gerald of Aurillac* will repay consideration. One episode showing Gerald as landlord, if carefully considered, suggests that seigneurial control was otherwise limited in reality:

> On one occasion he met a number of countrymen who had left their hold-ings, and were moving into another province. When he had recognized them and inquired where they were going with their household goods, they replied that they had been wronged by him when he had given them their holdings. The soldiers who were accompanying him urged that he should order them to be beaten and made to go back to the holdings from which they had come. But he was unwilling, for he knew that both he and they had one Lord in heaven, who was accustomed rather, in the words of the Apostle, to forbear threats [Ephesians 6.9], and who was not used to raise the hand of His might against the fatherless [Job 31.21]. He therefore permitted them to go where they thought they would be better off, and gave them permission to live there.

In an ill-organised countryside with a low population, the threat of on-the-spot physical violence may not have been much of a deterrent to opportunistic relo-cation as here. The extent to which control was possible given the poor commu-nication of the early and, indeed, later Middle Ages should always be considered if the period is to be properly understood. The other episode is the one for which the *Life* is best known: about Gerald and the Just Price. It takes us back to Italy:

> Once on his way back from Rome as he was going past Pavia he made his camp not far from the city. The Venetians and many others hearing of this immediately went out to him, for he was quite the most celebrated traveller on that road, and was known to all as a religious and generous man. When therefore the traders, as their manner is, were going about the tents and enquiring if anybody wanted to buy anything, some of the more considerable

among them came to Gerald's tent and asked the retainers whether the lord count (for so they all called him) would order some cloaks or spices. He himself called them and said, 'I bought what I wanted in Rome; but I should like you to tell me whether I bought wisely.' Then he ordered the cloaks that he had got to be brought out. Now, one of them was very valuable, and a Venetian looking at it, asked what he had given for it. When he had learnt the price, 'Indeed', he said, 'if it was at Constantinople it would be worth even more.' When the count heard this he was horrified, as though in dread of a great crime. Afterwards, therefore, when he met some Roman pilgrims whom he knew, he gave them as many shillings as the Venetian had said the cloak was worth more than the price he had given for it, telling them where they could find the seller of the cloak.

This was a context that Odo of Cluny would have been familiar with, for he had travelled to and from Italy. Pavia, unlike Lucca, was a centre for international commerce. Venice was in regular touch with Constantinople, and its merchants might be expected to know the prices of goods there. Odo presents Gerald not as wedded to the monastic virtue of poverty, but as aware of the Christian (originally Roman) notion of an inherent value of goods. European commerce was in its infancy.

Despite the touching fidelity to them of such as Gerald of Aurillac, the kings of France were now extraordinarily weak, and remained so until the twelfth century. Accordingly, little will be said about them in the rest of this book. However, the Carolingian king Charles the Simple (where *simplex* means 'straightforward') negotiated two outcomes that deserve attention and respect. In 911 he reached an agreement with Rollo, leader of a Viking army in northern France, whereby they would convert to Christianity, be settled at the mouth of the River Seine, and protect the area against other Vikings. Rollo became a count and royal vassal. This was the beginning of the end of the Viking Age on the Continent and the origin of the duchy of Normandy, the district of the Northmen, who of course took over a great deal more territory (see Map 7.4). As Northmen were wont to do, they assimilated well into the culture and ways of doing things where they settled, as will be seen later. In 921 Charles the Simple, king of the western Franks, also made a treaty of friendship with Henry I, king of the eastern Franks, recognising France and Germany as separate kingdoms and ushering in centuries of relative peace between them. Their common origin in the Carolingian kingdom and empire is shown by the royal titles. The kings met for this purpose on a ship in the River Rhine at Bonn, precisely on the border between their two kingdoms, in an interesting diplomatic expression of their equality. So, leaving the French crown to be disputed by the last Carolingians (including the unfortunate Charles the Simple, who was to die in prison) and the Counts of Paris until one of the latter, Hugh Capet, established the Capetian dynasty (987–1328), we turn to the success story of the tenth century, Germany and its kings and queens who would eventually become emperors and empresses.

The Rise of Germany

In 911, after the end of the line of Carolingian rulers in East Francia, its leading nobles met at a royal centre called Forchheim and chose as king one of their number, Duke Conrad of Franconia, who, if he was not a Carolingian, was at least a Frank. Conrad was not a particularly successful ruler, and before his death he indicated that the next king should be Duke Henry of Saxony, from the most powerful family in Germany. This family can be traced back to the married couple Liudolf and Oda. The oldest medieval person of whom I'm aware, living to the age of 107, Oda saw the formation of early Germany. Her husband Liudolf was duke of East Saxony in the middle of the ninth century. In contrast to the eighth-century dukes mentioned in Chapter 4, Widukind the leader of the Saxons and Tassilo who aimed for an independent Bavaria, Liudolf was a Carolingian military commander of a border region. Dukes were royal officials with responsibilities, especially military, over a larger area than that of counts. The effect of Carolingian governance on conquered regions was discussed at the end of the previous chapter and will be reiterated below. There is no doubt, however, that the grim military situation *c*.900 necessitated and promoted the power of dukes in East Francia. In particular, the disastrous defeats by Magyars between 907–10 included the deaths in battle of both secular and church leaders. The coronation of the first real king of Germany, Conrad, occurred the year before Oda died; Conrad was backed to be king by her elderly son Duke Otto of Saxony. She did not live to see her grandson Henry become king in 919. Henry was crowned in Frankish dress, stressing continuity with the Carolingian past. Henry's son, grandson and great-grandson all named Otto ruled for the rest of the century, and give the label 'Ottonian' to the dynasty and this period of German history. For what they ruled see Map 6.3.

The success of the dynasty was founded on military accomplishment. Henry I organised effective defence against the Magyars and won an important victory over them at Riade in 933. His use of a network of fortresses and forces maintained by agricultural production is reminiscent of Alfred the Great's defence of England toward the end of the previous century and influence is possible (note that his son married an English royal woman, Edith). Defence became offence, and there was also extensive campaigning of both sorts against the Slavs. Tribute and booty were an economic basis for early German royal and aristocratic power as well as the main one, peasant production. Henry's son Otto I defeated the Magyars so soundly at the Battle of the Lech in 955 that they settled down in Hungary, where the Magyar language is spoken to this day. Something of the grimness of the time can be glimpsed in the fate of Otto's son-in-law Duke Conrad the Red of Lorraine. Two years before the battle he had joined Otto's eldest son Liudolf in revolt. Now Conrad fought for Otto and was killed at the Lech; his body was sewn into a leather sack and brought back to Cologne for burial in the cathedral. Two months after that battle Otto I defeated the Slavs at the Battle of Recknitz. Writing a little later in the century, Widukind of the important monastery of Corvey describes how the battlefield was left after a

Map 6.3 The German Empire and its neighbours

night of slaughter in the enemy camp. The head of the leader of the Slavs 'was placed in the field, and around it seven hundred decapitated captives; their chief adviser with eyes torn out was deprived of his tongue and left for useless in the midst of the cadavers.' These victories had not only immediate practical results, but significantly contributed to the widespread reputation of the rulers who won them. The offer of an imperial crown to Otto I in 962, as had been the case with Charlemagne back in 800, was a consequence of his military success, although (also like Charlemagne) it followed on directly from his involvement in Italy, in circumstances to be considered presently.

Carrying on Frankish eastward expansion from which his own kingdom had originated, Otto I made major conquests of Slavs beyond the River Elbe, which he attempted to consolidate by their conversion to Christianity. Thus he created both bishoprics and marches on his eastern frontier. A march, again, was a border territory, and the German official placed over a march was known as a margrave (count [German *graf*] of a march, a much larger area than an ordinary county). Life on the eastern frontier can be examined by focusing on Margrave Gero and his family. Gero fought Slavs for many years, and received besides the profits of war extensive grants of land and, of course, his official position. The historian Widukind sums him up thus:

> Gero indeed was an experienced warrior, but he also possessed a good head for civic affairs. He was eloquent and knowledgeable and showed his prudence more in deeds than in words. Though adept at acquisition, he also displayed largesse, and what was best, zeal in religion.

Gero was responsible for the construction of bridges through the swamp at Recknitz which enabled King Otto's forces to reach and defeat the Slavs. Gero's warrior son Siegfried married 13-year-old Hathui but was soon killed fighting Slavs. Margrave Gero then founded a monastery for women at Gernrode (Gero's clearing; the eastern part of the church there is of tenth-century date) out of profits from war with the Slavs for his recently widowed daughter-in-law Hathui, who was its abbess for 55 years. Hathui commissioned a Life of the patron saint of the monastery to be written by the priest Nadda, who wrote its prologue to her, and there is known to have been an Old Saxon translation of the Book of Psalms at Gernrode. From the savagery of Recknitz to Hathui's cultural centre is a long way, but both belonged to the same environment. The eastern frontier was an asset for Ottonian Germany as its own territory had been for the earlier Franks, although the northeastern marches were lost in the great Slav revolt of 983 just before the death of Otto II. There was another asset in the silver mines of Saxony, the Ottonian heartland.

It is very important not to approach the early history of Germany retrospectively, reading into it characteristics of later periods. While eventually the German kingdom may be said to have had an 'elective' monarchy, with the rulers chosen by 'the princes', Ottonian kingship could hardly have been more dynastic. Otto I was named by his father as sole heir to the throne when he was in his teens, Otto II was crowned during the lifetime of his father when he was a child and Otto III actually succeeded his father as king when he was a toddler and grew up under a long regency of his mother, grandmother and aunt, of whom more will be said below. The great innovation of this family was to break with the Frankish tradition of dividing the kingdom among royal sons. There were consequent tensions which took the form of rebellions of bypassed (or at least anxious) sons and brothers allied with one or more dukes. Duchies were in any case given to other royal sons or associated with the royal family through marriage. Early Germany has been seen as an agglomeration of ethnic units that never quite knit together as a country. Yet whatever existed before the consolidation of Frankish control over the region was transformed by Carolingian administration. The reason why Germany did not enter the modern world as a unified nation may have more to do with the limitations of Carolingian governance than any weakness of Germany itself. Below its public institutions, but not separate from them, was a world of private power, lordship, family (feud was endemic) and subsistence farming. The following case is instructive. In a rebellion in 941, Erich, one of the conspirators against Otto I, was killed. Years later Erich's son Hildiward was chosen bishop and went down to Italy to do homage to Emperor Otto I and receive the staff of episcopal office (this is lay investiture, by the way, to be discussed in the next chapter). Otto gave him the staff, saying, 'take here the price for your father'. This is a reference to compensation given to a family for the loss of a family member: Erich had been killed by the supporters of Otto, so Otto refers to the bishopric as compensation given to Erich's son. No matter how exalted the context, the basic reality can intrude.

And then there was the empire. In the Carolingian break-up the imperial title logically enough attached to whoever ruled Italy, where Rome was; however, the discrepancy between this grand title and the minor rulers who bore it eventually became too much and it was not used after the death of Berengar of Friuli, king of Italy, in 924. To make sense of the following, refer to Map 6.3. The Carolingian Empire had broken up into not only France, Germany and northern Italy, but also, northwest of Italy, the kingdoms of Provence or Arles on the Mediterranean and Burgundy to its north. In the ensuing decades of contention for the rule of northern Italy, another Berengar, of Ivrea, seeking support became the vassal of King Otto I of Germany. Yet Berengar went too far: when King Lothar of Italy died in 950, Berengar took the kingship for himself and imprisoned Lothar's widow Adelheid (Adelaide), who asked Otto I for help. She was the daughter of the king of Burgundy, which Otto had protected against encroachments by the kingdom of Provence; so complex was the route to German involvement in Italy. Otto went to Italy to deal with his unruly vassal, married Adelheid and became king of Italy as well as Germany. He was now king of the Franks and the Lombards as Charlemagne had been.[3] The similarities between the two rulers do not end there. Otto went back to Germany with Adelheid, leaving Berengar to govern Italy for him. Ten years later, with Berengar encroaching on papal land, it was the pope who asked Otto for help. Otto and Adelheid came south to Italy and in 962 were anointed and crowned emperor and empress by the pope in Rome, after which Berengar and his wife Willa were ousted. Otto issued a charter known as the *Ottonianum*, written in letters of gold on parchment stained imperial purple, which confirmed the old Carolingian arrangements with the papacy.

This twice-revived Roman Empire in the West was to endure until 1806, as stated previously. In the long run it hindered the development of both Germany and Italy into coherent countries like France, England and Spain. Part of the problem lay in the future, with the emergence of an assertively independent papacy in the second half of the eleventh century which will be considered in the next chapter. The papacy did not want to be part of a strong secular power. The difficulty of governing Italy was there from the beginning of what is often called the German Empire. Whereas Charlemagne conquered a Lombard kingdom for which its rulers were still issuing laws in the eighth century, what Otto I took over in the tenth century had emerged from the break-up of the Carolingian Empire highly fragmented, principally into autonomous episcopal cities. Where public government still had some strength in Tuscany, the marquis supported the Ottonian king emperors. The Ottonians were to go beyond the Carolingians in attempting to rule all of Italy, but their control of it was tenuous even when the rulers were there rather than north of the Alps where their physical presence was also needed for governance. As was the case with Charlemagne, there was direct confrontation with Byzantine forces in southern Italy, where Saracens were now also to be opposed. Diplomacy between the empires of Byzantium and the West had its problems – the Ottonian envoy Liudprand of Cremona complained of everything in Constantinople starting with the Byzantines' reference to Otto I as 'king' (*rex*) rather than 'emperor' (*basileus*) – but eventually bore fruit in marriage alliances, as will be seen. For the Byzantine Empire as well as for Germany, the tenth century was a period of success, although the ultimate triumph of Emperor Basil Bulgaroctonos (the Bulgar-Slayer) came early in the next century. Competition for the great Slav mission field needs to be seen in this light. The Byzantines were angered when Otto I sent missionaries to Kiev in Russia, for they were about to consolidate the Byzantine commonwealth with the conversion of the Russian ruler Vladimir in AD 1000.

An interesting perspective on the life and times of Otto I is provided by Hrotsvitha of Gandersheim in Saxony. Her *Deeds of Otto I*, written between 965 and 968, contains the earliest statement of German imperial ideology, with its marked stress on the Ancient Roman background, and is, moreover, the first historical work by a woman.[4] It was requested by her abbess Gerberga, Otto's niece, who in 947 had been granted by Otto the right to have a law court, mint and army at Gandersheim. The monastery at Gandersheim had been founded in the ninth century by Duke Liudolf of Saxony and his extremely long-lived wife Oda, and no fewer than three of their daughters were its abbesses, in turn. In the mid-tenth century another family monastery of the rulers of Germany, which was also for women, was founded at Quedlinburg. Its abbess Matilda was the patron of the above mentioned tenth-century historian Widukind of Corvey. The monastery for women at Gernrode, founded by Margrave Gero, and its abbess Hathui should also be recalled here. These three monasteries were located in the region of the Harz Mountains in northern Germany, as were the main concentration of royal estates and the silver mines. All of this is to give context for Hrotsvitha's *Deeds of Otto I*, which is one of 17 short Latin works, including six plays written in the style of the Roman playwright Terence but on Christian subjects, of which she is the author. 'But I do not think it fitting for a frail woman abiding in the enclave of a peaceful monastery to speak of war, with which she ought not even to be acquainted,' writes Hrotsvitha in the *Deeds of Otto I*; however, she does so in a tricky situation. Her abbess Gerberga was the daughter of Otto's rebellious younger brother Henry, and the two were on opposite sides of the conflict that Hrotsvitha avoids describing through the statement just quoted. She was a clever woman.

Hrotsvitha's works tend to have heroines rather than heroes, and this even affects the *Deeds of Otto I*. Hrotsvitha seems, indeed, to be going out of her way to include every conceivable woman in Otto's life, and almost all of them are praised. In a text that would be about 20 pages of an ordinary paperback book, we find the following women mentioned, and in some cases discussed extensively: Matilda, second wife of Henry I; Edith, first wife of Otto I, her sister Adiva, her mother, and the ignoble mother of her half-brother the Anglo-Saxon king Athelstan (who isn't named); Judith, wife of Otto's brother Henry and mother of Hrotsvitha's abbess; the captive wives and dear children (some of whom were presumably female) of the Avar (read Hungarian) leaders defeated by Henry after Otto made him duke of Bavaria; Liudgard, daughter of the aforementioned Queen Edith; Ida, wife of Edith's son Liudulf; Adelheid (Adelaide), Otto I's second wife, and her unnamed lady-in-waiting; the unnamed daughter (mentioned with her unnamed brother) of Liudolf and Ida; and finally, in a list of subjects that Hrotsvitha says she will not go on to consider, there is Willa, 'wretched spouse' of Berengar in Italy. Particular attention is given to the above mentioned Adelheid, who was to marry Otto. According to Hrotsvitha, Adelheid showed considerable initiative in escaping from Berengar's prison before Otto came on the scene. They are subsequently described as ruling together. Why does Hrotsvitha include all these women in a work that explicitly sets out to chronicle Otto's achievements? Put simply, she had an interest in what women did, and was reasonably confident of their, and her own, abilities.

A contemporary counterpart of the *Deeds of Otto I*, by a male author, the same Liudpriand of Cremona who was cited above concerning his diplomatic mission to Constantinople for Otto I, makes an instructive comparison. Written in 964, it is much shorter than Hrotsvitha's work, and begins precisely where the latter leaves off. Liudprand too mentions a number of women, almost all negatively presented, it is true, but still there. Thus at the beginning of Liudprand's work is Willa, the 'wretched spouse' of Berengar at the end of Hrotsvitha's account. Women are mentioned at other points in his text: the widow of the pope's vassal Rainer, Stephana, and her sister, the widow Anna and the pope's niece, some man's wife outside Rome and others unspecified, with all of whom Pope John XII (whom Otto deposed) is said to have had sexual relations. There were also women pilgrims who he says avoided Rome and its predatory pope. Chapter 19 is worth quoting in full:

> Meanwhile the women, with whom the so-called pope John was accustomed to carry on his voluptuous sports, being many in numbers and noble in rank, stirred up the Romans to overthrow Leo, whom God and they themselves had chosen as supreme and universal pope, and bring John again back to Rome. This they did; but by the mercy of God the venerable pope Leo escaped from their clutches and with a few attendants made his way to the protection of the most pious emperor Otto.

Revolting women are rare in the Middle Ages and it is extraordinary that this passage was written at all. The point may be seen less clearly by younger readers who are not familiar with the extent to which women have been left out of traditional history, although there are still history books in print which include fewer women than these short works considered here.

All historians whether medieval or modern must write to some extent of women in treating of the final Ottonian decades of the tenth century, the very end of the First Millennium, and generally do so favourably. On 14 April, 972, in St Peter's Church in Rome Otto II, already king and emperor, married Theophanu, the niece of the Byzantine emperor, and she was crowned empress. In 973 the old King Emperor Otto I died. Shown in Figure 24 are Otto II, Theophanu and their son Otto III in a contemporary ivory made in Milan. Look carefully at the small figures at the feet of Christ: if they got up and stepped out of the composition, we might be able to see what these people looked like, at least as regards their Germanic dress. Otto II wears soft boots and gloves, his clothing apparently unadorned except by a shoulder clasp such as the saint above him is wearing. The sleeves of Theophanu's robe are decorated, probably with jewels rather than embroidery, for the design resembles the ornament on the cross in Christ's halo, only the carving on the sleeves is better. Otto III is dressed, as befits a child, in a thinner fabric which falls in many small folds. All are crowned. The composition of the figures is significantly symmetrical, with emperor and empress kneeling on an even plane. Otto II has the more honorific position below the right hand of Christ and is in close proximity to his foot, as if to kiss it. The top of Theophanu's head, and even more her eyes, are higher than her husband's, close to the hand of the Virgin Mary above her. She holds her child Otto III, whose finely carved hands also express veneration. The arrangement of the figures is somewhat paralleled by a plaque on a contemporary processional cross (not illustrated) in which Abbess Mathilda of Essen and her brother Duke Otto, the children of Liudolf and Ida to whom Hrotsvitha referred, stand opposite one another holding a cross, with the brother not a bit taller than the sister. That disaster did not soon overwhelm the Ottonian royal family was due to a considerable extent to its women.

When Otto II died in 983 the little king Otto III was only three years old, but there was no shortage of able regents. Circumstances could hardly have been

Figure 24 Ivory of Otto II, Theophanu and Otto III at the feet of Christ, *c*.980.
(Civiche Raccolte d'Arte Applicata, Castello Sforzesco, Milan; all rights reserved)

worse, especially as Slavic lands previously conquered by the Germans had
revolted just before Otto II's death; there was, unusually, some trouble to the
west, in Lorraine, as well; always Italy was intractable and the basis for the
Ottonian superstructure weak. First and foremost among the regents was
Theophanu but also, especially after Theophanu's death in 991, the elderly
Queen Empress Adelheid and her daughter Abbess Matilda of Quedlinburg.
There are features of the way Theophanu is referred to in documents that are
noteworthy. Theophanu's imperial title when her husband was alive was *co-imper-
atrix*, and after his death *imperatrix augusta*, Latin feminine forms of 'empress' to
suit her gender. Yet in one of two surviving charters in her own name, she is
Theophanius imperator augustus, Latin masculine forms of 'emperor' – she has

become an honorary man. In the charter she also refers to 'our investiture or *mundburdium*' or possibly 'the *mundburdium* of our empire', the phrase is ambiguous. *Mundburdium* was the 'protection' that men were always to have over women, and for a woman to be associated with it in any other way is perhaps the most extraordinary thing of all. The evidence must be kept in perspective. In 1002 another Byzantine princess, the emperor's own daughter, 'born to the purple', came to Italy to marry Otto III, but he had already died, and we are not even sure of her name. Ottonian women on whom we have been focusing owed their importance either to direct connections to men or to membership of families whose fortunes had been made by fighting men. Yet these women had real authority and power in the most successful state of their day, when Europe was at its most disorganised, its cultures were mixing in the rough, a new society was very much in process of formation, the Roman Empire, regardless of what they thought, was far in the past, and population had only begun to grow.

Towards 1000

Indeed, the rise in European population which, with a terrific check by the Black Death, has continued to the present day, is detectable before the end of the tenth century. Signs of expansion are as simple as taking new fields into cultivation. These are known as assarts and the process of assarting is well evidenced in the property charters of the monastery of Cluny which was discussed near the beginning of this chapter. Land was cleared of bush and sometimes drained. It was brought back into cultivation in the valleys of the Rivers Loire in France and Po in Italy, for example, and reclaimed from the sea along much more of the southern coast of the North Sea than just the Netherlands. Reclaimed land is fertile land. Thus expansion of population and increased agricultural production went together. These were assisted by basic technological improvements: a better plough that turned over the soil; the horse collar that allowed a horse to pull with its shoulders and horseshoes that improved the usefulness of this animal that is quicker than an ox; the spread of watermills for grinding grain. Also, advantageous farming practices were spreading: threefold crop rotation, which spread the benefits and risk with two crops per year and allowed the rest of the land to recover its fertility, and cultivation of legumes (beans), which nourished both people with protein and the land by nitrogen-fixing bacteria that live in nodules in the roots of these plants. All of this underpinned the eleventh-century transformation of Europe to be considered in the next chapter. With population growth, the nature of settlement could change as people clustered together, and a landscape of dispersed farmsteads came to have villages and even larger towns. This chapter began by examining cities in three areas of Europe when urban settlement was at a low point; the next chapter will pick up the rise of urbanisation to the point where town-dwellers developed a sense of their own interests and what to do about them. Unsurprisingly, Lucca was precocious: it was at war with Pisa by 1004.

In the crucible that was France, major social change was already being wrought. The extensive charters of Cluny indicate a late transition from recognisably Antique slavery to medieval serfdom, with the latter seen to maximise resources of the lords. The key distinction here is not one of legal status, the old categories of 'free' and 'unfree' still seen in the Carolingian estate record examined in Chapter 5 having fused together. Instead, it lay in the way that the peasants were living: like Actard and Eligilde in that document, on property that they could hand on to their children, rather than having nothing but the food and clothing that the lord supplied. Another development is the rise of the knight. In Cluniac charters from the third quarter of the tenth century on, the term *milites* 'soldiers' comes to be used instead of *nobiles* 'nobles' for lords, stressing the practical basis of their power. Armed horsemen had come to be seen as what counted in warfare, and this attracted prestige. Best of all was to have a castle, or rather a whole network of them like the counts of Anjou. For the dominant warrior aristocracy it was a highly competitive situation, and a violent one for everybody. Pleas for order came quickly, and took an interesting form. In the most chaotic region of fragmented France, the southwest, at the end of the tenth century bishops associated their flocks in collective oaths to keep the Peace of God by not attacking non-combatants. This spreading movement was motivated by the Church's concern for social peace and, indeed, social reform as well as to protect the interests of its own clerical non-combatants, but tapped into enthusiastic lay piety and a tradition of self-help. In a society where power was so often structured by oaths of submission, mutual oaths will have a surprisingly important role to play.

Recognition of these developments has led to another theory of historical periodisation to put beside the Pirenne Thesis, although typically of the late rather than early twentieth century it is the product of scholarly consensus rather than the idea of one individual. It proposes that the years around AD 1000 were a major historical threshold, even the end of Antiquity. The latter extreme position would deny the significance in the birth of Europe of a number of major developments which the reader may care to review at this point. One is the formation of several political units under barbarian rulers where there had been one Roman empire in the West, and the withering away of state taxation within them. Another is the complex effect of Justinian's Reconquest of the Western Mediterranean region which had only limited success in attaching part of it to the Roman Empire ruled from Constantinople and paradoxically encouraged the rest of the West to keep going its own way. Another is the new and different, limited but influential phenomenon of vibrant, Christian, learned culture coming from the British Isles. Another is the rise of Islam introducing a new political, religious and cultural dynamic to part of the Mediterranean and greatly lessening the influence of the Byzantine Empire, especially on Italy. Another, related to the latter, is the formation of the core of Europe within France, Italy and Germany, with the significant powerbases in the north of France and later Germany. What is certain is that Europe at the end of the eleventh century was a very different place than Europe at the beginning of the eleventh century, as we shall see in the next chapter, and that the long roots of these changes stretch back into the tenth century that we have been examining in this one. Likewise the tenth-century monastic reform fed into later reform of the Church, not least in promoting celibacy to the extent that the married priesthood of the West could no longer be tolerated.

Figure 25 Christ crucified on the Cross of Lothar, *c*.1000. (© Domkapital Aachen [photo: Ann Münchow])

Finally, there is only one contemporary statement of a belief that the world was going to come to an end in the year 1000. A later tenth-century writer, Abbo of Fleury, recalled a preacher saying so when he was a child. On the other hand, European leaders at the end of the tenth century were enthusiastically empire-building precisely *not* 'as if there were no tomorrow'. To the north in Scandinavia, which was converting to Christianity, the Danish conquest of England was being carefully planned and carried out at this time. Conversions of peoples to Christianity cluster remarkably around AD 1000: Norway, Iceland, Poland, Hungary and Russia. If the decision to convert was motivated by conviction and/or fear that the world was about to end, the sources do not say so. To the south in Rome, Emperor Otto III and his pope Sylvester II were attempting to revive the Roman Empire in a truer sense than anyone before. Let us pause to consider an image of Christian empire from the late tenth century, a sign of the success of early Germany. It is the Cross of Lothar, of which the front is decorated with jewels set in gold with a cameo of Augustus, the first Roman emperor, in the middle and the rock crystal seal of the Carolingian ruler Lothar II near the base. The reverse, which is illustrated here (see Figure 25), is plain silver with a beautifully simple incised figure of Christ crucified. An alternative significance of the year 1000 is apparent in the sources, which elaborate on the salvation of humanity resulting from what was, in the Christian view, the most important event in history: the incarnation of Christ. An example will be given at the beginning of the next chapter. In the Christian view, AD 1000 was the thousandth anniversary of God made man. Whereas the official church line was against tying the floating 1000 years of the New Testament Apocalypse down to any span of human history, there was a great positive message of hope in the historical fact of the millennium of Christ's birth.

The Eleventh Century:
Transformation of Europe

New Beginnings and Old Ways

Early in AD 1000 Otto III, 'servant of Jesus Christ and emperor of the Romans, Augustus, according to the will of God our saviour and liberator' as he is styled in his charters at precisely this time, travelled from Rome to Gniezno in Poland. This is one of the longest overland journeys recorded up to this point in the early Middle Ages. Entering the place with bare feet (in winter!), he prayed at the tomb of St Adalbert of Prague, who had been one of his advisers before being martyred by Prussians resisting efforts to convert them.[1] Emperor Otto then set up an episcopal structure in Poland and recognised its leader Boleslav, who gave him gifts including 300 armed soldiers. Going west to spend Easter, as Ottonian rulers were wont to do, at Quedlinburg, site of an important monastery for women in the heartland of Saxon royal power, Otto III thence proceeded to Aachen, where Charlemagne had established his capital and where Otto himself had been crowned as a child of three. There the young king emperor, who was not more than 20, ordered the bones of Charlemagne to be dug up secretly to confirm that they lay where people thought they did, finding a gold cross hung around his predecessor's neck and the clothes partly preserved. By tradition, the Carolingian manuscript known as the Coronation Gospels, which is shown on the frontispiece of the book you are reading and discussed in its Introduction, also came to light on this occasion. Its name derives from its customary use as the holy book on which the German emperors took their coronation oath. Then Otto III returned to Rome. Two years later he was dead. AD 1000 was not an ordinary year even in the life of this extraordinary man.

The emergence of the Christian kingdoms of Poland and Hungary at this time was of long-term consequence for European history, but the same cannot be said of Otto III's short reign as a whole. Establishment of the Magyar kingdom of Hungary and its Church organisation with imperial favour, but without an imperial visit, occurred most likely in 1001. Contemporaries would not have mistaken the political consequences of the emergence of Polish and Hungarian

Churches independent from the German Church, but Otto facilitated their separation. One can deeply empathise with the historian Francis Dvornik, who wrote in the late 1940s, when Europe lay in ruins:

> it is no exaggeration to say that Otto III was the only German Emperor who succeeded in mapping out for Central and Eastern Europe a scheme acceptable to both German and the new Slavonic and other nations, and comprehensive enough to shape the fate of this part of Europe to the benefit of all peoples concerned.[2]

Indeed a primary issue in the great wars of the twentieth century, including the Cold War, was still the consolidation of Europe's eastern lands. For our purposes here, the ambition of Otto III to be a real Roman emperor needs to be appreciated. He spent much of his short reign in Rome, where he had a palace on the Palatine Hill. He was aware that the Donation of Constantine, by which that first Christian emperor had supposedly handed the West to the pope, was a forgery, although the document was only discredited by Lorenzo Valla finally in the Renaissance. He worked in cooperation with the man whom he had appointed pope, his old tutor Gerbert of Aurillac, who took the name Sylvester II, after Constantine's pope Sylvester I. Otto III's *renovatio imperii Romanorum*, 'renewal of the Empire of the Romans', was an original concept of the Roman Empire as extended over kingdoms including Germany. Yet unitary rule from Rome was not where Europe's future lay. This is one of several respects in which the beginning and end of the eleventh century look very different.

Writing around 1030–45, the Burgundian monk Ralph Glaber presented the beginning of the century positively as a time of renewal in his *Histories*. From 'the thousandth year of the born Word [Christ] bringing life to everything' on, good men flourished. The following passage is often quoted, and rightly so:

> Just before the third year after the millennium, throughout the whole world, but most especially in Italy and Gaul, men began to reconstruct churches, although for the most part the existing ones were properly built and not in the least unworthy. But it seemed as though each Christian community was aiming to surpass all others in the splendour of construction. It was as if the whole world were shaking itself free, shrugging off the burden of the past, and cladding itself everywhere in a white mantle of churches. Almost all the episcopal churches and those of monasteries dedicated to various saints, and little village chapels, were rebuilt better than before by the faithful.
>
> (*Histories*, III.13)

Five years later, Glaber says, the relics of many saints came to light. These are very medieval expressions of renewal. The building of churches is a sign to modern historians of the rise in population and agricultural production, the quickening of economic activity, that were mentioned at the end of the previous chapter; and to art historians, of the rise of Romanesque architecture. There is, however, a darker side to Glaber, in whom can be seen the stirrings of a demonic obsession that would grow in succeeding centuries. In cultures long Christianised, the supernatural anxieties were internal ones within the Christian religion. The need to assert the power of the Christian God over external, pagan forces faded. The pagan gods were regarded either as demons, or else humans whom demons deluded people into worshipping as gods; either way, demonic power was not stressed in the centuries when most of Europe was being converted to Christianity and the faith consolidated there. This older attitude can still be seen in the writings of Glaber's contemporary, Burchard of Worms.

Bishop of Worms from 1000–25, Burchard made a compilation of church law that included a penitential called the *Corrector and Physician*. A text of this sort specifies what penances should be performed for what sins and/or for how long, and the title of this one in particular follows the traditional use of disease as a metaphor for sin. Penance is strictly speaking not punishment for wrongdoing, but (like asceticism, out of which it grew) exercises to improve a person's spiritual state. Since these normally included, as for the misdeeds cited below, a period of time on bread and water only, the distinction may be blurred. Burchard's penitential makes extensive reference to magical practices. These are interesting in their own right, but they are not necessarily based on observation of what people did in Burchard's own time, since they are drawn from a variety of sources. What is most important is the attitude toward these practices: *how* they were thought to be wrong. They are presented as vestiges of paganism: 'Hast thou consulted magicians and led them into thy house in order to seek out any magical trick, or to avert it; or hast thou invited to thee according to pagan custom diviners . . .?' Penance must be done for worship of sun, moon or stars or in the wrong places (springs, stones, trees, crossroads) or incantations unless directed to the right address: 'Hast thou collected medicinal herbs with evil incantations, not with the creed and the Lord's prayer, that is, with the singing of the "credo in Deum [I believe in God]" and the paternoster [our Father]?' Even Christian texts can be wrongly handled: 'Hast thou sought out oracles in codices or in tablets, as many are accustomed to do who presume to obtain oracles from psalters or from the Gospels or from anything else of the kind?'[3]

The problem of magic is one of misbelief. Burchard provides three variations on the theme of night-riding women which for all the murkiness of the topic are crystal clear as to what is going on. The women are deceived by the devil into thinking or dreaming that they ride with the witch Hulda or goddess Diana. Nothing actually happens, which is just as well:

> Hast thou believed what many women, turning back to Satan, believe and affirm to be true, as thou believest in the silence of the quiet night when thou hast gone to bed and thy husband lies in thy bosom, that while thou art in bodily form thou canst go out by closed doors and art able to cross the spaces of the world with others deceived by like error and without visible weapons slay persons who have been baptised and redeemed by the blood of Christ, and cook and eat their flesh and in place of their hearts put straw or wood

or anything of the sort and when they are eaten make them alive again and give an interval of life?

Only once does Burchard of Worms allow that magic actually works, interestingly enough in the case of impotency:

> Hast thou done what some adulteresses are wont to do? When first they learn that their lovers wish to take legitimate wives, they thereupon by some trick of magic extinguish the male desire, so that they are impotent and cannot consummate their union with their legitimate wives. If thou has done or taught others to do this, thou shouldst do penance for forty days on bread and water.

The same penance is specified for the following:

> Hast thou done what some women are wont to do? They take off their clothes and anoint their whole naked body with honey, and laying down their honey-smeared body upon wheat on some linen on the earth, roll to and fro often, then carefully gather all the grains of wheat which stick to the moist body, place it in a mill, and make the mill go round backwards against the sun and so grind it to flour; and they make bread from that flour and then give it to their husbands to eat, that on eating the bread they may become feeble and pine away.

Like the first example above, for which the 40-day fast had to be repeated for the next seven years (only for one or two years in the variants), this would be murder if anything happened, but it was not expected to; the penance for wilful murder was much more extensive, affecting the rest of a person's life. Note that although there is a tendency for magical practices to be associated with women in Burchard's penitential, this is by no means always the case. Among those wherein gender is not specified, the following example was probably directed at men:

> Hast thou made little boys' size bows and boys' shoes, and cast them into thy storeroom or thy barn so that satyrs or goblins might sport with them, in order that they might bring to thee the goods of others so that thou shouldst become richer? If thou hast, thou shalt do penance for ten days on bread and water.

This is trivialised paganism, which could easily take the form of the things that women did.

There is a significant pattern of difference between the early and later Middle Ages to be remarked here. Evidence for the early medieval centuries indicates an endemic belief in witchcraft; however, the Church did not encourage such a belief at the time and secular rulers can be seen to discourage it as well, although in an inconsistent way. The first passage quoted above is reminiscent of ones from a much earlier Irish penitential, a Lombard law code and a Carolingian capitulary all of which target the accuser: 'because it is in no wise to be believed by Christian minds that it is possible that a woman can eat a living man from within'. The Lombard law just quoted even penalises the judge who orders the death of a woman so accused. Nor are these the only early medieval sanctions to penalise the accuser rather than the accused. In the early Middle Ages people were not supposed to have anything to do with witchcraft: they were not to engage in what were seen as both ill-intentioned and unchristian practices that it entailed and they were not to believe in it, which included accusing others of it. Witchcraft accusation was also a means for a man to end a marriage and still keep the woman's property, and may for this reason as well have been seen as a threat to social peace as well as the stability of marriage. In other words, there were plenty of people in the early Middle Ages who believed in and were frightened by witchcraft and/or were prepared to accuse and/or kill witches; however, the prevailing attitude of the authorities was that witchcraft was pagan nonsense. The latter, at least, would change, as medieval Christianity internalised witchcraft. From the end of our period witchcraft was increasingly associated not with demonic delusion, but with frightening, active demonic power. By the fifteenth century the *Malleus Maleficarum (Hammer of Witches)* deemed it heretical to hold that witchcraft did not work. This contrast between early and later medieval attitudes toward witchcraft should always be kept in mind when considering the subject.

The Church in the Early Eleventh Century

Burchard of Worms was an outstanding churchman of the early eleventh century and he illustrates a number of characteristics of the Church in that period, to which we now turn. The reformed Benedictine monastery of Lobbes in the far northwest of what was then Germany, now Belgium, made a significant contribution to Burchard's education. He was appointed bishop by Emperor Otto III, who was impressed by his ability. His church of St Peter at Worms had extensive lands with a dependent population. Burchard made the *Decretum*, the collection of church law from the penitential portion of which we have been quoting, in order to improve things in his episcopal diocese. Such passages as were examined in the previous section represent an attempt to deepen the influence of Christianity over Europeans. Burchard was a keen reformer of the Church, through its councils and laws, and ultimately of society. He eloquently conveys the disorder of the times in this statement from the *Laws and Statutes of the Household of St Peter at Worms*:

> Every day murders in the manner of wild beasts are committed among the dependents of St Peter's. They attack each other through drunkenness, through pride, or for no reason at all. In the course of one year thirty-five serfs of St Peter's, completely innocent people, have been killed by other

serfs of the church; and the murderers, far from repenting, glory in their crime.

It reminds us of the large areas of early medieval people's lives that were not concerned with religion, and, by implication, that family honour and vengeance were not only the concern of the aristocracy. The eleventh-century transformation of Europe is nevertheless especially clear where the Church is concerned, and so extensive consideration will be given to religious affairs in this chapter. The aim in this section is to establish what the church changed from in the course of the century.

First, an overview, provided by Map 7.1, shows that by the early eleventh century Christianity was established in most of Europe, with the top-down conversion of Russia, Poland, Hungary and, progressively, of Scandinavia underway. In the lands along the southern coast of the Baltic Sea, however, resistance to Christian conversion, seen as linked to foreign conquest, hardened, and the Slavs and Balts there would not be converted within the period of this book. Parts of Europe had been Christian for a very long time, long enough for the conversion even of the countryside to become more than nominal, although, below the level of outright worship of pagan gods, there was still plenty of survival of trivialised paganism there. Eastern and Western Christianity had been growing apart for centuries with disagreements on practice and on authority (whether the pope of Rome or patriarch of Constantinople was head of the Church). We have seen evidence of suspicion through to conflict in the cases of Archbishop Theodore of Tarsus in the seventh century (pp. 67–8), the Iconoclast Controversy in the eighth century (p. 84) and Khan Boris in the ninth century (p. 122), but also Willibald attending church in the East in the eighth century (p. 79). Finally, by the early eleventh century a doctrinal difference was established throughout the Western Church with the addition of a single Latin word *filioque* to the Christian statement of belief known as the Nicene Creed. *Filioque* means 'and the son' (= Christ), and was used to say that the Holy Spirit came from the Father and the Son, thus emphasising the equivalence of the three persons of the Christian Trinity; that is, of God. Any meddling with the Creed was deplored by the Eastern Church, which had recently concluded centuries of dispute about how to express the nature of the Christian God. There was not yet a permanent split between the two Churches, however.

Within Western Christianity in the early eleventh century, key terms are 'Benedictine age', 'age of faith', 'proprietary church', 'episcopal church' and 'liturgical state'. The monastic reform begun in the tenth century continued in an age of flourishing Benedictine monasticism and influenced the eleventh-century reform of the wider Church. In the early eleventh century there were, as always, hermits, notably the long-lived Sts Romuald (950–1027) and John Gualbert (990–1073) in Italy, but in communal monasticism the Rule of St Benedict had no rival. References to various 'monastic orders' are anachronistic before the end of the eleventh century. Plenty of religious establishments were still in need of reform. The development of a great international reformed

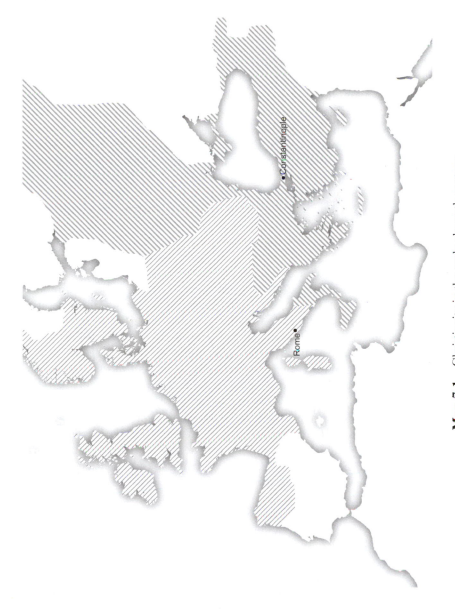

Map 7.1 Christianity in the early eleventh century

monastic network focused on the monastery of Cluny is essentially an eleventh-century phenomenon. By the end of the long abbacy of Odilo of Cluny (999–1049), there were 67 dependent priories, so called because each was under a monastic official called a prior; there was only one abbot over all, and he was responsible only to the pope. Centres of monastic renewal in northern Germany remained important. (See again Map 6.2.) Monastic reform was influential especially in promoting clerical celibacy. In the West priests were supposed to be sexually continent but early medieval priests, it will be recalled, were normally married. For example, in one family in eleventh-century northern England, son was succeeding father in the church positions of treasurer among the clergy of Durham cathedral and priest of a church at Hexham. These were the ancestors of Ailred of Rievaulx, famous abbot of the early twelfth century and the first of his line not to marry. The ban on clerical marriage was one way in which church reform marginalised women, seen as threats to clerical male virtue. Observe that Burchard of Worms imposed penance on anyone who would not receive mass and other Christian sacraments from married priests. Burchard's penance implies that pious people, perhaps under the influence of the stricter rules of monasticism, objected to married priests. But he was wary of undercutting the authority of the clergy, even of those who were unchaste.

The capacity of lay people for acts of piety and their interest in church reform are notable. If there is one period in the Middle Ages to which the overused phrase 'age of faith' can be applied, it is the early eleventh century. One expression of religious faith was founding and endowing churches and monasteries and contributing to their upkeep. The church rebuilding at the beginning of the century referred to by Ralph Glaber, as quoted earlier in this chapter, would have involved both clerical and lay supporters. Fulk Nerra, count of Anjou, established two monasteries for men and with his wife Hildegarde a monastery for women in the early eleventh century. He went more than once on pilgrimage to the Holy Land. The extent of travel for purposes of religious devotion at the time is striking. Even Robert the Devil, duke of Normandy, obviously with many sins requiring penance, was sufficiently concerned about his salvation to go to the Holy Land. Further down the social scale, two brothers in a later generation of the originally peasant family near Barcelona mentioned in Chapter 6 went on pilgrimage to Santiago (St James) de Compostela in northwest Spain and their eldest and most successful brother, to the Holy Land. Going on pilgrimage could enhance status, but it also entailed risk. The wills of the two brothers, drawn up in 1022 before they set off for Santiago, have been preserved, and indeed one of them is never again recorded in the family documents. There were mass pilgrimages to the Holy Land, all the way to the eastern Mediterranean, in 1010, 1025 and 1033, comprising people of varied social background. These can be tied in with mass meetings at church councils for reform and affirming the Peace and Truce of God.[4] Lay initiative at the highest level for church reform will be considered as a function of the liturgical state.

Some of the laity had another sort of interest, a proprietary interest, in the Church, which was itself a great proprietor. Staying with the example just mentioned, one of the brothers who went on pilgrimage to Santiago, his brother who went to the Holy Land and a third brother owned the local church, shared between them in fractions, yielding revenues from tithes and offerings and also local influence. The roots of such an arrangement go far back, to landlords building private churches on their estates throughout the early Middle Ages, to which they appointed priests, supposedly with episcopal supervision. This was the way most churches got built. By the early eleventh century a parochial system was developing whereby Europe was covered with churches, each with land and tithes, a tenth of produce due from primary producers on designated estates, for support. It may not seem the most interesting subject, but the parochial system affected the society and culture of millions, the parish becoming the main unit of identification for Europe's people. Like monastic proprietors, although not necessarily to the same extent, the churches of bishops were endowed with lands from pious bequests, especially from the estates of deceased aristocratic bishops. In a church, whether episcopal or otherwise, staffed by several priests (canons), they might share out the endowment in fixed portions (prebends). Hrotsvitha, the woman writer discussed in the previous chapter, technically lived at Gandersheim under such arrangements, which are hard to distinguish from monasticism if participants followed a rule. The proprietary church was intricately involved in manorial and feudal relationships. As an unusually conscientious example of the former, the above mentioned private legislation of Burchard of Worms for his serfs may be cited. Where the latter were in place, becoming a bishop involved receiving lands attached to the episcopal office as a fief from the ruler, to whom the customary feudal fee known as a 'relief' was paid. This was too close for comfort to the payment of money for church office, known as 'simony',[5] an old problem especially related to the power and prestige of bishops.

The church in the early eleventh century was ruled by virtually autonomous bishops. Each was the religious authority in his diocese. Bishop Burchard of Worms illustrates this at every point. He compiled the *Decretum*, the collection of church law of which the *Corrector and Physician* examined in the previous section is a part, for use in the diocese of Worms. Bishops occasionally met together in regional councils, or synods, at which important reforming initiatives could be taken. Burchard attended three such in the province of the archbishop of Mainz, within which Worms lay. The Church was not centralised. Only later would Burchard's *Decretum* make a major contribution to the developing body of canon law for the Church overall. Bishops normally owed their office to secular rulers. Burchard of Worms, as mentioned above, was no exception and neither was the bishop of Rome. Much of the time the papacy slipped into rivalry among the local nobility; the alternative was appointment by the German emperor. That so little has been said about the papacy in this account of the Church in the early eleventh century is significant of the limited role of the pope in the Church at that time. All over the West, the primacy of the bishop of Rome was recognised: the pope was the head of the Church. Burchard of Worms acknowledged this too, but his partners in church reform were German rulers (for example, Henry II, who presided over one of the reforming councils that Burchard attended) and not the pope, who figures little in the *Decretum*. Rome was not the nerve centre of the Church, for the papacy tended to focus on Italy and react to developments from elsewhere. Its late adoption of the Creed with *filioque* is one example. Another is the reform movement itself. The papacy in the earlier eleventh century had its ups and downs, but the downs were very low. Benedict IX bought the papacy in 1032 and sold it in 1045. Then Emperor Henry III initiated the reform of the papacy from outside.

By 'liturgical state' is meant the close association, on an ideological and practical level, of church personnel and thought with earthly government. Kings, anointed at their coronation with holy oil like bishops at their consecration, ruled as vicars (deputies, representatives) of Christ. Secular rulers normally called episcopal councils; we have just seen an example of a German king presiding over one. It was hard to distinguish between Church and State in the business of the late Anglo-Saxon royal council, the *witan*. Robert the Pious, weak like all French kings of the period, was said to be able to cure illness by touch and supported the monastic reform carried out by Cluny. Please look carefully at the accompanying illustrations of two German rulers crowned by Christ from the beginning of the eleventh century. Here an astonishingly bold portrayal of Otto III (see Figure 26) in the place of Christ has been modified in the representation of his successor Henry II the Saint (see Figure 27). This is political art, but revealingly religious in both context and content (Otto III appears in a gospel book and Henry II in a sacramentary, a book to accompany the Christian ceremony of the Mass). Some explanation of the iconography is required so that the comparison can be fully appreciated, starting with Henry and working back to Otto for greater clarity. Above Henry is Christ, sitting in a mandorla, an oval, all-around halo, pointed at the top (and would be, too, at the bottom where it intersects with Henry's shoulders and head being crowned by Christ), and also with a halo around his head that bears a cross, partly obscured. By contrast, it is Otto who sits in the mandorla, and his head at the top of it intersects with the round halo of Christ bearing a cross, which here is partly obscured by the hand of God crowning Otto. The equivalence of Otto with Christ is being unequivocally claimed. In reality, all German king emperors of the first half of the eleventh century were church reformers, Henry III (1039–56) crucially so because his reform of the papacy would after his death lead to a challenge to the system he was part of. Rulers ran the Church. In the early eleventh century very few churchmen objected to this state of affairs.

At this point consideration of the Church in the later eleventh century, in some respects strongly contrasting with the early-eleventh-century counterpart just described, will be deferred until later in the chapter, where it will lead into the First Crusade with which the chapter and the book end. Attention turns now to medieval and modern views of eleventh-century society, the impact of northern and southern developments in what has been called the Norman Century, and the beginning of the rise of towns in Europe. Some of this will take us up to the end of the eleventh century as well. This is an unusually long chapter, but it must be so given the degree and complexity of the changes that were underway in the eleventh-century transformation of Europe.

Figure 26 Otto III in the Liuthar Gospels, *c.*1000. (© Domkapital Aachen [photo: Ann Münchow])

The Three Orders and Feudalism

Writing in Old English at the start of the eleventh century, Archbishop Wulfstan of York came as close to social analysis as a medieval writer can in the *Institutes of Polity*. Most of the section 'Concerning the Throne' reads as follows:

> Every lawful throne which stands perfectly upright, stands on three pillars: one is *oratores*, and the second is *laboratores* and the third is *bellatores*. 'Oratores' are prayer men, who must serve God and earnestly intercede both day and

Figure 27   Henry II's Sacramentary, between 1002 and 1014, showing the German ruler himself. (Bayerische Staatsbibliothek)

night for the entire nation. 'Laboratores' are workmen, who must supply that by which the entire nation shall live. 'Bellatores' are soldiers, who must defend the land by fighting with weapons. Every throne in a Christian nation must stand upright on these three pillars. And should any of them weaken, the throne will immediately totter; and should any of them shatter, then the throne will tumble down, and that is entirely to the nation's detriment. But let them be diligently fixed and strengthened and made firm with the wise teaching of God and with worldly justice; that will be to the lasting benefit of the nation.

We have met before with these categories. King Alfred the Great was the first to use them as far as we know (see p. 128). A little later in the eleventh century they appear in the writings of the Continental authors Bishop Adalbero of Laon and the anonymous biographer of Bishop Girard of Cambrai, who is said to have spoken of them. Whatever the ultimate origins of the medieval concept of the Three Orders, the case is instructive for showing that, allowing for unusual features like writing as serious a work as the *Institutes of Polity* in the vernacular, the British Isles were part and parcel of Europe throughout the Middle Ages. The context for all of the above was one supporting kingship, although Gerald is said to have spoken of the support of each of these groups of people for the others. This medieval social analysis can be seen as a call for order in disorderly times. By the eleventh century external threats to the Continent had virtually ceased, whereas England was conquered by the Danes as will be explained in the next section of the chapter; however, powerful, internal, social forces were at work to challenge such stability as kingship on the old, Carolingian model had provided, as will be examined presently.

It is always good to consider a culture on its own terms, although to do so may prompt questions than an insider would not ask. Three such questions about the medieval division of people into the above mentioned three categories are posed here. In the depiction of Otto III discussed in the previous section, a pair each of soldiers and clerics stand respectively to the left and right below the ruler. This is a twofold division, in relation to which the Three Orders represent an innovation. Why were workers, manual labourers, brought into the picture? The same possibility exists as the reason why the Carolingian polyptyques we have examined recorded the primary producers in detail: because the very powerful people drew directly on the surplus of these labourers. Where does one place a fighting bishop, a common enough eleventh-century figure? Bishop Odo of Bayeux is featured sufficiently in the (very secular) Bayeux Tapestry, which visually tells the story of the Norman Conquest of England in 1066, to support the argument that it was made for him, but he is only once shown doing anything religious, when he blesses a meal of food looted by the soldiers on campaign. Odo appears in the thick of the battle of Hastings, rallying 'the boys (*pueri*)'. True, he does not have sword, lance or shield as they do, holding instead a *baculum* which can mean either a staff or a club, but in these respects he is just like his half-brother Duke William. Riding a big black horse, with chain-mail visible below the helmet and sleeves of the fine, probably padded-leather garment he wears, Odo is unmistakably a knight. He is not the only example where the boundaries between fighters, professional religious people and workers overlap or are blurred. Members of the invasion force are shown digging in order to make a mound on which the fortress at Hastings was built. Were women in the Three Orders? It is easy to assume that they were excluded from such a theoretical construct, and certainly they were not *bellatores*. Yet monastic prayers from both genders were valued and women and girls reckoned among the 'men of St Germain' in the Polyptyque of Irminon. One can be more certain that those who formulated the modern concept of feudalism did not have women in mind.

The Three Orders is too static and ideal a concept for modern enquiry, which wants an analysis of complex relationships in real society. After the Middle Ages, lawyers dealing with land transactions involving medieval property deeds frequently came across references to the fief (*feodum*) given by lords to vassals in return for service. The idea of the Middle Ages as characterised by an elite holding fiefs, having temporary use and enjoyment rather than outright ownership of land, was picked up by historians studying the period and presented as the feudal system, feudalism. This is not uniformly defined. Any historian who uses the term[6] would recognise as feudal institutionalised patronage among the elite, giving and receiving honourable service of military assistance, customary financial payments and counsel. Many distinguish sharply between feudalism and manorialism, which essentially comes down to the difference between vassals and serfs. If their fiefs were in land, vassals were themselves the lords of serfs on their estates or manors, manorial lords; if they had vassals of their own, they were themselves feudal lords. It should go without saying, but is being said nevertheless to make the contrast between serfs and vassals crystal clear, that serfs were never lords. By doing homage, vassals became the men of their lords in high-level dependency, in contrast to the low-level dependency of peasants such as the 'men of St Germain'. The dependency of homage (Latin *hominaticus*, a word which significantly appears in the early eleventh century, see below) is expressed by the initiating ceremony in which vassals placed their hands between the hands of their lords (compare the much earlier action of Duke Tassilo on p. 94), usually kneeling. Latin *homo*, plural *homines*, 'human being(s)', was used for either vassals or serfs in the Middle Ages, however. Some medieval historians define feudalism more broadly to incorporate manorialism. Marc Bloch wrote of a 'feudal society' (also the title of his book) bound by ties of dependency from top to bottom. Social relations on manors naturally feature in the concept of a 'feudal mode of production' or 'estate mode of production', relating economic production to power.

However defined, feudalism is seen by historians as fully developed by the eleventh century. In early eleventh-century France, private power triumphed as counts' public judicial courts ceased to meet. The office of count as the king's representative wielding delegated royal power had had a continuous existence from the beginnings of the kingdom, the county being the Roman *civitas*. Now the *bannum*, the right to tell people what to do, was usurped by any castellan lord. Service-contracts of vassalage ideally suited this highly competitive and violent situation, in which it was vital to gather supporters. In 1020, exactly when it might have been expected, the following account of fealty was written by Bishop Fulbert of Chartres for Duke William of Aquitaine. As a contemporary view at a crucial time, it is worth quoting in full:

> Requested to write something regarding the character of fealty, I have set down briefly for you, on the authority of the books, the following things. He who takes the oath of fealty to his lord ought always to keep in mind these

six things: what is harmless, safe, honourable, useful, easy, and practicable. *Harmless*, which means that he ought not to injure his lord in his body; *safe*, that he should not injure him by betraying his confidence or the defences upon which he depends for security; *honourable*, that he should not injure him in his justice, or in other matters that relate to his honour; *useful*, that he should not injure him in his property; *easy*, that he should not make difficult that which his lord can do easily; and *practicable*, that he should not make impossible for the lord that which is possible.

However, while it is proper that the faithful vassal avoid these injuries, it is not for doing this alone that he deserves his holding: for it is not enough to refrain from wrongdoing, unless that which is good is done also. It remains therefore, that in the same six things referred to above he should faithfully advise and aid his lord, if he wishes to be regarded as worthy of his benefice and to be safe concerning the fealty which he has sworn.

The lord also ought to act toward his faithful vassal in the same manner in all these things. And if he fails to do this, he will be rightfully regarded as guilty of bad faith, just as the former, if he should be found shirking, or willing to shirk, his obligations would be perfidious and perjured.

Notice how negative is this formulation: vassals are not to hurt lords, who can be seen to be 'protecting their backs' by the arrangement.

The following record of a feudal oath sworn in 1058 to the Count and Countess of Barcelona – from an area unusually well documented, as we have already seen, as well as being where the earliest use of *hominaticus* (homage) is recorded – has more than one feature of interest. It has just the same negative presentation of the vassal's obligations:

> I Richard Altemir, the son of Lady Ermengardis, swear that from this hour forward I will be faithful to you, the Lord Count Raymond, son of the Countess Sancia, and Lady Almodis, countess, the daughter of the Countess Amelia, without fraud or evil deceit or any deception, and I, the said Richard, from this hour forward will deprive you, the said Count Raymond and Countess Almodis, neither of your life nor of your members which are attached to your bodies, nor of the city which is called Barcelona, nor of the county which is called Barcelona, nor of . . .

and on and on with fortresses, cities, bishoprics, lands and revenues not to be taken by the vassal Richard, who only toward the end also swears to protect them for the count and countess. The oath is taken to the couple and is also notable for its use of matronymics at the beginning: the vassal and his lords are all identified as the offspring of their mothers. Identification of people by their mothers rather than fathers occurs in a small but interesting proportion of documents, peaking in the early eleventh century in the region. On the whole, feudal arrangements marginalised women from property and power. Fiefs were given primarily for military service and were not divided, but rather passed to the eldest son by primogeniture. The replacement of partible inheritance by primogeniture was part of wider family strategies to preserve, build up and consolidate the patrimony. Early medieval families had not cared overly much where their wealth came from and the opportunity for women to control it was considerable. Now society was becoming better organised on principles which included male domination.

Feudal ties structured the power relations of the dominant class, the people termed 'soldiers (*milites*)' in Latin, 'horseback riders' in French and German and eventually in English 'knights'. The eleventh century saw the rise of the knight, to the point where there was an initiating ceremony for knighthood as well. A feudal and knightly ethos can be seen in literature for the dominant class and lesser folk by the end of the century. The literature shows what these people were entertained by and is also a most useful source of information about their values, what they thought was important, their morality and outlook, everything that can be summed up in the word 'ethos' used above. About 1100 the Old French poem the *Song of Roland* was written down in a manuscript which survives at Oxford University. We looked briefly at the historical kernel of the story in Chapter 4: the defeat of Charlemagne's rearguard in the Pyrenees by Basques in 778. It would be frankly foolish to deny the subsequent development of oral tradition about the event, but we do not know what this was. In the *Song of Roland* the mountain Basques have become a great Saracen army, to whom Charlemagne's rearguard, commanded by Roland, has been betrayed by his stepfather Ganelon in revenge for the following incident. Background for it in a long-standing quarrel between the two men is provided at the end of the poem, when Ganelon says at his trial:

> 'In goods and gold Roland once cheated me'
> (*Song of Roland*, CCLXXII)

but his accuser says to Charlemagne:

> 'Though Roland may have cheated Ganelon,
> In your service he should have been secure;
> Betraying that is Ganelon's true crime,
> His perjury and treason against you.'
> (*Song of Roland*, CCLXXVII)

Personal vengeance is apparently all right, but not when it interferes with social obligations!

The feudal and knightly setting and ethos are apparent throughout the *Song of Roland*, including the incident in question, which comes near the beginning of the poem. Roland 'volunteered' his stepfather for a dangerous mission, an unexpectedly unfriendly act, given their relationship, which advertises the enmity between them. When Ganelon angrily points this out, Roland offers to go in his place;

> Said Ganelon: 'You'll never go for me.
> You're not my vassal, nor am I your lord.'
>
> (*Song of Roland*, XXI)

Feudal service might prompt such an offer, but in the circumstances Roland has just deepened the insult. Much later, when Ganelon proposes Roland as commander of the rearguard, Roland speaks *a lei de chevaler*, 'by the law of the horseman'; that is, according to the knightly code of conduct, and accepts the dangerous mission (LIX). When Charlemagne's army returns to France, they think of Roland and the rearguard in mortal peril back in the pass of Roncesvalles while they are coming back to what they value:

> Then, when they reached their mighty fatherland,
> They looked on Gascony, their lord's domain;
> And they recalled their honours and their fiefs,
> Thought of the maidens and their noble wives:
> Not one of them from pity does not weep.
>
> (*Song of Roland*, LXVI)

Roland and his companion Oliver are something of a contrast:

> Roland is valiant, Oliver is wise,
> And both are matchless in their chivalry.
>
> (*Song of Roland*, LXXXVII)

Here knightly prowess is summed up in a single word. Faced with impossible odds, Oliver sensibly advised Roland to blow his horn for assistance from Charlemagne's main force while there was still time, but Roland was too proud. Later Oliver reproaches him:

> And he replied: 'Comrade, the fault is yours,
> For prudent valour is not foolishness:
> Caution is better far than recklessness.
> The French are dead through your temerity,
> And our service for ever lost to Charles.
>
> (*Song of Roland*, CXXXI)

Mielz valt mesure que ne fait estultie literally means 'Measure (moderation) which doesn't do stupid things is better'. Roland's main fault is *démesure*, rashness, a serious one in warfare. The last line reminds us that the feudal ethos was one of honourable service, the feudal oath one of subordination, albeit at a high level.

The institutionalised patronage that we have been discussing was not established everywhere in Europe. In Anglo-Saxon England, for example, people could change their lords, whereas vassalage was permanent unless lords did their vassals an injury. The thoroughly feudalised Normans did much to spread these institutions north and south, and to them we now turn. First, the operation of what can be called the North Sea power complex, which includes the Norman conquest of England, will be examined, and then the fascinating Norman conquests in the Mediterranean.

The Norman Conquests

An analytical concern of this book has been the relative significance of the North and the South in early medieval European history. The break-up of the Carolingian Empire and the last invasions were very disruptive. For a time, the relative economic and political importance of the North beyond France was higher than before, or, excepting England, it would be again. Its high point is the rule of King Cnut (Canute) over the lands shown on Map 7.2 in the earlier eleventh century. Our interest is in relations between powers in the area: alliances, some by marriage (see the genealogy chart in Figure 28), attempts at conquest, all adding up to the North Sea power complex. In introducing the Vikings in Chapter 5, the point was made that consideration of their activity of kingdom-forming would be reserved for a later chapter. The establishment of political units on the European model in Scandinavia is a very important part of what the North Sea power complex was all about. Their conversion to Christianity was a vital part of this process. Norway was in no way a coherent kingdom before its top-down conversion, which was remembered as a rough affair. The career of its eleventh-century king Olaf the Stout Haraldsson will illustrate the operation of the North Sea power complex very well. The Danes wanted to rule Norway and had some Norwegian support, but the Viking Olaf established himself as king there in 1016. He had converted to Christianity in Normandy and proceeded to Christianise Norway by force. In 1026 he joined the Swedes in attacking Denmark. In 1028 he was ousted as king of Norway by King Cnut of Denmark and England and plenty of Norwegian opposition. Olaf took refuge in Russia, but returned to Norway in 1030 to try to get his throne back. He was defeated and killed at the Battle of Stikelstad, and although there were pagans on both sides of it, Olaf became the first Viking saint. Ultimately these warring political units in process of formation would become regular European kingdoms, but not yet.

At the beginning of the eleventh century England was still in the Viking Age, the object of a sustained and ultimately successful attempt at conquest by the kings of Denmark, the descendants of Harold Bluetooth who, his great rune-stone proclaims, had 'made the Danes Christian' in the previous century. The Anglo-Saxon king was Athelred the Unready, whose epithet is from Old English *unræd* meaning 'no-counsel'. England was relatively well governed for the time but ill defended. (This is the context in which Wulfstan wrote the *Institutes of Polity* previously referred to.) The huge silver payments made to the Danes to go away are evidence of the wealth of England, but times were desperate. Alfheah, archbishop of Canterbury, captured by Vikings in 1012, refused to appeal for his

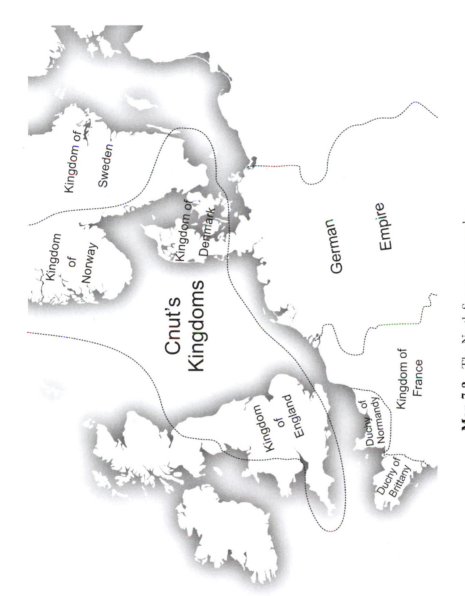

Map 7.2 The North Sea power complex

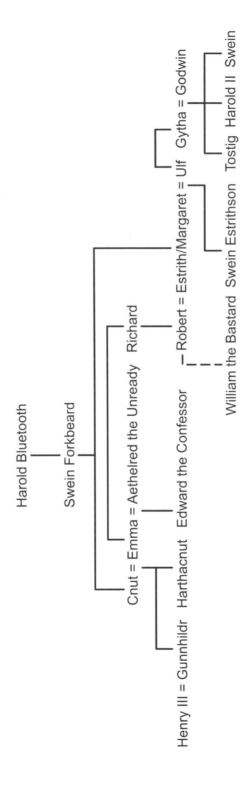

Figure 28 Genealogy of the North Sea power complex

ransom to be paid because of the suffering that such payments were inflicting on people and was duly martyred.[7] Athelred was married to Emma, the sister of the duke of Normandy, Richard II, descendant of Vikings settled by treaty in northern France almost a century earlier, as we have seen. The result of the Danish Vikings' campaign against England was that England accepted a member of the Danish royal house as king. Cnut married Emma, widow of Athelred (her sons by the latter went into exile in Normandy), made the greatest silver payment of all (80,000 pounds) to the Vikings to go away, and settled down to become a respected English king (1016–35). He even issued a law code, the work of Wulfstan, long after any Continental monarch had done so. This was not all Cnut was, though. He soon became king of the Danes on the death of his brother. Norway slipped in and out of the Danish orbit of power, as we have seen, and part of the Swedes came under his rule. Occasional reference to what Cnut ruled as an empire is modern not medieval, however; the empire in our period was Roman.

Cnut was a ruler of power and wealth, noted for his generosity, with international connections. We see him and Emma giving a great cross of gold and jewels to an English monastery in the illustration (Figure 29), which was drawn *c.*1020. Its iconography can be compared with the German illustrations shown and/or mentioned in the previous chapter. King Cnut also distributed gifts to people on the Continent, including Bishop Fulbert of Chartres whom we quoted about fealty above. Making his mark on Christendom, Cnut went on pilgrimage to Rome in 1027. In Rome he was present at the imperial coronation of the German ruler Conrad II, whose ally he was and whose son Henry III married his daughter Gunnhildr. The imperial connection testifies to Cnut's significance. This is what the eleventh-century historian Adam of Bremen says of these events:

> The Emperor Conrad at that time received the daughter of King Canute for marriage to his son Henry. In royal state he at once proceeded to Italy with them to do justice to that kingdom. Accompanying him on the expedition was King Canute, very dreadful in his power over the barbarian peoples of three realms.

About Cnut and the intricate family connections, Adam of Bremen is very precise, if not always accurate:

> Canute received Aethelred's kingdom and married his wife named Imma, who was a sister of Count Richard of Normandy. The king of the Danes give the latter his own sister, Margaret, in marriage by way of alliance, and when the count repudiated her, Canute gave her to Duke Ulf of England and married this Ulf's sister to another duke, Godwin, because he shrewdly reckoned that the English and Normans would prove more faithful to the Danes through intermarriage. In this reasoning he was not mistaken. To turn away Canute's wrath this Count Richard, indeed, set out for Jerusalem, where he died, leaving a son, Robert, in Normandy. Robert's son is the

Figure 29 Drawing (*c.*1020) recording the gift by King Cnut and Queen Aelfgyfu (Emma's English name) of an altar cross to New Minster, Winchester, in Stowe MS. 944, fol. 6. (© British Library Board. All rights reserved.)

William whom the Franks call the Bastard. By King Canute's sister, Ulf had as sons Duke Björn and King Svein. By Duke Ulf's sister, Godwin had Svein, Tostig and Harold.

These relationships can be followed on the genealogical chart as long as the error is realized: it is Count Richard's son Robert (the Devil) who married and divorced Margaret and went on pilgrimage. Margaret was also known as Estrith; from Swein Estrithson are descended all of the kings of Denmark down to the present day.

For years after the death of Cnut in 1035 we see the North Sea power complex in full operation, with England a prize. When Denmark was menaced by Norway, King Harthacnut, Cnut's son, made an agreement with King Magnus the Good (illegitimate son of Olaf the Saint) that they would leave each other's kingdoms alone but if either died without an heir, his kingdom would pass to the survivor. But Harthacnut brought to England from exile Edward, surviving son of King Athelred the Unready. By 1042 the sons of Cnut were dead and in that year Edward became king of England. There was some fear of invasion from Norway by the disappointed Magnus, but he was trying to snatch Denmark and died in five years. Edward is called the Confessor because of his ascetic lifestyle, an expression of the lay piety of the time. He was indeed a king with no heirs. He had been brought up in the Norman court: William the Bastard, now Duke of Normandy, was his friend. In 1051 or 52 William visited England where it is likely that Edward promised the English throne to him, making William his heir. Now at this time the King of Denmark was Swein Estrithson, Cnut's sister's son. The king of Norway was the classic Viking Harold Hardrada, who felt that he had inherited any broken promises made to his predecessor Magnus. When Edward the Confessor died, he left a young nephew, but the English crown went to Harold Godwinson, of the most powerful aristocratic family, distantly related to everyone else as the genealogical chart shows. Edward and the other nobles agreed to his succession at the time, 1066. On 25 September, Harold of England fought Harold Hardrada and his invading army at Stamford Bridge in the north of England and won. On 14 October King Harold of England fought Duke William, soon to be the Conqueror, and lost. In 1069–70 a Danish fleet under King Swein coming to northern England was repelled, though the Danish threat to England continued until 1085. The Viking Age was at an end. The Age of the Normans, who looked south for their institutions and contacts, had arrived.

The Norman Conquest of England resulted in a highly unusual situation there, which readers of English may well consider, mistakenly, to be normal in medieval Europe. King William considered all of England to be his property by right of conquest and proceeded to give it out as fiefs. In contemporary terms, those holding land directly from the king included noblemen and long-dead patron saints of monasteries and churches alike in feudal tenure. Thus a document associated with the Domesday Survey of England in 1086 lists the king's barons in one region of Cornwall as St Petroc, St Neot, the bishop of Exeter and the count of Mortain. As a detailed survey of landholding, Domesday Book is uniquely valuable. One can discover that the priests of St Neot held lands with 4 peasants, 1 ox, 20 sheep and 10 goats, or they were supposed to, but the Count had taken away all of their land and given it to one of his vassals, leaving them only one acre. We have seen an example of monastic estate records in Chapter 5, but Domesday Book supplies data on secular landholding as well. Aside from William and his successor, other eleventh-century European kings emphatically did not own all of the land in their kingdoms. Moreover, feudal institutions originated as an organic growth with long roots, as we have seen. People came to have more than one lord, a situation with which the practice of liege homage, attested from the mid-eleventh century on, arose to cope, for it specified the lord who took precedence over the others. The result was not a 'feudal pyramid', but something rather more like patterns made in a children's string game, which English speakers know as 'cat's cradle' but probably has names and variations all over the world. In Normandy the dukes worked to tighten the feudal structure under their control through to the mid-eleventh century. This meant that they spread feudal institutions in a particularly centralised form both to the north and to the far south.

The Norman conquest of the power vacuum that was southern Italy took many years. Map 7.3 shows the situation in which Norman opportunists flourished. They can be illustrated by their chess pieces (see Figure 30), on which their long stirrups, mixture of round and kite-shaped shields, chain mail and even the way the horse's fetlocks are rendered are comparable with depictions in the Bayeux Tapestry. North or south, Normans were Normans. Indeed, it was an elaborate board on which they played in southern Italy. South of papal Rome and its territory, more than 200 years after the Carolingian conquest of the Lombard kingdom, the Lombard duchies survived. Lombard cultural influence was everywhere predominant on the southern Italian mainland except in Calabria. There were also cities that had long been independent of Byzantine control. Benevento, Capua, Salerno, Naples, Amalfi and Gaeta had a long history of conflict. The far south was part of the Byzantine Empire, which still taxed. German imperial claims to rule southern Italy were ineffectual. Sicily was part of the Fatimid Caliphate when the eleventh century began, and the Saracens made their presence felt on the mainland; the Amalfitans were old allies of theirs. Southern Italy was neither feudal nor manorial. In the second decade of the eleventh century Norman mercenaries aided a Lombard rebel against Byzantines in Apulia with papal support, unsuccessfully. In the third and fourth decades Norman assistance to the rulers of first Naples, then Capua and then Salerno in struggles with each other was the origin of the Norman principate of Capua in 1058. Then entered the 12 sons of Tancred of Hauteville in Normandy, who fought for or against the Byzantines, the Lombards, the pope and the Saracens. From this emerged the Norman duchies of Apulia and Calabria, the county of Sicily, and ultimately in the next century the kingdom of Sicily, which took in the lot. The really outstanding sons were Robert Guiscard 'the Wily' and Roger 'the Great Count'.[8]

The Normans altered arrangements of great antiquity in southern Italy. The papacy, newly reformed – in circumstances which we will consider before long – but concerned as ever by threat to its territory, fought them with Byzantine, Lombard and German support at the Battle of Civitate in 1053 and lost. By 1059 the papacy, opposing secular control in a new way, as will also be seen, allied with the Normans. Richard, prince of Capua, and Robert Guiscard, 'by the grace of God and St Peter duke of Apulia and Calabria and, with the help of both, future duke of Sicily', became papal vassals. The phrase quoted here is the way that Robert was styled in his oath of fealty, which duly begins

Map 7.3 Southern Italy in the early eleventh century

Figure 30 Chess pieces from southern Italy depicting Norman knights, eleventh century. (Bibliothèque nationale de France)

with what he will not do to injure his papal overlord, gives a good statement of liege homage, and concludes with the promise to support the clergy and people of Rome in electing a new pope. In these circumstances eventual papal support for the Norman conquest of England is not surprising. For the Byzantines, 1071 was a terrible year in which they were defeated by the Seljuk Turks at the Battle of Manzikert, leading to the loss of most of Asia Minor (modern Turkey), and were driven completely out of Italy with the capture of Bari by Robert Guiscard. This was the end of Roman rule there which had been continuous since the beginning of the third century BC except for the mid-fifth to mid-sixth centuries AD. The Norman capture of Salerno in 1077 was the end of Lombard rule, which went back to the second half of the sixth century. Sicily had been in Saracen hands since the ninth century. Its conquest, significantly advanced by the taking of the major city of Palermo in 1072, was completed in 1091, ensuring Robert Guiscard's brother, Count Roger, an enduring place in Sicilian folk memory.

There seems to have been no limit to Norman ambitions in the Mediterranean. The betrothal of Robert Guiscard's daughter to the son of the Byzantine emperor became, upon the latter's overthrow, an excuse to invade the Byzantine Empire. The city of Durazzo across the Adriatic Sea was captured by the Normans in 1082, and Robert's son Bohemund[9] proceeded to make life miserable for Emperor Alexius Comnenus in the Balkans for years, as the emperor's daughter Anna Comnena tells us in the *Alexiad*. Anna Comnena gives no fewer than three descriptions of Robert Guiscard in the *Alexiad*, of which this is the first:

> This Robert was a Norman by birth, of obscure origin, with an overbearing character and a thoroughly villainous mind; he was a brave fighter, very cunning in his assaults on the wealth and power of great men; in achieving his aims absolutely inexorable, diverting criticism by incontrovertible argument. He was a man of immense stature, surpassing even the biggest men; he had a ruddy complexion, fair hair, broad shoulders, eyes that all but shot out sparks of fire. In a well-built man one looks for breadth here and slimness there; in him all was admirably well-proportioned and elegant. Thus from head to foot the man was graceful (I have often heard from many witnesses that this was so). Homer remarked of Achilles that when he shouted his hearers had the impression of a multitude in uproar, but Robert's bellow, so they say, put tens of thousands to flight. With such endowments of fortune and nature and soul, he was, as you would expect, no man's slave, owing obedience to nobody in all the world. Such are men of powerful character, people say, even if they are of humbler origin.

Anna regularly refers to Westerners as Kelts, showing her familiarity with Ancient Greek writings and bringing off an effective 'put-down' in that by so doing she is referring to them as the barbarians that Herodatus knew. Robert was, in fact, one of the 12 sons of Tancred of Hauteville in Normandy, a lesser noble whose sons would have had a problem even if he had had extensive lands and the Normans had not practised primogeniture. When Robert Guiscard died, his son Bohemund was rather left out of the inheritance. Unsurprisingly, he went on the First Crusade and established the Norman principality of Antioch in 1098 as the Norman century drew to a close.

North and south, the Norman conquests are a phenomenon between the last invasions of Europe and the beginning of European expansion in the Crusades. It is interesting to reflect that the Viking Harold Hardrada, before he became the 'Hard Ruler' of Norway, as a member of the emperor's Varangian guard served with Byzantine forces against Saracens and Lombards in Sicily and southern Italy from 1038–41, when the Normans were also active there. Norman rule is an important stage in the development of the two most sophisticated, best administered countries in medieval Europe: England and Sicily. In both cases existing arrangements which the Normans kept and developed were important. Anglo-Saxon England had relatively effective, even if primitive, public government (to which Cnut's law code is a witness) and the Italian south had both Byzantine and Muslim administration. The above mentioned Domesday Book is the most extraordinary product of Norman governance. Although nothing comparable has survived from Italy, there is evidence of written surveys based on Greek and Arabic documents in connection with granting fiefs in newly conquered Sicily. To both areas the Normans brought feudal centralisation. Culturally their impact was very great on England, which was brought into closer contact with the Continent. An example is the spread of Romanesque architecture in England. In the south of Italy and Sicily the Normans patronised existing architectural styles. One distinctive decorative feature can be observed in England and Italy: the zigzag ornament on columns in Durham cathedral in northern England has its counterpart in the cloisters at Monreale in Sicily; however, whereas the former would have been enhanced with paint, the latter are filled by mosaic tesserae. In southern Italy and Sicily the Normans were one more element to be assimilated into the vibrant cultural mixture of that area.

The Rise of Towns

Much closer to home, the Normans' takeover of the county of Maine, which adjoins Normandy on the south (see Map 7.4), and the rebellion of the inhabitants of Maine when William the Conqueror was away consolidating his rule over England are context for events in the city of Le Mans in 1070 which will be used to illustrate the rise of towns. Where appropriate, reference will be made to the three cities examined in the previous chapter. This can begin with the observation that what was occupying William in England involved the capture and recapture of the city of York in the context of English rebellion and allied Danish invasion, and the destruction of the countryside by William's forces. In general, as population grew and agricultural production increased in the eleventh century, people clustered together more in villages and cities. In the latter, supplied with food from the surrounding countryside, they engaged in specialised occupations. Le Mans had its workers in food, clothing, wood, stone, metal and wax, very much bringing to mind the old nursery rhyme about 'the butcher, the baker, the candlestick maker'. There is a contrast to be drawn with the Frisian quarter of Worms (later called the Jewish quarter) indicating that it was inhabited by outsiders engaged in long distance commerce, which in any case Le Mans had little to do with. On the other hand, in the occupation of its people Le Mans resembles tenth-century Lucca, which also was not a centre of international trade. Yet Lucca was more of an administrative centre and aristocratic place-of-residence than Le Mans. In the account that follows note that the nobles live in the countryside. Increasingly, local people were becoming involved in industry and trade; however, the vast majority of Europe's population were subsistence peasants. The urban growth from which modern 'Western' cities are directly descended was just beginning in the eleventh century.

The 'rise of towns' is concerned not only with physical entities: named, always walled settlements, some of which were very old. Like Worms, Le Mans was a Roman city that continued without a break as the seat of a bishop. Remains of the late Roman walls of Le Mans can still be seen, and the place was considered prosperous in Carolingian times. Terms for townspeople like *burg*ers, *burg*esses and *bourg*eois all refer to the town as a fortress, but it became more.

Map 7.4 Normandy and its neighbours

Towns developed into areas of freedom from the normal rights of lordship, with some measure of self-government. Townsfolk, though by and large descended from serf families, developed commercial interests. At the same time lords had sharpening interests of their own in exploiting the rights of *bannum* for profit. These, again, were originally royal rights of command delegated by kings to their public officials, which by the eleventh century were usurped and wielded in private lordship. The exercise of *bannum* could take the form of tolls, objectionable to those engaged in commerce, insistence that town residents use mills and ovens provided by the lord (for a fee of course), and above all private jurisdiction administered by the lord, who profited greatly thereby. Townsfolk didn't just object to regulations that served the old lord's interests, they wanted regulations that served their own commercial, artisanal and urban interests. The interests of lords and townsfolk were incompatible, except that everybody wanted to make money in an economy where its use was increasing. In negotiating an improved position, townsfolk sometimes formed a sworn association of mutual help and support known as a commune. The first that we know of was at Le Mans in 1070. As is typical of the later eleventh century, there was a lot going on at the same time and place: rebellion of the county of Maine against Norman rule, moves toward urban self-government, and direct action in the cause of social peace.

The account of 'The Deeds of the Lord Bishop Arnald' in *Acts of the Bishops Dwelling in the City of Le Mans* shows concern for the interests of that bishop and close knowledge of events. Like the source of the phrase about the Three Orders attributed to Bishop Girard of Cambrai, it belongs to a genre of episcopal biography that is usually written by one of the cathedral clergy. Its author shows an interesting inconsistency in the way he relates what happened in Le Mans that will be considered in due course; for now, his account will be condensed. It is the source of quotations in what follows unless otherwise specified. As already stated, William of Normandy had become count of Maine 'after the heirs to the countship were wiped out and completely destroyed'. Yet there was a surviving daughter of a previous count of Maine: her name was Gercendis, she was the wife of Atho, a marquis in northern Italy (of Liguria, not Tuscany), and they had a son called Hugh. This was her second marriage, 'divorce intervening' with the first one. When the leaders and people of Maine rebelled against the absent William who was otherwise occupied in England, they sent for this family and gave control of Maine to Atho. Bishop Arnald took himself off to King William in England, at which 'his adversaries' in Le Mans seized his possessions there and, when he returned from England, would not let him into the city at first, before the clergy and the adversaries came to an agreement. Subsequently, Marquis Atho developed doubts about the venture, along with a shortage of funds with which to buy support in Maine, and went back to Italy, 'leaving his wife and son in the hands of Geoffrey of Mayenne, a noble man of very shrewd disposition'. To Gercendis we shall return.

The action taken by the people of Le Mans when Geoffrey abused his position there must first be considered:

Therefore, when Geoffrey of Mayenne, her guardian and quasi-husband, levied certain imposts against the citizens and attempted to oppress them by certain new exactions, they took counsel as to how they might resist his evil attempts; neither would they suffer themselves to be oppressed unjustly by him or anyone else. And so, a conspiracy having been made, which they call a commune, they all bind themselves equally by oaths, and compel Geoffrey himself and other leading men of the same region, although unwilling, to be bound by the oaths of their conspiracy. By the presumption of this co-swearing, they committed innumerable crimes, condemning many everywhere, without any trial, tearing out their eyes for certain very slight causes, strangling others by hanging, truly – which it is abominable to relate – for a very light fault; indeed irrationally setting on fire nearby castles in the days of holy Lent, even in the time of the Lord's Passion.

Medieval institutions of this type, which also included guilds, city corporations and peace associations, were unfeudal in that they involved not dependent relationships, but the cooperation of equals. Participation in the commune of Le Mans cut across social groups. How Geoffrey of Mayenne and others of his ilk were brought into it is unclear, but presumably relates to the importance of the city in the rebellion against William. The commune constituted its own judicial system, as was especially desired in town self-government. The 'crimes' of the account are in fact punishments of hanging and blinding, judicial abuses. Town justice was characteristically rough. The account of the commune quoted here is negative, which makes what comes after surprising.

The conspirators of the commune of Le Mans got together an army to attack Hugh of Sillé, another 'one of the chief men of the same region' who had done them unspecified injuries and 'was opposing their holy ordinances'. The last term belongs to the movement for the Peace and Truce of God, and so does the nature of the force taking direct action against the opponent. It was 'an army of the multitude' 'of rustics'; later, when the expedition typically ended in disaster, the author writes of captives 'as much noble as ignoble, whom they seized for judgement: not only soldiers but even mere women far and wide through the fields, like little deer'. Most significantly, it was led by churchmen. 'After the army also had been assembled, with the bishop and priests of each of the churches with crosses and banners in the vanguard, in a furious assault they aimed for the castle of Sillé.' Now 'the adversaries' are in the castle and there is even a reference to 'our troops'. Geoffrey of Mayenne betrayed them. A rumour was spread that the city of Le Mans was in the hands of the enemy, 'that the city had been handed over to the party of the adversaries' and people panicked. The bishop himself was captured, but released by Hugh of Sillé. Naturally the author of the account is on the side of his bishop, of whose biography it forms a part. Perhaps he does not convey accurately the extent of Bishop Arnald's (or even his own) commitment to this disastrous expedition, the commune, or the rebellion against William, which, as we will see, did not succeed. Be that as it may, take special note of the interesting, mixed composition of the communal attack force, to which reference will be made again near the end of the chapter.

To one who is interested in the possibility of female initiative, Gercendis reads like what Gregory of Tours called a 'woman full of energy and resource'.[10] When, after the events just recounted, Geoffrey of Mayenne thought it prudent to send her young son Hugh down to join Atho in Italy and withdraw from Le Mans to a castle, Gercendis stayed in the city. There she plotted to bring Geoffrey back, in order, according to the account, to resume their sexual relationship. Gercendis is the key figure in the revolt of Maine: the link to its line of counts, the opportunity for her son to become count there (as he eventually did), and the means to restore family pride about which women cared at least as deeply as men. The entire episode may have been her idea. Geoffrey of Mayenne was allowed into one of the fortresses on the city wall, from which he was dislodged with great difficulty with help from Count Fulk of Anjou, the county that adjoined Maine on the south. The counts of Anjou were quite as ready as the dukes of Normandy to spread their influence over surrounding regions. The king of France is nowhere to be seen in all this, which is testimony to the weakness of the French monarchy in the eleventh century. When the author tells how, after Geoffrey's forces occupied certain houses, 'our forces unexpectedly cast fire onto the same houses albeit near the church, and compelled them to flee thence – not without great work defending the roofs of the church from so near a blaze' his personal concern is apparent. The circumstance of a local nobleman holding part of the city's fortifications against its citizens says a lot about disorder at the time.

The rise of towns by no means always involved communes, which were generally created in areas of less effective central control. The city of Worms stayed under German and episcopal governance and the needs of its townsfolk were accommodated without major strife. Likewise the citizens of York, as in other English cities, secured privileges from the English monarchy. In fragmented northern Italy, on the other hand, communes were common, and Lucca would be no exception; indeed, there were rural communes in its vicinity as well. What happened at Le Mans perfectly illustrates the point made at the beginning of this paragraph. When William the Conqueror appeared at Le Mans with a large army, there were negotiations between him and the leaders of the city, who accepted his rule 'after receiving oaths from him, as much concerning freedom from punishment for betrayal *as about preserving the ancient customs and judicial arrangements of the same city*'. In the phrase italicised here there was room for improvement in town conditions, given the medieval tendency to cloak change in statements of preservation. William, governing a realm from the southern border of Maine to the southern border of Scotland, did not want a rebellious Le Mans, he wanted a prosperous town generating wealth. It was an argument that could appeal to landlords as well when towns grew up on the manorial patchwork of Europe. The development of towns as privileged self-governing entities was only just beginning in the eleventh century. Another early example is Milan in northern Italy, which had its own consuls by 1097. There urban agitation coincided with the acute phase of church reform, to which we now turn.

The Church in the Later Eleventh Century

In the mid-eleventh century, the papacy was reformed and took control of the reform movement and of the Church. Historians commonly apply the label 'Gregorian Reform' to the whole movement, named for Pope Gregory VII (1073–85) who provoked an unprecedented dispute between Church and State. Yet Pope Leo IX (1049–54), who initiated the above mentioned takeover and set the papacy to operating in new ways, is at least as important. In the first year of his papacy Leo travelled extensively: to reforming synods at Pavia in Italy, Reims in France and Mainz in Germany where he acted, and was seen to act, as head of the whole Church. With Pope Leo IX and the advisers he appointed, which included Hildebrand, the future Pope Gregory VII, reform ideology from the North met papal ideology from the South. The reformers thought that they were restoring the papacy to a position of power which it had lost. In fact, the Church had never been centralised under papal control in the way that they were to bring about by the end of the eleventh century. The process impinged on the bishops, who had been virtually autonomous authorities in their dioceses; however, the ultimate power had been royal/imperial. As stated in the section on the Church in the early eleventh century, rulers then and previously ran the Church. All rulers 'worth their salt' felt that they had responsibility for right religion in the lands they ruled. Such was and remained the acknowledged role of the emperor of Byzantium. As well, rulers used and relied on the church and its personnel, especially its organisation, in governance. Naturally they wanted to appoint such important ministers of Church and State. In the second half of the eleventh century papal control sought to replace secular control of the Church, and the secular rulers were very resistant to this change. Ecclesiastical attitudes hardened toward lay participation in running the Church, which came to be seen overwhelmingly negatively. Lay abuses of the Church (including expropriation as illustrated on p. 000 above) eclipsed the fundamental lay contribution of Duke William of Aquitaine and Emperor Henry III in particular to church reform.

Popes Leo IX and Gregory VII contrast strongly in their relations with the German rulers. Leo cooperated closely with King Emperor Henry III, the keen church reformer who had appointed him. There was outright conflict between Gregory and King Henry IV, who deposed each other from office. Of the contrasting agendas of these popes, one could say that Leo IX attacked abuses of the system but Gregory VII attacked the system itself. That is, Leo opposed clerical marriage and payment for church offices, as did Gregory, but Gregory objected to the granting of church offices by laymen and to secular rulers running the Church. In between these popes comes radical change, especially associated with Cardinal Humbert, whom Leo IX appointed and whose ideas

Gregory VII followed. Humbert headed Leo's delegation to Constantinople, where the Eastern and Western Churches parted ways permanently in 1054; however, this split was inevitable once there was a strongly assertive papacy. In 1058 Humbert completed his *Three Books against the Simoniacs*, in the last of which he wrote against the appointment to, and conferral of, church offices by lay people. 'For how does it pertain to lay persons to distribute ecclesiastical sacraments and episcopal or pastoral grace, that is to say crozier staffs and rings, with which all episcopal consecration is principally effected and by which it functions and is sustained?' This is called 'lay investiture', a lay person clothing the appointee with the symbols of church office. (For an example see p. 148 above.) Early in 1059 a papal synod decreed: 'That no cleric or priest shall receive a church from laymen in any fashion, whether freely or at a price'. At the same time, Pope Nicholas II issued a decree about how a new pope should be chosen by the clergy of Rome, without secular influence. It was this independence that his Norman vassals were to guarantee. The Church looks very different at the beginning and end of the eleventh century and the same can be said of the crucial decade of change, the 1050s.

The active and forceful application of church policy against lay involvement in church appointments by Pope Gregory VII against King Henry IV of Germany in 1075 is what brings on the Investiture Controversy. It started over the disputed bishopric of Milan. King Henry IV appointed a bishop whom the ecclesiastical establishment there wanted, but he was not the one supported by local reformers and Pope Gregory VII. Gregory's alliance with the Patarini, who combined urban revolt with church reform, against the bishop whom Henry IV had appointed at Milan, associated him with the notion that impure priests could not confer valid sacraments, which the Church normally rejected. Again, there are several issues involved here: church reform, urban self-government, and, as well, German imperial rule of northern Italy, which the ecclesiastical establishment at Milan favoured but the townsfolk seeking self-government did not. Late in 1075 Gregory strongly objected to Henry's appointment of the bishop. Early in 1076 German nobles and bishops defied Gregory and called on him to resign as pope. Immediately Gregory excommunicated and deposed Henry as king and released his subjects from their fealty to him. Here we may pause to consider. His deposition of Henry IV as king of Germany was very difficult to support. Papal deposition of emperors could be justified on the grounds that the imperial office in the West was the pope's to bestow. The papacy had no such role in kingship. Gregory tried citing historical precedent, for one the deposition of the last Merovingian king in the mid-eighth century as an act of Pope Zacharias (see p. 000 above). The anonymous author of *On Preserving the Unity of the Church* in the late eleventh century pointed out exactly why Pope Gregory's argument was historically inaccurate. The exchange is an interesting use of the early medieval past by those much closer to it than we are, as well as an illustration of the debate provoked by the Investiture Controversy.

Pope Gregory VII can be viewed as having the same flaw as the hero of the *Song of Roland*: *démesure* or rashness. Yet he tried to prepare. Shortly before the

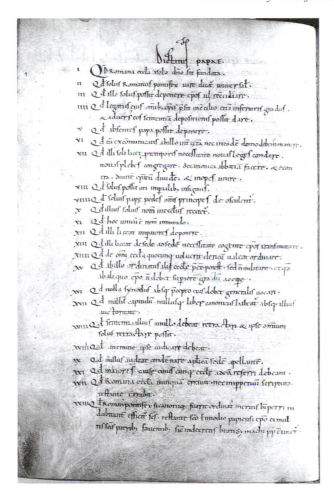

Figure 31 *Dictatus Papae, Sayings of the Pope*, 1075. Reg. Vat., 2, fol. 80v. (Archivio Segreto Vaticano)

Investiture Controversy broke out, 27 points headed 'Dictatus Papae', 'Sayings of the Pope' were written into the papal register of business. They are illustrated as they appear in the manuscript here (see Figure 31). These points are historically significant as an indication of what Gregory was thinking at the time. While a Saying like the ninth, 'That the Pope is the only one whose feet are to be kissed by all princes', may suggest that Gregory wanted to rule the world, the majority of the Sayings are about papal control of the Church, like the third, 'That he alone can depose or reinstate bishops'. That was the issue. The choice of bishops by the leading clergy of their diocese was a novelty, and papal advocacy of it a challenge to the *status quo*, which was appointment by secular rulers. As Wenrich of Trier eventually wrote:

That which is done concerning clerical benefices, namely the freeing of them from secular authority, and concerning bishops, who ought not to receive their bishoprics at the hands of a lay prince, all this creates bad blood at first through its very novelty, but there seems none the less to be a certain semblance of justice in it.

Here is a man working his way through change. The extent to which the lands that went with church positions were held feudally was a complicating factor: part of investiture was conferring the fief. In his struggle for reform Gregory always stressed the dignity of the papal office, and several Sayings, like the one first quoted, express this. The last Saying, 'That the Pope may absolve subjects of unjust men from their fealty', is a more mundane weapon that was actually used against Henry. Point 12 of the 'Dictatus Papae', 'That he may depose Emperors' would, as mentioned above, overshoot the mark. These were means to Gregory's ends that had brought him into conflict with secular power, not ends in themselves. Having investigated the nature of the Investiture Controversy, arising from the papal agenda to get control of the Church, it is time to resume the account of what happened.

Excommunicated (which deprived him of the support of churchmen on whom he relied) and about to be judged at a German council chaired by Pope Gregory VII, King Henry IV crossed the Alps to where Gregory was staying at the castle of Canossa. This was one of the extensive possessions of Mathilda, heir to the position and lands of the marquises of Tuscany, a supporter of church reform and in this case of church peace. It was January 1077. 'There, on three successive days, standing before the castle gate, laying aside all royal insignia, barefooted and in coarse attire, he ceased not with many tears to beseech the apostolic help and comfort . . .' Gregory wrote these words in an explanation to the German nobles of why he had given in, absolved Henry and recognised him as king. They were not pleased, for they welcomed the weakening of the kingship that the dispute with Gregory had brought about. From King Henry IV's point of view, the timing of the Investiture Controversy was disastrous. He had succeeded his great father Henry III (a hard act to follow) to the throne as a small child at a time when the German nobility was engaged in intensifying competition for wealth and power, with which Carolingian governance was ill equipped to deal. Now the practical and ideological role of the church in Carolingian governance were being undermined by the direction that the reform movement was taking. More specifically, Henry was faced after he grew up with the outbreak of revolt, especially involving Saxony in 1073. He won a great victory over the rebels in 1075, just before the struggle with Pope Gregory VII began. The Saxon War, which might otherwise have been over, continued until 1088. Right away in 1077, some German nobles elected a rival king, Rudolf of Swabia, at Forchheim, the place where the first king of Germany had been chosen at the beginning of the tenth century, another interesting reference to earlier history. Their self-conscious action can be seen as the true beginning of German elective monarchy. When Gregory eventually recognised Rudolf, Henry

IV came up with a rival pope, Clement, who crowned him emperor in Rome in 1084. Gregory died in 1085 among his Norman allies, who in rescuing him from Rome did a lot of damage in the city.[11] Successors would ultimately achieve his aims early in the next century by compromise.

The Church was on its way to recognition by rulers as a separate entity of some power. As Europe became more organised, the alternatives for the Church were to be part of coherent kingdoms or centralised under papal monarchy. Not surprisingly, the papal reformers worked for the latter, and not just because of institutional self-interest. Long standing papal fear of domination by secular power and thus concern for territorial independence would ensure that, while the Investiture Controversy involved France and England as well, relations with the German Empire would be especially prickly. By the end of the eleventh century there were signs that the future of Europe would not lie in universal empire. The dreams of Emperor Otto III and Pope Sylvester II at the beginning of the century would not come true. The papacy would make sure that this did not happen. The state of relations with the papacy – Clement the anti-pope was still alive – may not have encouraged German participation in the great venture at the end of the century, the First Crusade, but Germans went on it anyway, together with people from all over Christendom.

The First Crusade

The First Crusade (1095–99) will be examined here as an outgrowth of eleventh-century developments. It was the first stage of European expansion and resulted, for a time, in European colonies along the east coast of the Mediterranean (see Map 7.5). Increasing population and agricultural production underpinned the transformation of Europe in that century in all respects. For what it is worth, Robert the Monk includes a reference to population pressure in his version of Pope Urban II's appeal for crusade at the Council of Clermont in 1095. The Crusade was an expression of continuing lay piety in the tradition of the mass pilgrimages to Jerusalem (see Figure 32) mentioned when discussing the Church in the early eleventh century. Robert the Monk has Urban say:

> And we do not command or advise that the old and feeble, or those unfit for bearing arms, undertake this journey; nor ought women to set out at all, without their husbands or brothers or legal guardians. For such are more of a hindrance than aid, more of a burden than advantage. Let the rich aid the needy; and according to their wealth, let them take with them experienced soldiers. The priests and clerks of any order are not to go without the consent of their bishop; for this journey would profit them nothing if they went without permission of these. Also, it is not fitting that laymen should enter upon the pilgrimage without the blessing of their priests.

Going on crusade out of devotion replaced penance for any sins.

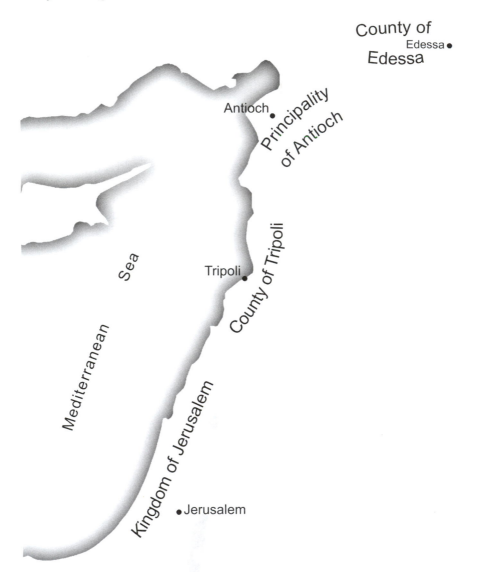

Map 7.5   First Crusade and the Crusader states

The role of lay piety in the First Crusade may have been more profound. Every account has Pope Urban proclaim the Crusade, but the earliest of them all, the anonymous *Deeds of the Franks* (*c*.1100) begins as follows:

When now that time was at hand which the Lord Jesus daily points out to His faithful, especially in the Gospel, saying, 'If any man would come after

Figure 32   The walls of Jerusalem in an early photograph. (After Charles Groeber, *La Palestine L'Arabie et la Syrie*, 1925; courtesy of Adrian Boas)

me, let him deny himself and take up his cross and follow me', a mighty agitation was carried on throughout all the region of Gaul, that if anyone desired to follow the Lord zealously, with a pure heart and mind, and wished faithfully to bear the cross after Him, he would no longer hesitate to take up the way to the Holy Sepulchre.

And so Urban, Pope of the Roman see, with his archbishops, bishops, abbots and priests, set out as quickly as possible beyond the mountains and began to deliver sermons and to preach eloquently . . .

This allows the possibility that the Crusade originated as a popular movement, a bandwagon on to which the pope jumped. It is not diminished by the early prominence of the itinerant preacher Peter the Hermit and Walter the Penniless who, with their motley followings, were the first to reach Constantinople. Their expedition ended in disaster. Given the way Church and society were developing in the eleventh century, the successful Crusade would henceforth be presented as a papal initiative: Urban called, Christendom came and delivered Jerusalem.

The earlier reform agenda can be seen in Fulcher of Chartres's account of Urban's speech at the Council of Clermont. It was a reform council, for example opposing simony, and a peace council affirming the Truce of God, the text of which is given elsewhere:

> Be it enacted, that monks, clergymen, women, and those who may be with them, shall remain in peace every day; farther, on three days, *viz.*, the second, third, and fourth days of the week, an injury done to anyone shall not be considered an infraction of the peace; but on the remaining four days, if any one injures another, he shall be considered a violator of the Sacred Peace, and shall be punished in the manner decreed.

But then the pope went further, pointing out that there were enemies of Christians, the Seljuk Turks, whom Christians should go and attack rather than each other. Urban had received a request from Byzantine Emperor Alexius Comnenus for assistance against them. The Byzantines got more than they had bargained for, especially when the Norman Bohemund showed up. Not all that long before, they had been fighting him. The historian Anna Comnena gives an entertaining account of the meeting of Bohemund and Alexius when the Norman passes through Constantinople on crusade. They converse politely, touch on their former enmity; Alexius gives Bohemund food, which the Norman suspects is poisoned, and rich objects, takes his oath of fealty and sends him on his way with other crusaders as quickly as possible. Anna is quite clear on Bohemund's lack of resources, which has prompted him to go on crusade. 'Apparently he left to worship at the Holy Sepulchre, but in reality to win power for himself – or rather, if possible, to seize the Roman Empire itself, as his father [Robert Guiscard] had suggested.' Of course Anna would know by the time she wrote this in the first half of the twelfth century that Bohemund got no further than Antioch, where he founded his principality (see Map 7.5).

One question that can be asked about the First Crusade is: what possessed people to 'up and go' on a venture like that? Here it is revealing to recall the army of the people of Le Mans and Maine, which comprised clergy and lay, noble and ignoble, men and women, and how 'in a furious assault they aimed for the castle of Sillé'. Compare the passage from Robert the Monk quoted first in this section, according to which Urban does not forbid women from going on crusade, but rather says that they are not to go unaccompanied by men. The Crusade can be seen as an outgrowth of such punitive expeditions. It is also an outcome of the rise of the knight, of course, and, together with the reconquest of Spain from the Muslims which was making significant advances in the later eleventh century, contributed to the ethos of chivalry as we saw in the *Song of Roland*. Chivalry had its limits. Crusaders beginning their overland journey to the Holy Land passed through towns on the River Rhine. Contemporary Christian and later Jewish sources agree in identifying those led by Count Emicho of Leiningen in Bavaria in particular as attacking Jews in these towns. In Worms, where an eleventh-century synagogue survives, the bishop like his counterparts elsewhere in the Rhineland protected the Jews, but townsfolk joined in the attack and many Jews were killed. The First Crusade was an astonishing success from the Christian point of view. On Friday, 15 July 1099 Jerusalem fell. The reference in one source to blood up to the horses' bridle reins is apocalyptic language from the biblical Book of Revelations 14:20, which suggests how the Crusade was seen; however, it was clearly an atrocious sack in which many men, women and children of various faiths were killed.

The Final Analysis

Europe was becoming more organised. External boundaries were developing, referred to by Pope Gregory VII as *fines Christianitatis*. At the end of our period, Christendom as a self-conscious, territorial entity had emerged, separate from lands inhabited by people who were stubbornly not Christians. Conversion was scarcely a motive for the First Crusade: the aim was to drive the Muslims out of the Holy Land. European society was also developing internal boundaries, distinguishing more sharply between 'us' and 'them'. Established Jewish communities in the Rhineland were persecuted by crusaders passing through, as we have just seen. On the whole, circumstances in the later Middle Ages were far more difficult for Jews in Europe than in the early Middle Ages. After the eleventh century heresy, religious dissent, about which so little has been said in this book because it was so relatively unimportant a problem, greatly increases. This does not mean that early medieval people were conformist; rather, heresy requires accusation of wrong belief. Such was more likely to be made in a centralised church. Also, the professional church was drawing a line around itself and saying to the laity, 'we run our own show'. The lay contribution to church reform had been considerable; ultimately lay folk would be squeezed out, but this had not yet happened by the end of the eleventh century. The principles of social organisation were male dominated. Church reform was male centred. While life could be very brutal for women in the early Middle Ages, they actually had *relatively* better access to wealth and power than women in the better organised periods before and after, that is in the early Roman Empire and the second half of the Middle Ages. Changing inheritance practices have been mentioned. After the eleventh century the reverse dowry fades away. People were not enlightened on the subjects of women and gender in the early Middle Ages. Spiritual equality of men and women was acknowledged, but women were held to be the weaker gender, were always to be under a man's guardianship, were not to hold public office or be clerics or be in authority over men in any way. In the early Middle Ages, however, public institutions were weak and so were the rules, or at least people tended not to adhere to them.

In the twelfth-century Crusader Kingdom of Jerusalem established as a result of the success of the First Crusade, women had more ability to inherit, heresy was unknown and there was even a leper king at a time when lepers were being strictly segregated in Europe. Perhaps the resemblance to early medieval Europe was one of frontier societies, or perhaps it was due to the extent of cultural diversity (most of the population of the Crusader States was indigenous) in comparison to the distinctive and original dominant culture now growing in Europe.

Epilogue

This book will conclude with a look at the world in the early centuries of the second millennium. To be conscious of the year 1000, or 2000 for that matter, one must use AD dating from the birth of Christ. In the whole world in AD 1000 only the more westerly parts of Europe used this dating system. In Constantinople or Byzantium, the greatest Christian city, it was not yet used. So our survey may justifiably begin with that part of the world where there was awareness of the turn of the first into the second millennium.

The years from 1000 to 1200 were exceedingly important for the development of Western European civilisation. The exasperatingly labelled Middle Ages were not a 'middle' but a beginning for Europe. Its basic culture had already been formed out of a fascinating combination of Christian Roman and indigenous European (Germanic, Celtic, Slavic) elements in the early medieval centuries before AD 1000; however, its most basic political and socio-economic institutions were defined in the period 1000–1200, from which their development has proceeded *without a break* up to the present day.

Take nation-states. Their destiny was by no means clear in AD 1000. Our period opens with the foremost monarch of the day, Emperor Otto III, ruling Central Europe from Rome and engaged to marry the daughter of the other emperor in Constantinople, who arrived in Italy shortly after her fiancé's untimely death. Yet Europe's political future was not to lie in a revived Christian Roman Empire, but in feudal monarchies like England and France. Starting from an appallingly weak position, the kings of France used the institutionalised patronage which we call feudalism to centralise their power with considerable success by 1200. In England, the Norman conquerors of 1066 took an already relatively well-organised monarchy and made it more so. By 1200 English legal and administrative institutions were on a firm footing; the feudal roots of modern representative democracy, arguably the greatest success story of the second millennium, reach back to this point.

The Western distinction between Church and State and the creative tension between them hardly existed in 1000 under Otto III, who ruled in close cooperation with the pope whom he had appointed. Yet, later in the century, reforming popes drew a line around the professional clergy and told everyone else to keep out of running the Church, and after that popes and emperors were usually at odds. So too were the English King Henry II and the archbishop of Canterbury Thomas à Becket, who ended up murdered in his cathedral in 1170. Wise rulers of Church and State avoided such perils and sought accommodation, but lines of demarcation were still being worked out in our period.

Take cities as economic powerhouses with some degree of self-government. These become visible in precisely the period AD 1000–1200. The towns which Ancient Rome had brought to Europe were more like, say, Canberra in that their administrative function was uppermost. Now merchants and tradesmen banded together in sworn associations of mutual help and support in pursuit of their own interests. Urban corporations with mayors and aldermen are their direct descendents, and so too is one particular type of guild first seen at the end of our period in Paris, Bologna and Oxford: universities.

This early European urban growth was underpinned by rising population and agricultural production which was underway at the beginning of the new millennium. Land was being reclaimed, simple technological advances like better ploughs and watermills were increasingly employed. The French historian Georges Duby refers to the period from 1000–1200 as one of 'peasant conquests'. The line of development of Western civilisation can be traced back to these humble beginnings.

Western European society, although still dreadfully violent, was getting a little better organised in our period. This was not without its down side. The opportunities for women to access wealth and power declined. Household, family and women were all marginalised by the growth of public institutions. As already seen, the laity were marginalised in the Church. Boundaries hardened. Outsiders – Jews, heretics, lepers – were more readily marked for exclusion. The English historian R. I. Moore has seen the 'formation of a persecuting society' in AD 1000–1200. In this respect, the worst was yet to come.

In comparison to its richer and more sophisticated neighbours, the Byzantine Empire and the Islamic bloc, Western Europe in AD 1000 could be called with some justification the Third World of its day (but only, as one of my students pointed out in an examination paper, if one focuses on the elite and ignores the masses of subsistence peasants common to all three areas). Within a hundred years the Crusades would give a taste of European colonialism to come, although the Holy Land was almost entirely lost before the end of our period when Saladin defeated the Crusaders at the battle of Hattin in 1187. Christian successes in the Western Mediterranean, the reconquest of Sicily and much of Spain from the Muslims, were permanent. This was the time when El Cid fought the Moors, those whom he was not allied with. Not all contacts were violent and 1000–1200 was a golden age of multicultural Muslim, Jewish and Christian scholarship and translation, out of which Greek philosophical texts transmitted through Arabic were reaching Western Europe by the end of the period.

What remained of the Ancient Roman Empire, after initial successes along its northern borders by Emperor Basil the Bulgar-Slayer, suffered a terrible defeat by Seljuk (not Ottoman) Turks at the Battle of Manzikert in 1071 and shrank back toward its capital Constantinople or Byzantium. Capturing that city was everyone's dream, the dream not only of Muslims but of Western Christians, who succeeded just after our period in 1204 when the Fourth Crusade 'went astray'.

The frontier peoples of the Muslim world between 1000–1200 demanded and got involvement in these struggles for position and power. The Seljuk Turks just mentioned conquered the Near East. Further east the Ghaznavids and their Afghan successors extended Muslim control over northern India in precisely our period, with consequences still felt to this day. Saharan peoples took control of North Africa and southern Spain.

South of the Sahara African cultures flourished on the salt for gold trade: in Ghana and in Nigeria, where the Ife people have left stunning portrait heads (see Figure 33). Janson's *History of Art* comments on one made of cast bronze: 'At the

Figure 33   Bronze Ife head from Nigeria, twelfth century. Like the Cappenberg head in Figure 34, the Ife sculpture probably depicts a ruler in a religious context. (After Leo Frobenius, *The Voice of Africa*, London, 1913)

Figure 34 Gilded bronze head of Frederick Barbarossa, twelfth century. If one's criterion of judging art is the natural representation of a human being, the Ife head is 'better' than this stylised portrayal of the ruler of the Holy Roman Empire. (Stiftskirche Cappenberg, D 59379 Selm)

time this head was produced, the twelfth century AD, nothing of comparable character can be found in Europe' (see Figure 34). In East Africa our period also saw the growth of coastal towns like Kilwa in Tanzania and the early stages of the inland settlement of Great Zimbabwe.

In China 1000–1200 falls within the Sung dynasty, a period in which significant social and economic innovations of the previous T'ang dynasty were developed and consolidated. The civil service examination became a routine challenge to generations of upwardly mobile Chinese until the early twentieth century. Although, as is also the case with India, many achievements of Chinese culture belong to earlier millennia, there was an explosion of technology, scientific and other intellectual creativity in eleventh-century China.

Certainly this was the world's most advanced civilisation as it is normally defined. China had three cities with a population of over a million. (Constantinople is unlikely to have had anywhere near that many, although greater Cairo may have done.) The Sung government issued paper money from the 1020s. (The ancient Chinese technology of paper production, earlier borrowed by the Arabs, had spread to Muslim Spain by our period.) Printing was well established, and even movable type was investigated. China set up a well organised navy. Contrary to a common misconception among even educated people, gunpowder was used *not* just for pretty fireworks, but in sophisticated weaponry.

One would be hard put to find any Great Wall of China in this period, as earlier fortifications had been allowed to break down. In 1127, from what is now Manchuria, Jurchen conquered northern China, establishing the Chin dynasty there. In the 1160s Genghis Khan was born, whose Mongol hordes would shake Eurasia in the next century.

The tradition of military government was established in Japan, where just before 1200 the shogunate was founded which lasted until 1867. The Japanese equivalent of our period was *mappo*, 'the latter days of the law', characterised by a social breakdown of Buddhist teachings. Eleventh-century women writers at the imperial court pioneered Japanese prose writing, when their male counterparts were still struggling to express themselves in the Chinese language and script. Murasaki Shikibu's *Tale of Genji* has been called the world's first psychological novel. Around 1000 Sei Shonagon wrote *The Pillow Book* and it is interesting that her lifetime may have overlapped with that of another woman author with court connections (although she lived in a monastery), Hrosvitha of Gandersheim, who, at the other end of Eurasia in later-tenth-century Germany, wrote plays and the first historical work by a woman, *The Deeds of Otto I*, grandfather of Otto III with whom this overview began.

Meanwhile in lands unknown to those surveyed so far, Maya civilisation had declined although the Maya were and are still around, and it was the turn of their northern neighbours the Toltecs to flourish in Central America. Beyond these, Indians in what is now the southwestern United States were building complex stone structures unparallelled in North America before the later nineteenth century; their descendants are today's Pueblo tribe. The Pacific Ocean is thought to have been fully colonised by AD 1000. There is evidence that Aborigines lived at Wattamolla in the Royal National Park near Sydney, Australia, within the period surveyed here, and some of us have unwittingly walked through one of their rock shelters on our way to the beach and lagoon there.

Notes

Prologue

1. Whatever was meant by this strange label, it can point us to a truth: the Roman Empire was already a Christian state when its Western half crumbled in the fifth century.

Introduction

1. For early medieval awareness of this, see p. 79.
2. Other dating systems were in use. For example, Hydatius, noting down events in fifth-century Spain (including his own capture by barbarians – *Hydatio capto* says the Latin briefly) still dated by Olympiads, even though the Ancient games at Olympia were no longer held.
3. Readers familiar with Peter Brown's published lecture, *Relics and Social Status in the Age of Gregory of Tours*, will recognize a similar conversion in his statement, 'That was written by one green in matters Merovingian'. Readers who have no idea what this note is about should put it aside.
4. See his articles in the journal *Africa* for 1962, 1971 and 1975.

Chapter 1: The Fifth Century: Kingdoms Replace the Western Roman Empire

1. This term is used to counter the common but misleading 'fall' for a process that lasted from 410 to 486. A good working definition is that the Roman Empire ended in a particular region when the army ceased to be paid. As was remarked in an altogether different context, it is hard to have a military dictatorship without a military.
2. This may be a Celtic loanword, in which case it comes from the Roman 'underworld' in more than one sense (see below); or a Germanic loanword, but it refers to no known ethnic group.
3. The exception at the beginning of the Middle Ages was Ireland, where the *Law of Adomnan* ended the practice as a social reform *c.*700.
4. To the northwest the Bretons still maintained their political independence, despite Frankish claims, as well as their identity.

5. He is said to have left out the Books of Kings because the Visigoths were warlike enough.
6. Alans, Huns, Picts and Scots are the exceptions.
7. Latin *puer*, 'boy', underwent a specialised development similar to *vassus*, and was still used to designate the Norman knights fighting the battle of Hastings in the Bayeux Tapestry, which records their conquest of England in 1066.

Chapter 2: The Sixth Century: the West Goes Its Own Way

1. These were the Amals. Family and ethnic pride are displayed in several of their names. Although Cassiodorus wrote a History of the Goths to show that Theoderic was descended from 17 generations of kings, only his father and uncle are known to have ruled.
2. The Gothic language survived in the Crimea throughout the Middle Ages.
3. Only in Britain was the survival of the *civitas*, plural *civitates*, limited, and even there they could become kingdoms. The *comes civitatis* is widely held to have been a very late Roman official, but if so it is curious that none can be shown to have served anyone other than a barbarian king.
4. Before the nineteenth-century nationalist revival, Hellenes, the word now used for themselves by the Greeks, were pagans. Eventually Constantinople came to be referred to just as 'the city', which is why the Turkish name is Istanbul, from the Greek for 'into the city'.
5. For a piece of evidence from the seventh century which suggests that the Franks always kept a close and wary eye on imperial intentions, see pp. 67–8 of the next chapter.
6. The better known title *History of the Franks* is not Gregory's and misrepresents his work, which is not a national history. It is deliberately avoided here.
7. The word 'chapel' originally designated the shrine where a piece of Martin's cloak (*capella*), which he was said to have cut in two and shared with a beggar, was preserved as a holy relic by the kings of France.
8. These are not illustrated here, but can be imagined easily enough from a verbal description. Each golden cover is taken up by a cross with a large, round sapphire in the centre and a rectangular-cut emerald further out on each arm of the cross (so that the four emeralds could be taken as the ends of a smaller cross within a cross), which is also decorated with pearls and other gems. Set between the arms of the cross are four reused Roman cameos of varying quality. The borders are of filigree and cloisonné inset mainly with garnet (see further the beginning of the next chapter).

Chapter 3: The Seventh Century: Cultural Watershed

1. The latter have been widely distributed. The writer was amazed to discover a replaced ship's rivet from Sutton Hoo in the minerals gallery at the Australian Museum in Sydney.
2. That these people came to be known as English rather than Saxons (as they are in the Celtic languages) may actually be due to the influence of Bede, who naturally used the label that applied to his fellow Northumbrians, the people who lived north

of the River Humber in England. Their origins he specifies in the *Ecclesiastical History* as having been in the land called *Angulus* (modern Angeln where Germany and Denmark come together), including the information that it 'is said to have remained deserted from that day to this', which receives some support from modern pollen analysis. The distinction of English from British in the text above may confuse modern readers but is normal in early medieval historiography.

3. The system of dating events from the *hegira* ('flight') of Mohammed from Mecca to Medina preceded the system of dating events from the birth of Christ first applied by Bede in the early eighth century. That these widely used ways of reckoning time both originated in the period under study in this book is noteworthy.

4. This was creatively edited by ibn-al-Tiqtaqa, *Al-Fakhri: On the Systems of Government and the Moslem Dynasties*, in 1302, from earlier accounts. Thus the camphor (prized as a medicine and quite mistakable for salt) story is found in *The History of Prophets and Kings* by al-Tabari (839–923) and *Futuh al-Buldan* ('Conquest of Countries') by al-Baladhuri (d.892), which also has the story of the 1000 dirhams but as the price not of a jewel, but of a woman captured in an earlier raid on Persia. The latter authors preface each tradition with an *isnad* listing its transmittors. The figure of 3 billion dirhams is from al-Tabari, who also cites an alternative version which says it was three times as much.

5. The reader is here referred back to what is said about the artificiality of historical periods in the Introduction, p. 5.

6. From the end of the second chapter of the second part of *Mohammed and Charlemagne*, published after Henri Pirenne's death from a draft which he completed in 1935. The article previously cited is Anne Riising, 'The Fate of Henri Pirenne's Thesis on the Consequences of the Islamic Expansion', *Classica et Medievalia*, 13 (1952), pp. 87–130.

7. 'King Reccesuinth offers (this crown to God).' It was part of buried treasure from Guarrazar not far from Toledo, the Visigothic capital.

Chapter 4: The Eighth Century: Formation of the Core of Europe

1. The Frisian language, the closest to English, is still spoken on the Frisian Islands off Holland and Germany

2. For an early medieval globe, see the equestrian statue of a Carolingian ruler in the next chapter. Contrary to what is so widely believed, the learned view in the Middle Ages, inherited from Ancient cosmography, was that the world was round. The only flat-earther among medieval writers is the Byzantine Cosmas Indicopluestes (= 'who has sailed to India').

3. St Waldburg's reputation for holiness was ultimately unable to overcome the pagan associations of her feast day, the 1st of May, and *Walpurgisnacht* is the great gathering of witches on the eve of May Day in German tradition.

4. Its usual title, *Hodoeporicon* (Greek for 'On the Road'), was given to it not in the early Middle Ages but in the Renaissance, presumably because its similarity to a travel genre popular at that time was recognised.

5. Ascribing ownership/lordship to the original saintly founder in this way is typically medieval.

6. So argues Janet L. Nelson, whose paper 'Making a Difference in Eighth-Century Politics: The Daughters of Desiderius', in *After Rome's Fall* ed. Alexander Callander Murray (Toronto, 1998) is a fine example of what can be achieved by bringing women into even the most traditional historical subjects.

Chapter 5: The Ninth Century: Expanding the Boundaries

1. The initial application of 'holy' to the revived Roman Empire came only in the twelfth century, was taken from Ancient pagan usage and did not please the papacy.
2. Louis is the same name as Clovis. It did not take the Carolingians long to adopt the name of the great king who had founded France and the dynasty which they had ousted. Louis was called 'the Pious' because care of the Church was what he was good at.
3. The younger son may have fared better; see p. 137, n. 2.
4. As will be seen in the next chapter, in the tenth century the Magyars settled down in Hungary, where Magyar is the native name of the Hungarian language. Despite appearances, 'Hungarian' derives not from the Huns, but from the Onogur Bulgars, another steppe nomad people whose identity was partially subsumed in that of the Magyars.
5. At this time the term 'Varangians' was not yet used; likewise Rurik's base would have been at the site later replaced by Novgorod, which means 'new fort' in Slavic. While Scandinavian mercenaries in foreign service were possible at any stage, the Varangian Guard of the Byzantine emperor came into being late in the next century, and was still in existence when the *Russian Primary Chronicle* was compiled.
6. The word for 'leader' in the Turkish group of languages to which the original language of the Bulgars belonged.
7. For further discussion of this medieval social analysis, which appears here for the first time, see pp. 167–9.

Chapter 6: The Tenth Century: Nadir to Take-Off

1. Reference is to his book *In Small Things Forgotten*, the title of which is a quotation from a seventeenth-century American document. A distinction should be made between the deliberate assembling and burial of finds as occurred at Sutton Hoo (see pp. 53–6 above) and the discarding, disregarding or loss of items as normally occurred at the York sites; an exception to the latter is the rich and rare eighth-century Anglian helmet deposited in unknown circumstances at Coppergate.
2. The name of her younger son is unknown, but could easily have been Bernard after his father. The dates of William's father Bernard Hairy-feet are right for him to have been Dhuoda's son, as is the circumstance that he tried to kill Charles the Bald but was pardoned (see above, p. 109).
3. *Rex Francorum et Langobardorum*; the title *Rex Teutonicorum*, king of the Germans, originated later with the papacy not the rulers themselves.
4. At least in the West. For Hrotsvitha in a world context, see the Epilogue.

Chapter 7: The Eleventh Century: Transformation of Europe

1. The recognition of Adalbert as a saint is the first example of anything like a centralised process of canonisation which has become normal in the Catholic Church. The people he was trying to convert were the equivalent of those with whom the Englishman Wulfstan traded in the Baltic in the late ninth century (see above p. 128).
2. Francis Dvornik, *The Making of Central and Eastern Europe* (London: The Polish Research Centre, 1949), p. 183.
3. Even Gregory of Tours can be caught doing this at a moment of crisis (*Histories*, V.49).
4. For the Truce of God see p. 196 at the end of Chapter 7.
5. So called from Simon the magician, who offered money to apostles spreading Christianity so that they would confer the power of the Holy Spirit, of God active in the world, on him (Acts 8:9–24).
6. The great R. W. Southern deserves honourable mention as one who did not.
7. That a twelfth-century writer, Eadmer, had to go out of his way to explain why this man deserved sainthood shows a difference between their way of thinking and ours.
8. That one of their contemporaries was called William 'the Good Norman' probably says a lot about the reputation of people of this ilk.
9. His (nick)name was that of a giant, given because his mother was so hugely pregnant with him. Somehow knowing that the Normans could give a child a pre-natal name makes them seem more human.
10. *Histories*, III.22, in reference to Deuteria who gave her town and herself to King Theudebert. The interpretation of Gercendis offered here is supported by two charters from the period in question that show her acting like a count in Le Mans.
11. One of the best places to visit there, the church of San Clemente, was rebuilt upon its predecessor which had suffered on this occasion.

Glossary

This is primarily a glossary of terms, but it includes any names of peoples and places about which confusion may arise and thus an explanation is needed. If there are words in a definition that you do not understand, these are probably also glossed.

Aachen or **Aix-la-Chapelle**   Charlemagne's capital, located in what is now Germany; it has alternative German or French names.

Abbasid dynasty   Caliphs from 750 on who ruled from Baghdad; the Abbasid period does not extend beyond the ninth century due to the fragmentation of the Islamic world and loss of power of these caliphs after that time.

abbots and **abbesses**   Male and female heads of monasteries.

acclamation   Here used for the formula of words shouted by people, which made a Roman emperor; however, Charlemagne was first crowned by the pope and then acclaimed by the crowd in St Peter's Church in AD 800.

acculturation   Taking on the characteristics of another culture.

advocate   Here the protector of a church or monastery; lay advocates were members of the nobility whose position presented opportunities for exploitation of the institution(s) in their care.

Alamannia or **Swabia**   Although the Alamanni/Alamans and the Suevi/Sueves were two Germanic peoples, Alamannia and Swabia are two alternative names for the same duchy in southwestern Germany; *Allemagne* is the French word for Germany.

allod; **allodial tenure**   An allod is an estate of land owned outright rather than held as a fief from anyone; allodial tenure is this sort of landholding as distinct from feudal tenure.

Amals   Ostrogothic ruling family; King Theoderic was an Amal.

amber   Petrified resin that washes up on the shores of the Baltic Sea and can be polished and used in jewellery; widely traded.

Ancient, **Antiquity**   Refers to the historical period before the Middle Ages; on where to draw the line between these periods, *see* pp. 65–7 and 154. *See also* late Antiquity.

Anglo-Saxons, **Angles**, **Angeln**, **East Anglia**   Anglo-Saxons refers to Germanic migrants to Britain from the Continent, their descendants and all who took on their identity. The Angles came from Angeln, a region on the North Sea coast where modern Germany and Denmark come together, and established East Anglia and other northern English kingdoms (*see* Map 3.1). Their name gave rise to English and England (*see* below). *See also* Saxons.

annals   Yearly entries of historical events; often used in titles of medieval historical texts, for example *Annals of Lorsch*.

Anno Domini (AD)   '(In the) year of the Lord', the Christian dating formula, reckoning how many years an event is/was from the birth of Christ; equivalent to modern CE, Common Era.

anointing   The ritual in which holy oil was poured on a new king, queen, emperor or empress as part of their coronation ceremony; likewise in the consecration of bishops.

ansange   A portion of the lord's own fields (demesne) on a manor assigned to a peasant family for cultivation on the lord's behalf.

anthropology, anthropological, anthropologists   The study of human beings and their societies; here anthropological applies to theories arising from such study by anthropologists.

Antiquity   *See* Ancient and late Antiquity.

apostles, apostolic   The 12 followers of Christ told by him to spread Christianity; anyone who brings Christianity to a region for the first time, especially the Apostle Paul, who did so in the Mediterranean in the later first century AD. Apostolic here refers to the popes, the bishops of Rome, who claimed to wield the authority of Peter, the chief apostle.

Arabs, Arabia, Arabic   Originally the peoples in, and north of, the Arabian peninsula in the Middle East; the early Islamic conquests (*see* Map 3.2) extended the Arabic language and identity much further. *See also* Saracens.

archaeology, archaeological   The study of the material remains of human activity; here archaeology designates such evidence as distinct from texts, although archaeological finds may include writing (*see* Figure 11).

archbishop   A more authoritative bishop.

Arian, Arianism   Arian Christianity, in emphasising the humanity over the divinity of Christ, was regarded as wrong by the Catholic majority of Christians. Arius was a Roman, but his heresy spread widely among the northern barbarians.

Arles, kingdom of   *See* Provence.

Armorica, *Tractus Armoricanus*, *Arborychoi*   Although Armorica is normally thought of as the northwest peninsula of Gaul/France, what is now Brittany, the late Roman *Tractus Armoricanus* covered the whole northwest quadrant of Gaul beyond the Loire River. The sixth-century Byzantine historian Procopius called the inhabitants *Arborychoi*.

arpent   A unit of measurement of land, often used for vineyards.

artefact   An object made by human beings.

ascetic, asceticism   The Greek word *ascesis* refers to exercises intended to improve the spiritual rather than physical fitness of Christians. Ascetics were keen Christians who altered their lifestyle in order to achieve salvation.

Asia Minor   The peninsula lying between the Black Sea and the Mediterranean Sea; modern Turkey.

assarts; assarting   Pieces of land newly cleared or reclaimed and taken into cultivation; the process of doing this.

augustus, augusta   The name of the first Roman emperor which became a title designating emperors thenceforth. Augusta is the feminine form: empress.

Avars   A nomadic people from Western Asia who came further west to the region of the Danube River; sometimes referred to by the name of their predecessors, the Huns.

Balts   Peoples living south of the Baltic Sea, here used in reference to the original Prussians.

***bannum*, *bannus*, banal**   The right to tell people what to do; originally delegated by kings to their representatives, banal rights eventually were claimed by any powerful noble.

barbarian, barbarous   Originally a negative designation by the Greeks, then the Romans, of people who were uncivilised in language and lifestyle (*see* pp. 18–19); eventually identified with pagan.

basileus   Greek title of the Byzantine emperor.

Basques   A people on both sides of the Pyrenees Mountains whose language has resisted acculturation by the Romans and everyone else; equivalent to the Gascons.

Bavarians, Bavaria   An identity formed on the upper Danube, the Bavarians were ruled by dukes over whom the Franks claimed control that was not effective until Charlemagne made it so. Bavaria was later one of the duchies of Germany.

bellatores   Latin for 'those who fight', one of the Three Orders of medieval society.

Benedictine monasticism   *See* monasticism and rule (monastic).

beneficium   Literally 'a benefit' with a wide range of early medieval meanings, including land let on easy terms.

Berbers   People of North Africa who kept their native speech and were thus called by the Romans 'barbarians', whence their name.

Bible   The holy book of the Christian religion, most of it the scriptures also sacred to Judaism (Old Testament), followed by the New Testament.

bishop   The leader of a Christian community, having control of the finances of the Church everywhere except Ireland. *See also* episcopal, diocese, see, archbishop, cathedral, consecration, synod.

bloodfeud   Violent reprisal for injury between families; also called vendetta.

bonnier   A unit of measurement of land.

bride-price   Customary payment in Germanic societies from the family of the husband to the family of the bride; in time it dovetailed with the reverse dowry and came to be paid to the bride.

Britain, British Isles, British, Britons, Bretons, Brittany   The British Isles are part of Europe comprising Britain and Ireland. In early medieval history the English inhabitants of Britain are distinguished from the British or Britons, speakers of Celtic languages (*see* Map 3.1). The Bretons originated in migration from mainly southwest Britain to the Continent opposite, transforming Armorica into Brittany. *See also* Insular.

bucellarii   Late Roman private armies were made up of 'biscuit men' so-called from their rations.

Bulgars   A nomadic people of Western Asia, part of whom came further west, settled in and ruled over what became Bulgaria, where most of their subjects were Slavs; other Bulgars on the Volga River converted to Islam.

burg (*burgus*)   A fortress, often used in the names of towns.

burgers, burgesses, bourgeois   Townsfolk.

Burgundians, Burgundy   A Germanic people settled in Gaul by treaties with the Romans. The Burgundian kingdom in southeast Gaul was absorbed by the Franks in the sixth century, but reappeared after the break-up of the Frankish Empire in the ninth century. Early medieval Burgundy was further south than late medieval Burgundy.

Byzantine Empire, Byzantium   What remained of the Roman Empire after its western half crumbled in the fifth century. Byzantium was the old name of its capital, Constantinople, and is sometimes used for the whole Byzantine Empire.

caliphate, caliphs   The Islamic empire, ruled by the caliph as successor to Mohammed.

canon, canonical The basic meaning of canon is a rule, so canonical means 'according to rule', as in the canonical hours at which prayers were to be said in a monastery. Canon has various derivative meanings: decrees of church councils were called canons, as were priests serving a church as a group. Canon law is church law.

Capetian dynasty The family of the Counts of Paris who replaced the Carolingian family as kings of France; so called from Hugh Capet (987–96), after whom the Capetian succession was unbroken until after the end of our period.

capitularies Decrees of the Carolingian rulers of France.

Caroline script The reformed handwriting sponsored by Charlemagne.

Carolingian From the Latin for Charles (*Carolus*), used to designate the family of Charles Martel and Charlemagne who ruled France and more generally the eighth and ninth centuries of French history.

Carolingian Renaissance The rebirth of learning sponsored by Charlemagne from the late eighth century with results lasting for most of the ninth century.

cartage Obligation of peasants to carry goods from place to place for their lord.

cathedral The church of a bishop.

Catholic Literally 'universal', in the sense of the whole church everywhere; used to designate the belief thereof, its meaning is equivalent to orthodox.

celibacy Not marrying because of ascetic abstinence from sexual intercourse. Clerical celibacy means priests not marrying.

Celts or **Kelts, Celtic** Peoples speaking Celtic languages, whose art may continue to display the principles of earlier Celtic (La Tène) style. The label is rarely used in the Middle Ages, and always in learned contexts, by authors who knew their Ancient sources. Anna Comnena uses Kelts for all Westerners, in the tradition of Herodatus.

chapel A lesser place of Christian worship than a church.

chivalry Conduct befitting a knight.

Christendom The part of the world that is Christian.

Christianity, Christian A monotheistic religion focused on Christ.

chronicle A form of historical writing especially concerned with the reckoning of time.

church 1. All Christians. 2. All Christian institutions. 3. A place of Christian worship.

city A relatively large cluster of population, normally walled. Any place with a bishop was a city by definition. *See also* town.

civilisation Traditionally incorporating the notion of a civilised as opposed to an uncivilised lifestyle, this word has come to be applied to any culture.

***civitas* (city territory)** An urban centre with its rural hinterland, the unit of Roman local/regional government often persisting in the early Middle Ages as the county and diocese.

Classical Fully developed Graeco-Roman civilisation.

clergy, clerical Professional churchmen, divided into minor and major clerical orders, the latter comprising subdeacon, deacon and priest.

clientship, client Dependency of one person (the client) on another (the patron).

cloisonné Technique of decoration, of Roman origin, by filling little metal compartments with garnet, glass or enamel.

cloister The covered walk around a courtyard attached to a monastery.

Cluny, monastery of; Cluniac A monastery founded in Burgundy in 910 which became a centre not only of monastic reform but also of a network of reformed monasteries, which were technically all priories under the abbot of Cluny, who was answerable only to the pope.

codex, plural codices A manuscript book.

coloni (plural), *colonus*, *colona* Peasants who were free tenants on estates.

commune A group association for mutual help and support in gaining self-government for a town.

condominium As used on p. 12, a way of living together.

consecration, consecrated A ceremony making something or someone holy: new churches and new bishops are consecrated.

Constantinople Originally the city of Byzantium, refounded by Emperor Constantine the Great to be a new Rome and capital of the Eastern Roman Empire, Constantinople was the greatest city of the early Middle Ages; now Istanbul in Turkey.

consul, consulship The most honourable office under the Roman emperor; there were still consuls in Ostrogothic Italy; the name was later revived, for example as applied to the heads of the city of Milan.

Continental Relating to the European mainland as opposed to the British Isles.

conversion A process of religious change, here to Christianity or Islam.

Coptic, **Coptic Egypt** The Copts were the indigenous inhabitants of Egypt; the label designates Christian Egyptians.

coronation The ceremony of crowning a king, queen, emperor, empress; often includes anointing.

counsel Advice; one of the things that vassals owed their lords.

count (*comes* or *graf*), **count of the city** (*comes civitatis*), **count of the Goths** (*comes Gothorum*), **county** (*civitas* or *gau*) A public official representing the king. On the part of the European Continent that had been within the Western Roman Empire counts were associated with the city territories. The *comes civitatis* in France had broad responsibilities, judicial and military in particular, for everyone in his county, whereas counts in Italy looked after the Ostrogoths. The Franks extended counts and counties beyond the boundaries of the former Roman Empire; in Germanic-speaking areas the count was the *graf* and the country the *gau*. *See also mallus*.

creed Christian statement of belief, beginning *credo*, 'I believe'. *See also* Nicene Creed.

crozier A symbol of episcopal office based on the shepherd's crook; *see also* investiture.

crusades; **crusaders** Armed pilgrimages intending to establish or maintain Christian control over the Holy Land; the people who went on them, so called because they sewed crosses on to their garments.

culture, cultural The total characteristics of a human society: language, lifestyle, creativity, everything.

Cyrillic alphabet Letters for writing the Slavic language modified from the Glagolitic alphabet devised by the Byzantine missionary Cyril for this purpose.

Danes Inhabitants of Denmark; Vikings mainly from Denmark. Note that Denmark at this time included what is now southwestern Sweden.

dar al-Islam Literally 'the house of Islam': the Muslim world.

Dark Ages Originally applied to the whole of the Middle Ages and then just to the early Middle Ages, this term is not in favour because it obscures the immensely significant developments that were underway in the period that saw the birth of Europe.

deacon The clerical order below priest.

Deeds (*Gesta*) A type of historical and biographical writing in the Middle Ages.

de facto; *de iure* Latin terms contrasting what is done 'in fact' with what is done 'by right'.

demons, demonic Evil spirits recognised by Christianity.

denier   A Frankish silver coin; the name derives from the Latin *denarius*.

devil   Evil spirit, in particular the chief one, the Devil, recognised by Christianity.

diminuendo effect   The use of progressively smaller letters at the beginning of a section of manuscript text (*see* the frontispiece of this book).

diocese   The area over which a bishop has authority.

dirham   A Muslim silver coin; the name ultimately derives from the Greek drachma.

divining, **divination**; **diviners**   Seeking information about the future or anything else by magical means; those who do so.

DNA   Deoxyribonucleic acid: the pattern of genes that shapes all living things; human DNA can be analysed to reveal the history of human populations.

doctrine, **doctrinal**   Christian religious teaching and belief.

Domesday Book, **Domesday Survey**   A recorded enquiry in AD 1086 into land-holding in England before and after the Norman Conquest, so called with reference to the day of reckoning at the Last Judgement, Doomsday, in Christian belief.

domesticus   Palace official in the kingdom of the Franks.

dowry, **reverse dowry**   Transfers of wealth associated with marriage; the reverse dowry, from the man to the woman, was the more significant payment in the early Middle Ages.

duke (*dux*, plural *duces*); **duchy**   A public official especially with military responsibilities; a duchy was larger than a county.

dynasty   An important family or line of rulers.

early Middle Ages   The period of European history dating from *c.*450 to *c.*1050.

East   A geographical designation of a region varying to some extent according to the context or direction of communication and influence: East–West contact would be across the Mediterranean and/or across Europe.

Eastern Christianity   Christian churches (in the sense both of the faithful and institutions) which neither used the Latin language nor recognised the bishop of Rome as their head. The only exception to this definition in the period of this book would be Arian Christianity in the western kingdoms, but this did not survive the seventh century. *See* Maps 4.1 and 7.1, but note that there were extensive Christian populations under Muslim rule and a scatter of Eastern Christians all the way to China.

Eastern Roman Empire   The part of the Roman Empire that did not crumble in the fifth century and survived throughout the period of this book. It was ruled from Constantinople, and from the original name of this city, Byzantium, it is usually called the Byzantine Empire; Byzantium can also be used for the empire as a whole.

East Francia   *See* Franks.

ecclesiastical   Of the church (Latin *ecclesia*).

emir   A Muslim ruler of what would originally have been a breakaway portion of the caliphate.

empire, **emperor**, **empress**   The Roman state and its ruler (Latin *imperator*, military commander), whether applied to its continuation in the East (the Byzantine Empire) or to its revival in the West (the Frankish Empire, later the German Empire). The Latin for empress is *imperatrix*. *See also augustus, augusta.*

endemic   Persistently characteristic.

English, **England**   Derived from the name of the Angles, one of the Continental Germanic peoples who settled in eastern Britain, but eventually applied to all of the Anglo-Saxons and their land. Distinguished here from the Celtic-speaking British whose kingdoms lay to the west and north of the English ones (*see* Map 3.1).

episcopal   Of bishops (from Latin *episcopus* via its adjective *episcopalis*).

ethnic, **ethnically**, **ethnicity**   An ethnic group comprises people with enough cultural characteristics in common to be given an identifying label. Earlier modern sources will sometimes use 'race' in this sense, but that term is avoided because associated with features of appearance, especially skin colour, which were of negligible significance to the people under study here.

ethnogenesis   The formation of an ethnic group, used especially in the sense of one growing up more or less on the spot, as people take on the identity of their rulers (*see* p. 17).

ethos   A value system, code of conduct, as in the ethos of chivalry.

etymology   The derivation of words, a matter of interest to, but much misunderstanding by, educated people in the early Middle Ages.

Eurocentric, **Eurocentrism**   Focused on Europe, even to the extent that history means only European history.

Europe   The western end of the Eurasian landmass. The notion of a Continent of Europe is as much cultural as geographical. It arose from the perspective of Mediterranean-centred civilisation: to the north was Europe, to the south was Africa and to the east was Asia; the other continents were unknown.

evangelium   *See* gospel.

evidence   Writings, artefacts or anything else that testifies to a state of affairs or supports an argument.

exarch, **exarchate**   A Byzantine official who combined political and military functions in governing an area, the exarchate.

excavation   Archaeological investigation carried out by digging and meticulously recording what is found.

fasting   Voluntarily limiting one's intake of food in order to keep the body in its (lower) place and train the mind to think on spiritual (higher) things.

fealty   Faithfulness (Latin *fidelitas*), formally sworn by vassals to their lords.

feodum or *feudum*   *See* fief.

ferial   Designates ordinary days which are not festivals of the Church and its saints.

feud   *See* bloodfeud. Note that these words have nothing to do with those glossed in the next two entries.

feudal; **feudalism**   Literally relating to fiefs (*see* next entry), feudal tenure being temporary use and enjoyment of land received by a vassal from a lord rather than outright ownership of it. Feudalism is best defined as institutionalised patronage; on the variety and complexity of meaning of this modern historical construct *see* p. 170.

fief   Originally *feodum* or *feudum* meant movable property, but came to designate the fief: maintenance, usually in the form of temporary use and enjoyment of land, provided by a lord to a vassal in return for service. Through the adjective *feodalis* or *feudalis* come feudal and feudalism.

field survey   Archaeological investigation carried out by looking at surface features (and surface indications of subsurface features) rather than by digging.

filigree   A decorative technique in metalwork involving the application of lines of tiny beads of precious metal.

filioque   Latin for 'and the son', words added to the Christian creed in the West in order to emphasise the likeness of the three persons of the Christian Trinity (God): the Holy Spirit proceeded from the Father and the Son.

frankincense   The hardened sap of trees which grow in the southern part of the Arabian Peninsula that gives off a beautiful scent when burned; used in religious worship.

Franks, **Frankish**, **France**   An ethnic identity that emerged in the region of the lower Rhine river and was taken on by a widening group of people, giving rise to the French and France. East Francia was that portion of the Frankish kingdom and empire that ultimately became Germany. Because of the prominence of the French in the First Crusade, 'Franks' came to be used by their Muslim opponents for all Europeans and still has that meaning in Arabic and Arabic-influenced languages.

Gallocentric   Focused on Gaul or France.

Gascons   *See* Basques.

gata   The Old Norse word for street, the origin of street names ending in –gate in the city of York.

Gaul, **Gallo-Roman**   The Roman name for what later became France. The Gauls were Celtic-speakers; their descendents in the Roman Empire are referred to as Gallo-Romans.

genealogy, **genealogical**   The tracing of family relationships.

Germans, **Germany**   The Romans distinguished Celts from Germans, and bequeathed the concept of *Germania* to the early Middle Ages and beyond. The kingdom of Germany grew out of East Francia. Its rulers were crowned Roman emperor by the pope from the mid-tenth century on.

Glagolitic alphabet   The original alphabet devised by Cyril in the ninth century to write the Slavic language, which was soon superseded by what came to be known as the Cyrillic alphabet.

gospel   From the Old English translation of Latin *evangelium*, 'good news'. The Gospels of Matthew, Mark, Luke and John, the evangelists, are the first four books of the New Testament in the Christian Bible, which record the life and teachings of Christ.

Goths, **Gothic**   Originally the easternmost of the Germanic peoples, divided into Ostrogoths and Visigoths. The Gothic language acquired prestige from Ulfila's translation of the Bible into it. Gothic occasionally appears as Getic through misidentification with an earlier people in Roman sources. Note that the use of Gothic for the architecture of the great cathedrals and later medieval art is an inaccurate, postmedieval reference, meaning barbarian, and has no relevance to the early Middle Ages.

Graeco-Roman   Refers to the two main cultures of the Ancient world, recognising the extent to which the lands around the Mediterranean Sea were a cultural unity.

Greek   The predominant language and culture of the Eastern Roman Empire, whose citizens and emperor were sometimes referred to by early medieval Western Europeans as Greeks, rather than Romans.

Gregorian chant   The music of worship sung in the churches of Rome, regularised by Pope Gregory I, which was taken as a standard for Western Christianity especially through its prescription by the Carolingian rulers for their empire.

Gregorian Reform   The movement for improvement of the Western Church in the eleventh century, named for Pope Gregory VII, who sparked its most acutely controversial phase.

hagiography   Writing about holy people, saints.

heathen   Non-Christians: dwellers on the heath, in remote places to which Christianity was slow to spread; the English equivalent of Latin *pagani*, dwellers in country districts, pagans.

hegemony   Dominant influence. Cultural hegemony can arise from, reinforce, but go well beyond the territorial limits of, political control. The Romans were past masters of it.

hegira   The flight of Mohammed and his followers from Mecca to Medina in Arabia in AD 622, from which point in time the expansion of Islam took off and the Muslim calendar is reckoned.

Hellenistic   The expanded Greek culture that took in the eastern Mediterranean region as a result of the conquests of Alexander the Great in the fourth century BC and persisted for many centuries thereafter.

heresy   A persistently held interpretation of Christianity that is judged to be wrong by the Church.

herisliz (**army splitting**)   Not individual desertion, but where a leader on a joint campaign departs with his forces for reasons of his own, leaving the rest in the lurch; a crime among the Franks.

hermits   Individual Christian ascetics living on their own, separate from ordinary society, rather than in monastic communities.

Hiberno-Norse   Refers to the culture that resulted from Viking settlement among the Irish.

hinterland   Land that is peripheral to a cultural, economic, social and/or political centre, be it the rural territory around a city or the Roman provinces away from the coastline of the Mediterranean Sea around which Roman civilisation was centred.

historical periodisation   The division of the past into chronological sections by historians and others, whose interpretations of the past may influence both the divisions made and the labels attached to them.

historiography   The writing of history and the study and interpretation that lies behind it.

holy   Religiously good, powerful, awesome, in essence or by association.

Holy Land   Israel/Palestine at the eastern end of the Mediterranean, of immense religious significance in Judaism, Christianity and Islam.

Holy Sepulchre   The tomb of Christ in which he rose from the dead according to Christian belief, contained within the principal Christian church in Jerusalem. The Holy Sepulchre was the specific goal of the First Crusade.

homage (*hominaticus*)   Doing homage was the ceremony by which a vassal became the man (*homo*) of a lord in high-level dependency.

homo   Although traditionally translated by English 'man, men', Latin *homo, homines* meant 'human being(s)'. It was applied to both vassals, who were usually men, and serfs, both men and women, of a lord.

honours (*honores*)   Public offices.

horseshoe arch   A curved architectural feature in which the ends turn inwards that is characteristic of Spain before and after the Muslim conquest.

Humanists; Humanist script   Participants in the principal cultural movement of the Renaissance dedicated to the study and revival of the culture of Ancient Greece and Rome; the style of handwriting they favoured in imitation not of Ancient (as they thought), but Caroline script.

Huns   A nomadic people whose western conquests starting in the later fourth century destabilised the barbarians settled north of the Roman Empire.

icon, Iconoclast Controversy, Iconoclasm   An icon is a picture of a holy person used as a channel for religious devotion to God in Eastern Christianity; iconoclast here is used in its original and literal meaning of someone who destroys icons, considering their use to be idolatry. This was a burning issue in the eighth and ninth centuries.

iconography   Artistic conventions by which the usually religious meaning of pictures was conveyed.

identity   Here used primarily in the sense of belonging to a group and presented as fluid rather than fixed. Identification with the ruling group is a key component of ethnogenesis.

idol, idolatry   The image of a god and worship thereof, normally associated with polytheism.

imperator*, *imperatrix   *See* empire, emperor, empress.

incantations   Forms of words said to produce supernatural effects.

Insular   Of the British Isles, in contrast to 'Continental' for the mainland of Europe. Insular script was also used in Brittany, however, before it was replaced by Caroline script.

investiture, Investiture Controversy   The formal bestowing of office and the lands that went with it, on bishops in particular, who were given crozier, ring and staff in the ceremony. Lay investiture was this being done by persons who were not professional churchmen, rulers in particular. The Investiture Controversy (1075–1122) arose when the papacy objected to lay investiture.

Ireland, Irish   The island west of Britain and its people, who also established colonies on the west coast of Britain, principally in southwest Scotland, at the beginning of the Middle Ages. *See also* Scots.

Islam, Islamic   A monotheistic religion focused on God (Allah) as revealed to his prophet Mohammed.

isnad   The line of transmission of early Muslim historical events which occurs as a list of sources prefaced to the events in early Muslim historiography.

jet   A form of coal that can be cut, polished and made into jewellery.

Judaism, Jewish, Jews   The monotheistic religion originally of the people of Ancient Israel at the eastern end of the Mediterranean Sea, but Jews were scattered from one end of the Mediterranean to the other and beyond by the early Middle Ages.

Justinian's Reconquest   A series of military campaigns (533–54), ordered by the Roman/Byzantine emperor Justinian I, that regained control of most of the western Mediterranean coast, much of which could not be held, however.

Just Price   The notion, inherited by the Church from the Romans, that there was a fitting price for each item offered for sale, regardless of variations in supply and demand. In effect the Just Price was the going price.

khagan or **khan**   The word for 'leader' in the Turkish group of languages, applied to Eurasian rulers across a wide area and over a long period of time.

king (*rex*)   The man of highest authority; early medieval kings were normally referred to as rulers of people rather than rulers of territory: for example, *rex Francorum*, king of the Franks rather than king of France.

knight, knighthood   A mounted warrior (French *chevalier* and German *Ritter* both mean horseman literally, while Latin *miles* was originally any soldier); by the end of the period of this book knighthood was a status of distinction conferred in an initiation ceremony.

laboratores   Latin for 'those who work' (with their hands, manual labourers), one of the Three Orders of medieval society.

Last Judgement   The final event of human history in Christian belief, when Christ will return to reckon the deeds of the living and the risen dead and so determine who will be saved and go to heaven and who will be condemned and go to hell.

late Antique, **late Antiquity**, **late Roman**   A period including at least the third to sixth centuries AD of Roman history and culture.

Latin   The language of the Romans and their empire in Antiquity, which evolved into the Romance languages: French, Spanish, Portuguese, Italian, Romanian and more than one language in the Alps. In, and long after, the early Middle Ages Latin survived in recognisably Antique form as an international language of the Church, learning and administration.

law, **law code**   Laws are the rules observed in society. A law code is the more or less systematic record of the laws followed by a particular group. Codification of law was a Roman activity imitated by barbarian kings.

lay, **layman**, **laity**, **layfolk**   Christians who are not in the professional Church; that is, not clergy, monks or nuns.

Levant   The lands on the east coast of the Mediterranean Sea.

limonite   A mineral, basically a fancy name for rust; what the rivets of the Sutton Hoo ship turned into.

liturgy   Formal Christian worship. The term 'liturgical state' used in Chapter 7 refers especially to the quasi-priestly status claimed by kings and eventually challenged by the Church in the eleventh century.

livery   As used in the document quoted on p. 103, it is short for 'delivery': the peasant family pays money instead of having to supply provisions for an army on campaign.

lord   A man of wealth and power, who could be a lord of vassals and/or a lord of serfs; institutions could also play these roles, as in the case of the monastery of St Germain-des-Prés which was the lord of the peasants discussed on pp. 103–4.

***Lotharingia* (Lorraine)**   Bears the name of Charlemagne's grandson Lothar, who received the middle region between West and East Francia (France and Germany) as well as Italy and the imperial title when the Carolingian Empire was divided in AD 843. It became part of early medieval Germany.

magic, **magical practices**   Attempting to bring about results in the natural world by supernatural means. While magical practices as such were usually associated with paganism in the early Middle Ages, some were incorporated into Christianity.

Magyars   Steppe nomads who established themselves in the Danube valley, raided from Eastern to Western Europe from the end of the ninth to the middle of the tenth centuries, and settled permanently in, and gave their alternative identity (Hungarian) and language (*Magyar*, pronounced Mahjjar) to, Hungary. *See further* pp. 112–14.

maior palatii   *See* mayor of the palace.

mallus   The court where counts administered public justice until the early eleventh century in France.

mandorla   A halo, representing the light of holiness, which completely surrounds a figure rather than just the head in art; it takes the form of an oval pointed at the top and bottom. *See* Figures 26 and 27.

manor, **manorial**, **manorialism**   A landed estate of a lord, normally with a dependent population of subsistence peasants; it may be divided into what is directly the lord's (demesne), cultivated by peasant labour, and what is the peasants', for which they owe the lord dues and services. In any case the lord lives off the surplus of their labour. The accumulation of such surpluses is the main, direct basis of wealth and power in early medieval society. Manorialism is a modern historical construct comprising all of the above.

manuscript   A handwritten text, usually on animal skin (parchment). Often used in the sense of codex, a book of pages bound together.

march   A border region organised for war under the command of a powerful military leader, like a margrave or marquis.

mare nostrum   Latin for 'our sea', what the Mediterranean was called by the Romans, whose empire surrounded it completely, deriving unity and focus therefrom.

margrave   German for 'count of the march', but generally a more important official than an ordinary count given the military responsibilities of command over border regions.

marquis   Like margrave, an official set over a march or border region.

Mass   *See* sacraments.

mayor of the palace (*maior palatii*)   Latin *maior*, literally 'greater one', here designates the top official of the Merovingian kings of France. From the mid-seventh until the mid-eighth centuries the mayors of the palace dominated the Merovingian kings and reduced them to figureheads.

medieval   Of the period of European history from the fifth to the fifteenth centuries AD, from the Latin *medium aevum*, the 'middle age'; in other words, it is the adjective for Middle Ages. It is occasionally applied to the history of other regions besides Europe because of some perceived similarity there to what was going on in medieval Europe, although the time periods may not be the same; care should be taken in such cases to determine what period is meant and to what extent the analogy with European history is valid or helpful.

Mediterranean   The sea that lies between Europe, Africa and Asia and, often in this book, the lands around that sea.

mercenary   A soldier who fights only for pay.

Merovingian   The dynasty of Frankish kings descended form Clovis, the great king who made France, but named for a still earlier ancestor Merovaeus; more generally the later fifth through seventh centuries of French history.

Middle Ages   The period of European history from the fifth to the fifteenth centuries AD. *See* p. 3.

millifiori   A decorative technique in which rods of multicoloured glass are fused together so as to make a pattern when cut in cross section; the little cross-sections are then used in decoration including cloisonné.

missus, missi dominici   *Missus* is literally 'one sent'; these were royal/imperial agents of the Frankish ruler Charlemagne and his successors.

mission, missionaries   Although these terms literally refer to a sending, they are used for any agents of religious conversion including the self-motivated.

monastery, monastic, monasticism   A place where Christians who have left ordinary society constitute a new society strictly ordered for achieving the goal of Christian salvation. Monasticism refers to this 'super-Christian' lifestyle and institutions; men who followed it were called monks and women who did so were called nuns. *See also* ascetic, abbot and abbess, hermits, and rule.

Moors, Moorish   Northwest Africans who enthusiastically converted to Islam and played an active role in Muslim Spain. In a Spanish context Moor is equivalent to Muslim.

mosque   Muslim place of worship.

muid   A barrel.

mundburdium Protection; women were always supposed to be under the *mundburdium* of a man.

Muslim, **Moslem**, **Moslim** A follower of the religion of Islam.

mawali 'Clients' of the Arab conquerors, the status assumed by non-Arab converts to Islam and their descendants.

Nicene Creed The version of the Christian statement of belief attributed to Emperor Constantine I when he presided over the Council of Nicaea in AD 325.

nobility, **noble** The wealthy and powerful; not a closed caste in the early Middle Ages.

nodfyr, ***niedfyr***, '**needfire**' Fire made by rubbing two sticks together, listed as a pagan practice among the Continental Saxons.

Norman Conquest of England The series of events, principally the Battle of Hastings, by which Duke William of Normandy made good his claim to the English crown in AD 1066.

Norse Scandinavians, Vikings; sometimes used of Norwegians rather than Danes. Old Norse is the language of Scandinavia in the Viking Age.

North A geographical designation of a region varying to some extent according to the context or direction of communication and influence: northern France, northern Germany, the British Isles and/or Scandinavia may be meant.

North Africa, ***Ifriqiyah*** Africa between the Mediterranean Sea and the Sahara Desert. Egypt is normally labelled separately. Following Roman usage, Arabic *Ifriqiyah* designated the part that is roughly modern Tunisia.

Northmen, **Normans**, **Normandy** The standard contemporary designation of the Vikings, including the original settlers of what would become Normandy in northern France.

numerology The 'science' of number symbolism.

octaves Liturgically, the week after a church festival.

Office Monastic communal prayer and psalm-singing at three-hourly intervals.

orthodox Correct in Christian belief.

Olympiads A system of dating by four-year periods between Olympic games, which continued in use even after the Ancient Olympic games were discontinued.

oracle A supernatural pronouncement.

oratores Latin for 'those who pray', one of the Three Orders of medieval society.

Ottonian The first dynasty of German kings, all but one of whom were called Otto, and the tenth century of German history when they ruled.

pagan Non-Christian, from the Latin for country dweller because pre-Christian practices tended to continue in the countryside.

palimpsest A manuscript where a previous text has been (partially) erased and written over with a new text.

panegyric Formal, rhetorical works of praise; hagiography (saints' Lives) is a subgenre of ancient panegyric.

pannage The right to run pigs in the forest of a manor, for which peasants paid. This was the standard way of keeping pigs in the Middle Ages; in particular, they ate the acorns there.

papacy, **papal** The institution of the bishops of Rome, always acknowledged in the West as the most authoritative bishops in the church, but papal control of the Church was limited before *c.*1050.

parchment   Prepared skins of sheep or cattle on which texts were written.

parish, **parochial system**   A defined territory of one or more landed estates, from the tithes (one-tenth of the produce) of which a priest was supported to minister to the religious needs of the parishioners. Europe was eventually covered with a network of parishes so that everyone had a church of which they were supposed to use the services. This is what is meant by parochial system.

Patarini   Radical church reformers in Milan in the later eleventh century.

paternoster   The most common Christian prayer, recommended by Christ to his disciples, that begins with the words 'Our Father', Latin *Pater noster*.

patriarch of Constantinople   The bishop of Constantinople. Patriarchs were the most authoritative bishops. Rome was a patriarchal see as well, but its bishop was traditionally called the pope; the word for 'father' lies at the root of both 'pope' and 'patriarch'.

patrician, **patriciate**   Originally a Roman imperial rank not an office, it took on some of the characteristics of the latter when applied to the military strongman under the Western Roman emperor in the fifth century. This was perhaps the sense in which Kings Pepin and Charlemagne of the Franks were given the title patrician of the Romans by the pope as protectors of the papacy. In any case, the patriciate had previously been the emperor's not the pope's to bestow.

patronage   Looking after someone else's interests, entailing dependency of the client on the more powerful patron. Rural patronage (*patrocinium*) was extended by landlords over peasants whom they protected from Roman taxation, and as such was a factor in the development of manorialism. Feudalism is best defined as 'institutionalised patronage'.

Peace of God and **Truce of God**   An attempt to counter the violence in society, the movement for the Peace and Truce of God began just before the year AD 1000. It involved the taking of oaths not to attack non-combatants and to limit fighting to certain days of the week (the Truce of God, *see* p. 196).

peasants   People who lived off the land by their own labour, *laboratores*, the vast proportion of the population in the early Middle Ages.

penance; **penitential**   After people confessed their wrongdoing to a priest, the priest would prescribe appropriate penance, exercises to be done by the penitents to improve their spiritual state and make sin less likely in the future. Penitentials were guides for priests as to what penance should be prescribed for sins and for how long.

perch   A unit of measure of land.

pilgrimage (*peregrinatio*)   Self-exile for ascetic/penitential religious reasons and/or travel to holy places for the same reasons.

Persia; **Persian Empire**   The original Iran, the other Great Power of the Ancient world, revived in the third century AD and often at war with the Roman Empire. The rise of Islam ended the Persian Empire.

persona non grata   Literally 'person not pleasing', someone who is unwelcome in a particular context.

Pirenne Thesis   The theory of the early twentieth-century Belgian historian Henri Pirenne that the rise of Islam marked the end of Antiquity and beginning of the Middle Ages.

plague   A vague term for serious epidemic disease in the past. Here the bubonic plague that spread from east to west in the Mediterranean and beyond in the sixth century.

plenitudo potestatis   The 'fullness of power' claimed by Pope Leo I for the papacy in the mid-fifth century.

polyptyque   Literally having several leaves, a fancy Greek name for a book.

pope   Traditional title (from Latin *papa*, 'father') of the bishop of Rome, who was acknowledged in Western Christianity as the most authoritative bishop in the Church.

prebends   Portions of church revenue that supported priests serving a church as a group.

precarium; **precarial tenure**   Land let on easy terms; the use and enjoyment of land rather than outright ownership of it.

primogeniture   Inheritance by the eldest son only.

princeps, **prince**, **principality**, **principate**   A convenient title for a ruler who was not a king, although it could also be applied to the latter. Literally meaning the first among equals, it was used as an alternative title by the Roman emperors and was applied to Frankish mayors of the palace; Lombards and Normans in the south found it useful as well. The meaning of a royal son who has not yet succeeded to the throne is not found in the early Middle Ages.

prior, **priory**   The monastic official second in authority to the abbot. In the monastic network of Cluny, there was only one abbot (of Cluny) and priors were the heads of all the dependent monasteries (technically priories).

private power   Ability to tell other people what to do and have them do it that comes from a person's own resources of wealth, status and supporters rather than from any position in an established government.

proprietary church   Normally refers to the Church as a source of revenues to lay owners or feudal lords of churches but as used in Chapter 7 also includes the Church itself as owner or holder of property.

Provence   The far southeast of present-day France, Provence was part of the first barbarian kingdoms of Italy (Odoacar's and the Ostrogoths') before being ceded to the Franks after Justinian's Reconquest of Italy began. The kingdom of Provence or Arles emerged from the break-up of the Carolingian Empire and was later joined to the kingdom of Burgundy (*see* Map 6.3), which was bequeathed to the German ruler in the eleventh century. The subsequent history of Provence was also complex.

psalter   The Book of Psalms, songs to God, in the Jewish and Christian (Old Testament) scriptures. Monastic communal worship involved extensive singing of psalms.

public power   Ability to tell people what to do and have them do it that attaches to any official position in an established government.

pueri (**'boys'**)   Among other things this designated the private armed followers of a lord. *See also vassi.*

Quran, **Koran**, **Alcoran**   Meaning 'Recitations', the Muslim holy book, in which the revelations of God to the prophet Mohammed are recorded.

racism   Although it can be found used with a broader meaning in traditional historiography, the term 'race' is avoided here because of its connotations of classification by appearance, especially skin colour, into categories thought to have a biological basis, categories unrecognised by the societies studied in this book. This is what is meant by the statement in Chapter 1 that the Ancient worldview 'lacked our racism'.

regent   Someone who rules for a king who is unable to rule, usually because of being still a child.

regimen   Governance, that, for example, which a bishop has over his flock.

relief   A payment by a vassal to a lord on receiving a fief.

'**religions of the Book**'   The acceptable status of Judaism and Christianity in Muslim belief.

Renaissance   The Renaissance is the period of history marked by a self-conscious 'rebirth' of (Ancient) 'civilisation' after the Middle Ages. It began in thirteenth-century Italy and spread north in Europe. Modern historians have applied the term to cultural rebirths in the Middle Ages; on the Carolingian Renaissance *see* pp. 95–6, 105, 109.

renovatio imperii Romanorum   Latin for 'renewal of the Roman Empire', the stated policy aim of King Emperor Otto III AD *c.*1000.

reverse dowry   *See* dowry.

Roman; Romans   Of the Roman Empire, including the eastern portion thereof which is also called the Byzantine Empire; its citizens. Also used of the city of Rome and its inhabitants, as should be clear from the context.

Romance languages   The European languages that Latin turned into: Italian, Spanish, Portuguese, French, Romanian and more than one language in the Alps.

Roman Empire   The ultimate extent of conquest by the city of Rome, completely surrounding the Mediterranean Sea and extending north as far as Britain; the eastern portion thereof that did not crumble away in the fifth century, also known as the Byzantine Empire; the revival thereof in the West with the papal coronation of Charlemagne in AD 800 and Otto I in 962.

romanesque architecture   A style of building based on Roman models, with indigenous European decorative input, that flowered in the eleventh century.

romanisation   The long-term cultural effect of being in the Roman Empire.

romanitas   The Roman way of life.

Romano-British   Of the Roman province(s) of the island of Britain, including the population thereof.

Rome   A city in central Italy, also used for the empire that originated in the conquests by that city; also used for the papacy, the bishops of Rome.

rune, runestone   An alphabet, based on Mediterranean prototypes, employed by Germanic-speakers before and after Christian conversion brought them Latin textual literacy in the Roman alphabet. The carving of runes on stones set up for the purpose of displaying their message is characteristic of (especially eastern) Scandinavia in the Viking Age.

rule (monastic)   The systematic ordering of the monastic life. Originally there were various rules and variations thereon; however, the Rule of St Benedict was normally followed in Western monasticism by the early eleventh century.

Rus, Russia   Scandinavians who went east in the Viking Age, from whom Russia is named. *See* pp. 116–17.

sacraments; sacramentary   Christian rituals that confer divine benefit, such as the Mass that commemorates and re-enacts the sacrifice of Christ; a sacramentary is a book of rituals for the latter.

saint   A holy person. Almost all of the saints mentioned in this book owed their status purely to local reputation.

Salian   Designates Franks who lived near the mouth of the Rhine river, whose name attaches to Salic Law.

Saracens   An ethnic name for the inhabitants of Arabia that predates the rise of Islam. Afterwards applied to all Muslims.

Saxons, Saxony   A people of northern Germany, some of whom migrated to Britain, where they established Wessex and other southern kingdoms. *See also* Anglo-Saxons. On its own 'Saxons' in this book normally refers to the Continental inhabitants of Saxony.

223

Scandinavia, **Scandinavians**   The northernmost part of Europe, including Denmark, Sweden and Norway, homelands of the Vikings.

Scots, **Scotland**   Originally the Scots were the Irish at home or abroad. Their principal colony established at the beginning of the Middle Ages was in what is now southwest Scotland, and in the ninth century its rulers became kings of what is now Scotland. Their Scottish identity was taken on by, and ultimately transferred to, the inhabitants of northern Britain.

script   Handwriting, classified into types like Insular script or Caroline script.

secular   From Latin *saeculum*, 'the world' or 'time', used as a term of distinction from what is more 'religious' because Christians were supposed to be in the world, but not of the world, with their minds focused on God and eternity.

see   The place from which a bishop wields his authority; this term and 'cathedral' both derive from the word for 'seat', in Latin and Greek respectively.

serf, **serfdom**   An unfree agricultural labourer; use of particular plots of land was inherited by families of serfs in distinction from Ancient slaves who were centrally maintained by their masters (Latin *servi* applies to both).

servitium   Latin for 'service'. Vassals owed honourable service of fighting, counsel and financial aid to their lords.

Shia   A sect of Islam originating with Muslims who maintained that the caliphs must be of the family of the prophet Mohammed and refused to accept the legitimacy of the Umayyad caliphs who were not so descended. Ultimately other differences of belief and practice developed between Shia and Sunni Muslims.

simony; **simoniacs**   The payment of money for church office; those who do so. For an explanation of the origins of the term, *see* note 5 to Chapter 7.

Slavs, **Slavic**, **Sclavinia**   Peoples of Eastern Europe speaking related languages over an area from the Baltic Sea to the Balkans. The Bulgars were originally not Slavic, but adopted the language and culture of their Slavic subjects who took on the identity of the ruling group.

society   Human beings living in relation to each other; their relations can be the subject of analysis.

solidi   At first gold coins, but after these ceased to be struck the *solidus*, from which French *sou* is derived, became 'money of account' in which prices were given rather than real money.

South   A geographical designation of a region varying to some extent according to the context or direction of communication and influence, but always including at least some Mediterranean lands.

spindle-whorl   Disk with a hole in the middle that weighs down the lower end of a spindle for making thread; as these needed to be heavy they were made of durable material and survive to be recovered by archaeologists.

steppe nomads   Dwellers on the grasslands where Europe and Asia come together.

Sunni   The Muslim majority who accepted the legitimacy of the Umayyad caliphs, in contrast to the Shia who insisted that the caliph must be from the family of the prophet Mohammed.

synagogue   Jewish place of worship.

synod, **council**   A meeting of bishops, normally summoned by the secular ruler in the early Middle Ages.

Three Orders   Those who pray (*oratores*), those who fight (*bellatores*), those who work with their hands (*laboratores*): the medieval social analysis; *see* pp. 167–9.

town   A relatively large cluster of population, normally walled. Here used more or less interchangeably with 'city', than which 'town' may seem the more appropriate term, given the small size of early medieval cities. Some specialisation of commercial and industrial functions is expected in towns, and ultimately self-government.

Treaty of Verdun   The agreement in AD 843 between the sons of Louis the Pious that split the Carolingian Empire between them (*see* Map 5.1).

Trinity   The Christian doctrine that God comprises Father, Son (Christ) and Holy Spirit.

Truce of God   *See* Peace of God.

Turks, Turkish   Peoples of Western Asia who converted to Islam. The Seljuk Turks came west to Asia Minor and the Levant in the eleventh century. It was against their control of the Holy Land that the First Crusade was directed.

Tuscany   Carolingian border region in north-central Italy, which long retained Carolingian traditions of public government under its marquis.

Umayyad dynasty, caliphate; house of Umayya   Descendants of the Meccan aristocracy rather than the family of Mohammed, rulers of the undivided caliphate until 750.

umma   The community of all believers in Islam.

uncial script   Late Roman handwriting used in manuscripts of high quality.

urban, urbanised, urbanisation   From the Latin word *urbs*, 'city', these terms all refer to city/town life: people living, working and exchanging ideas in close proximity to one another; and thus the presence of cities/towns.

Varangians   Western Europeans, from a Russian and Byzantine point of view. The Byzantine emperor's Varangian Guard was formed in the late tenth century, drawn especially from Viking and later, after the Norman Conquest of England, English warriors.

vassal (*vassus*, *vassalus*), vassalage   This term and what it represented rose on the social scale to designate the permanent dependant of a lord who owed the lord honourable service of fighting, counsel and financial aid (*see* pp. 25, 93–4, 170–3). Vassalage is the essence of feudalism as it is most commonly defined.

vendetta   *See* bloodfeud.

vernacular   The native speech of a people, used for languages other than Latin or Greek in the early Middle Ages.

vicar   Deputy for a higher authority; its representative.

Vikings, Viking Age   Their quintessential activity was piracy, but they did much else (*see* p. 000) and are broadly defined here as Scandinavians active in the period from the end of the eighth to the later eleventh centuries, the Viking Age.

villein   An unfree peasant, a serf.

votive crown   A decorated crown given to a church where it hung as an ornament.

Vulgate   The translation of the Christian Bible into Latin by Jerome in the late fourth century, which became the standard version of the Bible in medieval Western Christianity.

Walpurgisnacht   The eve of the feast of St Waldburg; that is, the eve of the 1 May (*see* note 3 to Chapter 4).

Welsh   Mainly associated with the people and language of Wales in Britain, it derives from the word which in Germanic languages (e.g., Anglo-Saxon *wealh*) designated Romanised Celts on the Continent as well as in Britain.

West   A geographical designation of a region varying to some extent according to the context or direction of communication and influence: East–West contact would be across the Mediterranean and/or across Europe. The West is used for the area north of Islam and west of Byzantium, where the core of Europe was formed (*see* Chapter 4).

Western Christianity   Christian churches (in the sense both of the faithful and institutions) which acknowledged the pope to be the most authoritative bishop in Christendom and used Latin as an ecclesiastical language.

Western Roman Empire   The part of the Roman Empire that crumbled in the fifth century.

witan   The royal council of the unified Anglo-Saxon kingdom of England.

witch; **witchcraft**   A person who attempts to bring about results by accessing supernatural power from the 'wrong address' (not the Christian God), and what they do.

York, *Jórvik*, *Eoforwic*, *Eboracum*   Respectively the modern, Viking, Anglo-Saxon and Roman names for the same city in northern England. There does not seem to be continuity of urban function from the Roman to Anglo-Saxon periods there.

Primary Source Translations

These are given chapter by chapter in the order in which the quotations appear; any translations not referenced here are the author's own. In a few cases quoted translations have been slightly and insignificantly altered. It is hoped that these references may provide a start for further reading.

Introduction

Cyril Edwards, 'German Vernacular Literature: A Survey', in *Carolingian Culture: Emulation and Innovation*, ed. Rosamond McKitterick (Cambridge: Cambridge University Press, 1994), pp. 164–5.

Chapter 1: The Fifth Century: Kingdoms Replace the Western Roman Empire

Sidonius. Poems and Letters, trans. W. B. Anderson, vol. 2 (Cambridge, MA: Harvard University Press; and London: William Heinemann, 1965), pp. 519, 521.

Sidonius. Poems and Letters, trans. W. B. Anderson, vol. 2 (Cambridge, MA: Harvard University Press; and London: William Heinemann, 1965), pp. 261, 263.

Sidonius. Poems and Letters, trans. W. B. Anderson, vol. 1 (Cambridge, MA: Harvard University Press; and London: William Heinemann, 1980), p. 273.

The Writings of Salvian, the Presbyter, trans. Jeremiah F. O'Sullivan (Washington, DC: The Catholic University of America Press, 1947), p. 130.

Ausonius, trans. Hugh G. Evelyn White, vol. 2 (London: William Heinemann; and Cambridge, MA: Harvard University Press, 1967), p. 343 (Paulinus of Pella, *Eucharisticus*).

Ausonius, trans. Hugh G. Evelyn White, vol. 2 (London: William Heinemann; and Cambridge, MA: Harvard University Press, 1967), p. 329 (Paulinus of Pella, *Eucharisticus*).

Sidonius. Poems and Letters, trans. W. B. Anderson, vol. 2 (Cambridge, MA: Harvard University Press; and London: William Heinemann, 1965), pp. 137, 139.

Victor of Vita: History of the Vandal Persecution, trans. John Moorhead (Liverpool: Liverpool University Press, 1992), p. 27.

Gregory of Tours, *History of the Franks*, trans. Lewis Thorpe (London: Penguin Books, 1974), p. 129.

St Patrick: His Writings and Muirchu's Life, trans. A. B. E. Hood (London and Chichester: Phillimore, 1978), p. 57.

St Patrick: His Writings and Muirchu's Life, trans. A. B. E. Hood (London and Chichester: Phillimore, 1978), pp. 58–9.

Gregory of Tours, *History of the Franks*, trans. Lewis Thorpe (London: Penguin Books, 1974), p. 131–2.

Gregory of Tours, *History of the Franks*, trans. Lewis Thorpe (London: Penguin Books, 1974), p. 93.

St Patrick: His Writings and Muirchu's Life, trans. A. B. E. Hood (London and Chichester: Phillimore, 1978), p. 51.

Chapter 2: The Sixth Century: The West Goes Its Own Way

Cassiodorus: Variae, trans. S. J. B. Barnish (Liverpool: Liverpool University Press, 1992), pp. 42–3.

Ammianus Marcellinus, trans. John C. Rolfe, vol. 3 (London: W. Heinemann; and Cambridge, MA: Harvard University Press, 1952), p. 545 (*Anonymi Valesiani Pars Posterior*).

Procopius, trans. H. B. Dewing, vol. 3 (London: William Heinemann; and Cambridge, MA: Harvard University Press, 1961), p. 121.

The Conversion of Western Europe, 350–750, ed. J. N. Hillgarth (Englewood Cliffs: Prentice-Hall, 1969), p. 75.

The Conversion of Western Europe, 350–750, ed. J. N. Hillgarth (Englewood Cliffs: Prentice-Hall, 1969), p. 78.

Ammianus Marcellinus, trans. John C. Rolfe, vol. 3 (London: W. Heinemann; and Cambridge, MA: Harvard University Press, 1952), pp. 549, 551 (*Anonymi Valesiani Pars Posterior*).

Gregory of Tours, *History of the Franks*, trans. Lewis Thorpe (London: Penguin Books, 1974), p. 154.

Procopius, trans. H. B. Dewing, vol. 4 (London: William Heinemann; and Cambridge, MA: Harvard University Press, 1924), p. 333.

The Rule of Saint Benedict, source of translation (from a book of readings for students) unknown.

Gregory of Tours, *History of the Franks*, trans. Lewis Thorpe (London: Penguin Books, 1974), pp. 546–7.

Lucien Musset, *The Germanic Invasions*, trans. Edward and Columba James (University Park: The Pennsylvania State University Press, 1975), p. 80.

Gregory of Tours, *History of the Franks*, trans. Lewis Thorpe (London: Penguin Books, 1974), pp. 409–12.

The Chronicle of John Malalas, trans. Elizabeth Jeffreys, Michael Jeffreys, Roger Scott et al. (Melbourne: Australian Association for Byzantine Studies, 1986), p. 228.

The Chronicle of John Malalas, trans. Elizabeth Jeffreys, Michael Jeffreys, Roger Scott et al. (Melbourne: Australian Association for Byzantine Studies, 1986), p. 130.

Paul the Deacon, *History of the Lombards*, trans. William Dudley Foulke (Philadelphia: University of Pennsylvania Press, 1974), p. 166.

Alfred the Great: Asser's Life of King Alfred *and Other Contemporary Sources*, trans. Simon Keynes and Michael Lapidge (Harmondsworth: Penguin Books, 1983), pp. 126–7.

Chapter 3: The Seventh Century: Cultural Watershed

Jonas, *Life of St Columban*, trans. Dana Carleton Munro, *Translations and Reprints from the Original Sources of European History*, vol. 2, no. 7 (Philadelphia: The Department of History of the University of Pennsylvania, 1895), pp. 3–4.

Aldhelm, the Prose Works, trans. Michael Lapidge and Michael Herren (Cambridge: D. S. Brewer; and Totowa: Rowman & Littlefield, 1979), p. 163.

T. W. Arnold, *The Preaching of Islam*, 2nd edn (London: Constable, 1913), p. 6.

T. W. Arnold, *The Preaching of Islam*, 2nd edn (London: Constable, 1913), p. 12.

ibn-al-Tiqtaqa, *al-Fakhri: On the Systems of Government and the Moslem Dynasties*, trans. C. E. J. Whitting (London: Luzac, 1947), p. 79.

Bede's Ecclesiastical History of the English People, ed. Bertram Colgrave and R. A. B. Mynors (Oxford: Clarendon Press, 1969), p. 333.

Isidore of Seville's History of the Kings of the Goths, Vandals and Suevi, trans. Guido Donini and Gordon B. Ford, Jr (Leiden: E. J. Brill, 1966), p. 1.

*The Visigothic Code (*Forum Judicum*)*, trans. S. P. Scott (Boston, MA: The Boston Book Company, 1910), pp. 169–70.

Chapter 4: The Eighth Century: Formation of the Core of Europe

The Anglo-Saxon Missionaries in Germany, trans. and ed. C. H. Talbot (London: Sheed & Ward, 1954), pp. 76–8.

The Anglo-Saxon Missionaries in Germany, trans. and ed. C. H. Talbot (London: Sheed & Ward, 1954), p. 91.

The Anglo-Saxon Missionaries in Germany, trans. and ed. C. H. Talbot (London: Sheed & Ward, 1954), p. 162.

The Anglo-Saxon Missionaries in Germany, trans. and ed. C. H. Talbot (London: Sheed & Ward, 1954), p. 161.

The Anglo-Saxon Missionaries in Germany, trans. and ed. C. H. Talbot (London: Sheed & Ward, 1954), p. 170.

The Anglo-Saxon Missionaries in Germany, trans. and ed. C. H. Talbot (London: Sheed & Ward, 1954), p. 156.

The Anglo-Saxon Missionaries in Germany, trans. and ed. C. H. Talbot (London: Sheed & Ward, 1954), p. 95.

*The Lives of the Eighth-Century Popes (*Liber Pontificalis*)*, trans. Raymond Davis (Liverpool: Liverpool University Press, 1992), p. 58.

James Thayer Addison, *The Medieval Missionary* (New York and London: International Missionary Council, 1936), p. 52.

Einhard and Notker the Stammerer, *Two Lives of Charlemagne*, trans. Lewis Thorpe (Harmondsworth: Penguin Books, 1969), p. 63.

P. D. King, *Charlemagne: Translated Sources* (Kendal: P. D. King, 1987), pp. 113–14.

P. D. King, *Charlemagne: Translated Sources* (Kendal: P. D. King, 1987), p. 168.

P. D. King, *Charlemagne: Translated Sources* (Kendal: P. D. King, 1987), p. 90.

Wendy Davies and Paul Fouracre (eds), *Property and Power in the Early Middle Ages* (Cambridge and New York: Cambridge University Press, 1995), p. 245.

The History of Feudalism, ed. David Herlihy (New Jersey: Humanities Press; and Sussex: Harvester Press, 1970), p. 86.

P. D. King, *Charlemagne: Translated Sources* (Kendal: P. D. King, 1987), p. 123.

Brian Pullan, *Sources for the History of Medieval Europe from the Mid-Eighth to the Mid-Thirteenth Century* (Oxford: Basil Blackwell, 1971), p. 28.

Stewart C. Easton and Helene Wieruszowski, *The Era of Charlemagne* (Princeton: D. Van Nostrand, 1961), p. 173.

Stewart C. Easton and Helene Wieruszowski, *The Era of Charlemagne* (Princeton: D. Van Nostrand, 1961), p. 175–6.

Einhard and Notker the Stammerer, *Two Lives of Charlemagne*, trans. Lewis Thorpe (Harmondsworth: Penguin Books, 1969), p. 77.

Stewart C. Easton and Helene Wieruszowski, *The Era of Charlemagne* (Princeton: D. Van Nostrand, 1961), p. 178.

Chapter 5: The Ninth Century: Expanding the Boundaries

P. D. King, *Charlemagne: Translated Sources* (Kendal: P. D. King, 1987), p. 93.

P. D. King, *Charlemagne: Translated Sources* (Kendal: P. D. King, 1987), p. 339.

Einhard and Notker the Stammerer, *Two Lives of Charlemagne*, trans. Lewis Thorpe (Harmondsworth: Penguin Books, 1969), p. 81.

P. D. King, *Charlemagne: Translated Sources* (Kendal: P. D. King, 1987), p. 339.

Einhard and Notker the Stammerer, *Two Lives of Charlemagne*, trans. Lewis Thorpe (Harmondsworth: Penguin Books, 1969), p. 82.

Einhard and Notker the Stammerer, *Two Lives of Charlemagne*, trans. Lewis Thorpe (Harmondsworth: Penguin Books, 1969), pp. 163–4.

P. D. King, *Charlemagne: Translated Sources* (Kendal: P. D. King, 1987), p. 259.

Pierre Riché, *Daily Life in the World of Charlemagne*, trans. Jo Ann McNamara ([Philadelphia]: University of Pennsylvania Press, 1978), p. 100.

Georges Duby, *Rural Economy and Country Life in the Medieval West*, trans. Cynthia Postan (London: Edward Arnold, 1968), pp. 368–9.

The Letters of Lupus of Ferrières, trans. Graydon W. Regenos (The Hague: Martinus Nijhoff, 1966), p. 16.

Carolingian Chronicles, trans. Bernhard Walter Scholz ([Ann Arbor]: The University of Michigan Press, 1972), p. 154.

Carolingian Chronicles, trans. Bernhard Walter Scholz ([Ann Arbor]: The University of Michigan Press, 1972), p. 143.

Carolingian Chronicles, trans. Bernhard Walter Scholz ([Ann Arbor]: The University of Michigan Press, 1972), p. 167.

Dhuoda, *Handbook for William: A Carolingian Woman's Counsel for Her Son*, trans. Carol Neel (Lincoln and London: University of Nebraska Press, 1991), p. 100.

Dhuoda, *Handbook for William: A Carolingian Woman's Counsel for Her Son*, trans. Carol Neel (Lincoln and London: University of Nebraska Press, 1991), p. 26.

Carolingian Chronicles, trans. Bernhard Walter Scholz ([Ann Arbor]: The University of Michigan Press, 1972), p. 159.

The Letters of Lupus of Ferrières, trans. Graydon W. Regenos (The Hague: Martinus Nijhoff, 1966), p. 49.

James F. Kenney, *The Sources for the Early History of Ireland: Ecclesiastical* (Dublin: Pádraic Ó Táilliúir, 1979), p. 582.

Gwyn Jones, *A History of the Vikings* (London: Oxford University Press, 1968), pp. 194–5.

Bertil Almgren et al., *The Viking* (Gothenburg: Tre Tryckare, 1966), p. 81.

The Annals of St-Bertin, trans. Janet L. Nelson (Manchester and New York: Manchester University Press, 1991), p. 44.

Conquerors and Chroniclers of Early Medieval Spain, trans. Kenneth Baxter Wolf (Liverpool: Liverpool University Press, 1990), p. 174.

Conquerors and Chroniclers of Early Medieval Spain, trans. Kenneth Baxter Wolf (Liverpool: Liverpool University Press, 1990), p. 176.

Alfred the Great: Asser's Life of King Alfred *and Other Contemporary Sources*, trans. Simon Keynes and Michael Lapidge (Harmondsworth: Penguin Books, 1983), pp. 118–19.

Alfred the Great: Asser's Life of King Alfred *and Other Contemporary Sources*, trans. Simon Keynes and Michael Lapidge (Harmondsworth: Penguin Books, 1983), p. 75.

Alfred the Great: Asser's Life of King Alfred *and Other Contemporary Sources*, trans. Simon Keynes and Michael Lapidge (Harmondsworth: Penguin Books, 1983), p. 125.

Alfred the Great: Asser's Life of King Alfred *and Other Contemporary Sources*, trans. Simon Keynes and Michael Lapidge (Harmondsworth: Penguin Books, 1983), p. 126.

Two Voyagers at the Court of King Alfred, ed. Neils Lund and trans. Christine E. Fell (York: William Sessions, 1984), p. 18.

Alfred the Great: Asser's Life of King Alfred *and Other Contemporary Sources*, trans. Simon Keynes and Michael Lapidge (Harmondsworth: Penguin Books, 1983), p. 91.

Two Voyagers at the Court of King Alfred, ed. Neils Lund and trans. Christine E. Fell (York: William Sessions, 1984), p. 23.

Alfred the Great: Asser's Life of King Alfred *and Other Contemporary Sources*, trans. Simon Keynes and Michael Lapidge (Harmondsworth: Penguin Books, 1983), pp. 132–3.

[Figure 23 caption] *Alfred the Great: Asser's* Life of King Alfred *and Other Contemporary Sources*, trans. Simon Keynes and Michael Lapidge (Harmondsworth: Penguin Books, 1983), p. 135.

Jo Ann McNamara and Suzanne Wemple, 'The Power of Women Through the Family in Medieval Europe, 500–1100', in *Women and Power in the Middle Ages*, ed. Mary Erler and Maryanne Kowaleski (Athens, GA, and London: The University of Georgia Press, 1988), p. 93.

Chapter 6: The Tenth Century: Nadir to Take-Off

St Odo of Cluny, trans. and ed. Gerard Sitwell (London and New York: Sheed & Ward, 1958), p. 33.

St Odo of Cluny, trans. and ed. Gerard Sitwell (London and New York: Sheed & Ward, 1958), p. 102.

St Odo of Cluny, trans. and ed. Gerard Sitwell (London and New York: Sheed & Ward, 1958), p. 103.

St Odo of Cluny, trans. and ed. Gerard Sitwell (London and New York: Sheed & Ward, 1958), p. 118.

St. Odo of Cluny, trans. and ed. Gerard Sitwell (London and New York: Sheed & Ward, 1958), p. 116.

St Odo of Cluny, trans. and ed. Gerard Sitwell (London and New York: Sheed & Ward, 1958), p. 117–18.

Boyd H. Hill Jr, *Medieval Monarchy in Action: The German Empire from Henry I to Henry IV* (London: George Allen & Unwin and New York: Barnes & Noble Books, 1972), p. 117.

Boyd H. Hill Jr, *Medieval Monarchy in Action: The German Empire from Henry I to Henry IV* (London: George Allen & Unwin and New York: Barnes & Noble Books, 1972), p. 116.

K. J. Leyser, *Rule and Conflict in an Early Medieval Society: Ottonian Saxony* (London: Edward Arnold, 1979), p. 33.

Boyd H. Hill Jr, *Medieval Monarchy in Action: The German Empire from Henry I to Henry IV* (London: George Allen & Unwin and New York: Barnes & Noble Books, 1972), p. 126.

Boyd H. Hill Jr, *Medieval Monarchy in Action: The German Empire from Henry I to Henry IV* (London: George Allen & Unwin and New York: Barnes & Noble Books, 1972), p. 137.

Liudprand of Cremona, *The Embassy to Constantinople and Other Writings*, trans. F. A. Wright, ed. John Julius Norwich (London: J. M. Dent; and Rutland, VE: Charles E. Tuttle, 1993), p. 171.

Chapter 7: The Eleventh Century: Transformation of Europe

Rodulfus Glaber, *Historiarum Libri Quinque*, ed. and trans. John France (Oxford: Clarendon Press, 1989), pp. 115, 117.

John T. McNeill and Helena M. Gamer, *Medieval Handbooks of Penance* (New York: Columbia University Press, 1990), pp. 329–30.

John T. McNeill and Helena M. Gamer, *Medieval Handbooks of Penance* (New York: Columbia University Press, 1990), p. 330.

John T. McNeill and Helena M. Gamer, *Medieval Handbooks of Penance* (New York: Columbia University Press, 1990), pp. 331.

John T. McNeill and Helena M. Gamer, *Medieval Handbooks of Penance* (New York: Columbia University Press, 1990), p. 339.

John T. McNeill and Helena M. Gamer, *Medieval Handbooks of Penance* (New York: Columbia University Press, 1990), p. 340.

John T. McNeill and Helena M. Gamer, *Medieval Handbooks of Penance* (New York: Columbia University Press, 1990), pp. 340–1.

John T. McNeill and Helena M. Gamer, *Medieval Handbooks of Penance* (New York: Columbia University Press, 1990), p. 335.

The Lombard Laws, trans. Katherine Fischer Drew (Philadelphia: University of Pennsylvania Press, 1973), pp. 126–7.

Marc Bloch, *Feudal Society*, trans. L. A. Manyon (Chicago: The University of Chicago Press, 1961), pp. 411–12.

Anglo-Saxon Prose, ed. and trans. Michael Swanton (London: J. M. Dent; and Rutland, VE: Charles E. Tuttle, 1993), pp. 189–90.

The History of Feudalism, ed. David Herlihy (New Jersey: Humanities Press; and Sussex: Harvester Press, 1970), p. 97.

The History of Feudalism, ed. David Herlihy (New Jersey: Humanities Press and Sussex: Harvester Press, 1970), p. 99.

The Song of Roland, trans. D. D. R. Owen (London: Unwin Books, 1972), p. 118.

The Song of Roland, trans. D. D. R. Owen (London: Unwin Books, 1972), p. 120.

The Song of Roland, trans. D. D. R. Owen (London: Unwin Books, 1972), p. 34.

The Song of Roland, trans. D. D. R. Owen (London: Unwin Books, 1972), p. 47.

The Song of Roland, trans. D. D. R. Owen (London: Unwin Books, 1972), p. 54.

The Song of Roland, trans. D. D. R. Owen (London: Unwin Books, 1972), p. 69.

Adam of Bremen, *History of the Archbishops of Hamburg-Bremen*, trans. Francis J. Tschan (New York: Columbia University Press, 1959), p. 100.

Adam of Bremen, *History of the Archbishops of Hamburg-Bremen*, trans. Francis J. Tschan (New York: Columbia University Press, 1959), p. 92.

Brian Tierney, *The Crisis of Church and State, 1050–1300* (Toronto, Buffalo and London: University of Toronto Press in association with the Medieval Academy of America, 1988), p. 44.

The Alexiad of Anna Comnena, trans. E. R. A. Sewter (Harmondsworth: Penguin Books, 1969), p. 54.

Gregory of Tours, *History of the Franks*, trans. Lewis Thorpe (London: Penguin Books, 1974), p. 183.

Brian Tierney, *The Crisis of Church and State, 1050–1300* (Toronto, Buffalo and London: University of Toronto Press in association with the Medieval Academy of America, 1988), p. 40.

Brian Tierney, *The Crisis of Church and State, 1050–1300* (Toronto, Buffalo and London: University of Toronto Press in association with the Medieval Academy of America, 1988), p. 44.

Brian Tierney, *The Crisis of Church and State, 1050–1300* (Toronto, Buffalo and London: University of Toronto Press in association with the Medieval Academy of America, 1988), p. 49.

Gerd Tellenbach, *Church, State and Christian Society at the Time of the Investiture Contest*, trans. R. F. Bennett (Oxford: Basil Blackwell, 1948), p. 115.

Brian Tierney, *The Crisis of Church and State, 1050–1300* (Toronto, Buffalo and London: University of Toronto Press in association with the Medieval Academy of America, 1988), p. 50.

Brian Tierney, *The Crisis of Church and State, 1050–1300* (Toronto, Buffalo and London: University of Toronto Press in association with the Medieval Academy of America, 1988), p. 49.

Brian Tierney, *The Crisis of Church and State, 1050–1300* (Toronto, Buffalo and London: University of Toronto Press in association with the Medieval Academy of America, 1988), p. 63.

The First Crusade: The Chronicle of Fulcher of Chartres and Other Source Materials, ed. Edward Peters (Philadelphia: University of Pennsylvania Press, 1971), pp. 4–5.

The First Crusade: The Chronicle of Fulcher of Chartres and Other Source Materials, ed. Edward Peters (Philadelphia: University of Pennsylvania Press, 1971), pp. 5–6.

The First Crusade: The Chronicle of Fulcher of Chartres and Other Source Materials, ed. Edward Peters (Philadelphia: University of Pennsylvania Press, 1971), p. 18.

The Alexiad of Anna Comnena, trans. E. R. A. Sewter (Harmondsworth: Penguin Books, 1969), p. 329.

Index